Watershed Days

MERCER
UNIVERSITY PRESS

Endowed by
TOM WATSON BROWN
and
THE WATSON-BROWN FOUNDATION, INC.

Watershed Days

Adventures (a Little Thorny & Familiar)

in the Home Range

Thorpe Moeckel

MERCER UNIVERSITY PRESS | *Macon, Georgia*

MUP/ P507

© 2015 by Mercer University Press
Published by Mercer University Press
1501 Mercer University Drive
Macon, Georgia 31207

9 8 7 6 5 4 3 2 1

Books published by Mercer University Press are printed on acid-free paper
that meets the requirements of the American National Standard for
Information Sciences—Permanence of Paper for Printed Library Materials.

The poem, A Quiet Life by Baron Wormser, on pages 117-118 is used with
permission.

ISBN   978-0-88146-531-0
Cataloging-in-Publication Data is available from the Library of Congress

for Kirsten, Sophie, and Tommy

Contents

Acknowledgments

Thanks to everyone named in this book. Thanks to my family and all of our critters. Thanks to the birds, beasts, and flowers. Many thanks as well to, in no particular order: Boaters of the 434/540, Frank Burroughs, John Lane, Jon Guy Owens, Gillian MacKenzie, Peter Relic, The Five Hole Gang, and my colleagues at Hollins University and UNC-Chapel Hill.

Thanks to the editors of the following journals, where some of these chapters appeared or are forthcoming, sometimes in slightly different form: *Adventum, Aethlon, Alabama Literary Review, ISLE (Interdisciplinary Studies in Literature and the Environment), Lost Magazine, Permaculture Activist, storySouth, Taproot, The Cleanest Line, The James Dickey Review,* and *Yale Angler's Journal.*

"Nature does not like to be observed,
and likes that we should be her fools and playmates."
—Emerson

2005–2006

With Cousin Alex in the Waves

My cousin Alex hops to a crouched position on his surfboard and digs an edge in the curl, his left foot back, right forward. I watch him from a place further down the wave. He stands fully now, a silhouette on a horizon of whites and blues. Sun lights our place in the ocean, but you can see the clouds and the shade they make not too far in either direction. We are in a pocket of light and everything is muted and shining. The tropical depression, also named Alex, has stalled off the coast twenty or so miles south and east of us. The darkness of those clouds is exhilarating. Curtains of rain tail beneath the mass.

The wave grows soft and Alex steers off the back of it, falling in the water oceanward of his board. He climbs on the nine-foot funshape and strokes for deeper water. He ducks under a wave. I look toward the beach and see by the houses that the rip has dragged us a half-mile from our entry point. Another good ride and I'll take to the sand; I'll walk to a place beyond the enclave of our family and enter the ocean again. It has been a good, wild year—a new job, a move to the country—since I last saw the ocean or rode a surfboard, and I intend to surf today until I am too waterlogged to see crooked or straight or even see at all.

Our families mosey about the beach, attentive to kindred swells. They ride waves of novels or gauge the sand's slope for the projected path of a bocce ball. They chat, catch up with one another—ten people who live in five different states and a foreign country. They daydream, think. They watch the other beachgoers. They listen to the surf and examine the clouds and cover their books when the squalls spit brief showers of rain.

I check the horizon again for humps, a set of waves. Nothing gives. I like the waiting, the watching. I like it as well as the wave riding. Two weeks ago, my wife, Kirsten, and I, we closed on that land, those eighteen acres and that barn and that drafty old house. But I'm not really thinking about that—see, the wind shifts now and then from offshore to sideshore, creating a chop that wrinkles the faces, making them bumpy and wedged, harder to read.

Three peaks build—dark, long walls approaching. It appears the last wave is the tallest; that has been the pattern today. Alex sits on his board. He watches, touches the water with his hands. The water is tepid but refreshing with the moil of salt and motion. I let the first wave pass. The second looks good, but the third towers as though peek-a-booing over its shoulder. I wait for it.

It's hard to discuss surfing without falling victim to the wistful, decidedly useless sentiment that plagues any treatment of the act that doesn't involve doing it. Yet I secretly love such sentiment and the feelings of superiority it breeds. It is a fine tonic to traffic in nouns like *dude* and *barney*, adjectives such as *rad, meaty, gnarly,* and *killer*. It is especially pleasing to say them with a surfer's drawl, the bratty, nasal one Sean Penn made famous in *Fast Times at Ridgemont High*. Recently I watched a surf flick—*Step Into Liquid*. While a feast of scrumptious cinematography, I wished several times that it had been muted. The narration was imbecilic, but my feelings of superiority were equally imbecilic and rewarding.

Surfing has a mystical side and it might be fair to say that such energy fertilizes the sport's weedy vernacular, fashion lines, music, and art. Such is America. We love our primitive side to death. There's probably some truth when I say that being in the water with my cousin connects me to a wave-riding family that extends back to the ancients of Polynesia and other coastal regions; that I feel a kinship with dolphins and manta rays and all the other large and small creatures—jellyfish, seaweed, plankton—that use waves to travel, feed, flee, mate, play, or die; that I'm in touch with light and sound, too, all that travels in waves.

The more tangible truth is I'm sitting on a board off an island where high-dollar homes in what used to be the dunes make the beach look almost like an afterthought, something a landscape crew installed. My father's wife Donna happens to own a house here. She's a beautiful, loving lady, and they are happy together—what else can you ask for.

Riding waves is simple. There's little gear involved save a board and some trunks, maybe a wetsuit. It is also effective; among gravity sports, surfing is unsurpassed in my experience for the way it empties your mind, demanding focus and attention and rushes of adrenaline, punctuated by calm and a gentler focus as you wait and watch for the next wave.

One of the more dangerous aspects of the sport is the way, for any surfer, the sound of breaking waves and the taste of salt water stoke the fire of memory. As much as you want to worship irony and avoid the grip and itch of nostalgia's wool turtleneck, past surf trips and surf companions always merge with the present one. It just happens. There are all the strangers with whom you've paddled and sat and stood in water off beaches from Tortola to Nova Scotia. You see their faces, their stances, the shapes and graphics on their boards. You see the folks from your favorite surf magazines and surf flicks. Of the big-wave riders in Hawaii, Gerry Lopez, from the best surf movie ever made, *Big Wednesday*, comes to mind. There are many others. I think of J. T. McMillan. We are at Otter Cove in Acadia National Park with the beast of Hurricane Bonnie stalled five hundred miles off Hatteras, sending fifteen foot swells into the Gulf of Maine, as it has for three days straight. He takes off, drops. He carves into a hasty, almost graceful turn, avoiding the chunk of ledge and then banking off the wall and speeding down the curl, spilling into the channel after another nice ride.

Memory is more than image, of course, more, too, than taste and smell and feeling. It is sounds of peeling surf and sounds of names— Bomba's, Wrightsville, Higgins Beach, Small Point, Hurricane Bonnie, Hurricane Fran. Because we face long periods of nearly flat ocean, East Coast surfers are perhaps more dependent on storms than waveriders elsewhere. I remember a nor'easter in Nova Scotia, conifers bending on that point near Lawrencetown where we'd set up camp. Ted Gilbert,

Andrew Herring, and I—college kids on fall break—are in the water the day after the storm. It is cold, but the locals are friendly, generous with the long, strong waves.

The first surfboard I rode belonged to Alex's father. My uncle and namesake Thorpe is my dad's younger brother. Like my father, he is cordial and outgoing such that you're not sure who he is. There are worse traits than elegance. You won't find two more generous, enigmatic people. In my youth, we made summer beach trips for a week or two at my grandparents' place in Jersey. Each year, I eyed Uncle Thorpe's graceful La Jolla Surf Systems single fin collecting dust in the corner of the garage near the fishing rods. Around age twelve, I started to flail on it in the waves in front of the convent at 111th Street—*Villa Maria by the Sea*. God Beach, Uncle Thorpe called it; it had been his hallowed surf ground before back trouble prohibited him from riding the board. Women in their habits often walked the beach. My little brother James referred to them quite innocently as penguins when he was a tyke. It took time, humiliation, and a few scars for me to gain proficiency on that board. Snippets of advice from other surfers made all the difference. "Move up on your board when you're stroking for a wave," a guy told me after another nasty nosedive. It helped.

I stroke four or five times. The wave, last of the set and a good one, approaches, sculpts itself and then takes me as though I were bait. It has a left-forming curl and I dig the rail to carve that direction once I stand. There is a gray wall ahead of me now and a gentle trough forming. The wave is soft and slow. I shuffle back on my board to stall it, to try not to get too far ahead of the shoulder. Now I shuffle forward and trim the board to generate speed for a bottom turn. If it sounds dramatic, it is. Yet it isn't. I slide the board for the shoulder and set a rail to turn it back to the trough, but I have come too far. The wave kisses me goodbye.

My favorite part of surfing might be the paddling out, and not because picking your way through and under the waves is a condensed version of life, which it is. There are times when you don't make it out and then there are times when you think you'll never make it, when wave after wave pushes you beachward, and you dive and dive, and your arms burn and your chest, and your sinuses are all salt with another nasal douche, and then you emerge from a dive, the energy of the wave lingering, having passed through as much as over you, and there is an opening, a lane of calm water extending beyond the impact zone, and you take it, and, yes, though you may be coughing, it is easy again, and you breathe and you stroke calmly and rest. That is all well and good, but I like paddling out because the reward is great—you get away from the mainland, and, best of all, you get to catch a wave. After all the hoopla, surfing is simply a glorious escape.

The surf isn't bad today. To have waves at all in South Carolina is lucky. Waist-high sets, maybe a few waves at the chest—they approach from the north. If the forecasters are correct, the tropical storm will threaten the Outer Banks tonight. Sea oats sway in the breeze. Clouds billow like marshmallow puff above the palmettos and crepe myrtles that picket the beach houses.

We ride one after another. The waves are long and hold their shape well. The southerly rip seems to be diminishing a bit. The walls are smooth with a light offshore wind. Alex is after another one. No longer my little cousin politely munching his Thanksgiving dinner or glimpsed, like a shadow, as he's whisked to or from football or hockey practice—he's eighteen now and headed to college on a lacrosse scholarship. He's more than a cross between Liam Nielson and Russell Crowe, and to say there's as much antelope in him as bluefish and bear is reductionist too, but that's what comes to mind as I watch him crouch to race the curl of another playful juicer. It tickles me in all the right places; watching my cousin surf is as fun as riding the waves.

I see my family, small figures on the beach. Though I like to think otherwise, we are not unusual. We are an edgy, fragile lot, as dependent as our independent facades are honed. Love and despair course through our motions, the disagreements spoken or not. Nobody mentions politics for long anyway. We laugh at each other. We can make each other cry without meaning to or knowing it. If it is brutal, it is tender, too. We need beach trips, the sun to bleach us out, the salt to mend our sores and season our tenderness. The relaxation of rest and bracing activity stills our bonds, both calls and quiets us to the beauty in one another.

It is afternoon. It has felt like afternoon all day. People walk on what's left of the beach, a few bending now and then to gather shells. The storm makes for a flood tide. A sudden rain slackens to drizzle and then is gone. I sit on my board, a 1960s Cutlass longboard, the deck misshapen from water damage. The board, great for smallish waves, was a gift from Ted Gilbert with whom I cofounded the surf club at a small college in Maine, a harebrained endeavor if there ever was one—we weren't even close to a club, much less a society or gang or ministry. Ted found the board rotting under a house in Wellfleet on Cape Cod in 1993. Fiberglass patches dot the board's deck. It weighs nearly thirty pounds and requires a good bit of shuffle up and back for it to turn. It is too heavy for a leash and the skeg is triangular, solid and similar in shape to a shark's fin. Though I don't ride it as much as I used to, once or twice a year now, I am always learning new ways to love and hate it—especially as it leans against the shed at our home far inland, as it does most of the year, shade for crickets and spiders and slugs.

Alex and I visit briefly with one another as we sit beyond the breakers. It is hard to say much in the ocean. My cousin, for instance, doesn't say, "You and Kirsten, you've bought a farm."

And I don't say, "Yes."

And he doesn't say, "How big?"

And I don't say, "Eighteen acres."

And he doesn't say, "You're not a farmer."

And I don't say, "Yes."

And he doesn't say, "Why?"

And I don't say, "It's beautiful there."

I don't say, "It felt right."

I don't say, "It was a good deal." Though it was a good deal.

And he doesn't say, "Are you going to grow your own food?"

And I don't say, "Yep."

And he doesn't ask, "What are you going to do for fun?"

And I don't tell him about the rivers and woods and plants and trees and critters, or how the mist rises off the Upper James many mornings like a second dawn, sound of the coal trains thicker with that moisture.

And I don't say, "I got this job teaching at a university, a good job. And if I don't get away from all that and get my hands dirty and get my face licked by river waves and see my daughter coming back from the barn with a pail of goat milk and see my wife in the garden, wearing one of those Jackie O-Goodwill numbers, the wind blowing her hair, tangling it among the sunflowers, and if I don't dig in the soil and try to learn something from that place and the people of that place, and cut some wood and build some sheds and butcher some deer and hogs and hook some trout and run some trails, that good job's going to swallow me up."

And he doesn't say, "Something swallowed you up a long time back."

We are on surfboards in the ocean, so talk is technical, of equipment, weather, and the demeanor of the waves. Our words lose their meaning as soon as we utter them, and maybe we say them just to feel the pleasure of that happening. Mostly, we speak through our motions, our choice and style of rides, and the way we watch the horizon. We communicate with all the innocence of two toddlers in a playpen, though there is something of hunters in our bearing as well—the wait, the stalk, the chase. Still, the beach houses are not far away, the trappings of modern life almost as close as the epoxy, fiberglass, and foam in the boards we ride.

A good wave approaches. Four pelicans soar a few feet above the wave's ridge. I look at Alex to see if he's going for it. We have been taking turns with wave choice. Not looking at me, he says, "Let's ride it together."

"Yeah, dude," I say, promptly lying on the board, stroking beachward. There is a long shoulder to the right. Once on my feet, I glance at Alex. He stands two arm's lengths away. He's locked into the wave with all the amped attention of those cars on the electric racetrack I had as a kid. Riding a wave is not often a social event, less often a family affair, and maybe this explains why the ride feels slower than normal. Everything is quite loud and quiet, too. With telling smiles and nods of our heads, we both put our hands behind our rumps and arch our spines backwards in matching, goofy poses. It isn't entirely inappropriate.

Boogie Water

Our rain gauge, a simple plastic version, stands stuck in the soil of a pot frizzy with rosemary. When, a few Saturdays ago, I woke early to heavy rain after an evening and night of the same and saw the water in the gauge had reached the three-inch mark, all the rivers in me turned green. I did a little jig. Kirsten, used to these fits, rolled over with passion and faced the wall. I squiggled into clothes like somebody in a fire drill and then set off to check the level of the creek down the road.

We moved to this nook of the Upper James River watershed a few months ago in July. It rained the first day we were here. That was the last rain. An inch and a half fell in an hour—a real gusher. The thunderstorm would have been a nice break from moving furniture and boxes had water not poured through the ceiling vent in the kitchen. As I stood entranced, Kirsten had the sense to move a trash can under the spout. Several gallons later, the rain stopped and then the leak. We laughed but it was forced. I spent some time the next day on the roof, caulk gun in hand, gooing the cracks where someone had smeared the asphalt shingles with the aluminum-based coating made for metal roofs. The view of our land and the lands beyond was good from that height. I looked and soaked up what was there and all that we hoped to make of what was there. It was as frightening as it was wonderful. We had a lot of work on our hands. I told myself that we were right on schedule but only half believed it.

So Jennings Creek was boisterous that three-inch morning, running dark and full where since midsummer it had been a clear trickle you could cross most anywhere without wetting your shoes. I was thrilled. To see a creek in flood that you've known exclusively in low water is like seeing a band play live after you've fallen in love—I mean come to need—hearing their music on the stereo. Yes, it was Saturday, the creek was cranking, the kitchen was dry, and there were no commitments that couldn't be put on hold. Things were just right.

Jennings drains the west slope of the Blue Ridge opposite Peaks of Otter. Three healthy tributaries—McFalls, Middle, and North creeks—support its flow. From its sources near the Blue Ridge Parkway, Jennings drains around twenty square miles, most of it National Forest land. It's an area of rugged ridges and slopes pocked with cliffs and hardwoods, laurel and pines. There's something very intestinal about the topography, especially when you study the contour lines on a map of the area.

I discovered Jennings Creek in our ragged Delorme Virginia Atlas & Gazetteer shortly after accepting a job in the Roanoke Valley last spring. When I drove up from our home in the North Carolina Piedmont to fill out paperwork for the new employer and to scout for a place to live, I camped on a beach just above North Creek's confluence with Jennings. After a nice morning stalking rainbows with a frayed deer hair caddis, I saw a For Sale sign as I drove out Arcadia Road. One thing led to another in the convoluted way things do when you're buying a farmstead and relocating a family and starting a new job. But here we are.

It is a mile and a half from the house down Arcadia Road to the bridge over the James River. The James was higher than I'd seen it as I putted across the bridge, boat and bike in the four-cylinder's bed. The water looked to be slower with no rocks visible and the mist and the rain hanging over it. I stashed my bike in the cedars near a bridge piling. In such weather, you never know who might be around—this area and its people are not the fair-weather type.

The drive from there was fun. Butterflies and moths burst from their cocoons against my ribs with every turn of the crankshaft. I was half watching the road through the smears of bad wipers and half watching the creek. There was more than enough water. You could feel the energy of the churning, of the velocity and friction, even in the truck. At a pool where we'd been swimming a few times, there was a massive wave train, with reactionary haystacks pulsing from where the water met its match in a school bus-sized, upturned bed of quartz-conglomerate sandstone, lichen-riddled and dripping madly. I had a vision of the Appalachians eons before—before Appalachians was a word—the volcanic activity, the plates colliding. Scale does something to the imagination, and whatever it does, I like it.

I parked on a gravel spur several miles up Jennings Creek from the James. This was roughly six miles from our driveway. The Appalachian Trail crossing was a bridge or two downstream and the confluence of Jennings and McFalls Creeks a bridge above. It was still dumping rain, but the air was warm for October. I don't like to paddle alone on a river or creek when I am running it for the first time, but it is best to do so when the air is warm and the water too. A wool riverdriver shirt under a now vintage sprayjacket with shorts and the usual helmet, lifejacket, sprayskirt, and paddle ensemble seemed like enough.

I hadn't paddled since the prior spring when we were living in the North Carolina Piedmont. There are a couple of runs in that area that almost compare with Jennings Creek, but they are neither as remote nor wild nor the rapids as continuous. So it took a little deep breathing and stuff—ferries and braces and torso twists in the swift pool by the road— to start feeling close to at home in the boat again, an old Dagger Cascade decked canoe.

Before I headed downstream, I remembered my friend Holwood and his advice to think like a Dixie Cup as he led me down Overflow Creek twelve years ago, him in a Corsica and me in a Slasher C-1. I thought of another buddy, Forrest, who showed me down the Watauga and Tellico and Chauga, and who once paddled the Green Narrows in an old, slicey Perception with no lifejacket or helmet because he'd left them at the rafting outpost where we lived and worked. It was comforting to feel the examples of these folks in me.

I like to pay homage to those with whom I've shared the pleasures of wild water before going downriver. Part of me is conscious about it, another isn't. To say that paddling, like many gravity sports, has a tribal aspect to it is sort of corny, but that has been my experience. So Chaz Zartman, Pat Hinchey, Orea Roussis, Ron Brabson, Chip Hogan, Snuffy Hall, Forrest Chewning, Lance Ellis, Steve Higgins, Mike

Woodruff, Jeanine Cheek, Hobbit Hawes, and others were all there, too, a surrogate family; and our river trips in North Carolina, West Virginia, Maine, Idaho, were there—many places, many good people, many trips. All of this ran through my head like so many baitfish and bad swims and good drops and shuttle drives and moldy polypro and sweet runs under a full moon—a kind of prayer, rave-like and fine.

But in the meantime there is the water, there is its motion, its music, its erosion, its reek. Jennings Creek was a flush. All but the largest boulders were buried. It sounded like a busy airport, and it smelled like when you're digging the twentieth posthole of the day, only cleaner than that and wetter.

The lines, the routes, were clear. At twenty feet across, there wasn't much room for messing around. But paddling is all about messing around. I should mention the wood. Trees, or parts of trees—hemlocks, mostly—lay across the creek in too many places. Limbs and stumps drifted, toppling or not, in the channels. Some of them hung on nearly submerged boulders. The loss of hemlock trees to the woolly adelgid aphid is one of the great tragedies of our time. It is quaint to raise such an issue in this context, but life's like that—the trivial and the tragic often share the same bed.

So I watched for eddies like I watched for trees. It might be healthy to round a bend or crest a horizon line to find a tree fallen riverwide and no eddy to catch. I don't know. It does something to your bladder. It does something to your eyes, too. Within the first four miles, I scouted three blind drops and twice I portaged due to wood.

The water was rising. The waves and holes were thick and tall. The boat rocked and lifted me from trough to peak or punched the maw, drenching my torso and often my face. Did I mention I was smiling? I was smiling. Traffic's "Mr. Fantasy" came to mind, and I sang it out loud. The water was singing louder. The rain needed a time-out, it was so totally careless and intense. I'd like to be ecologically correct and name the varieties of trees and mosses and shrubs that were part of the little rock opera, but the way I noticed them—blur, detail, blur—seems more related to velocity than Linnaeus.

River runners call such a run boogie water. You know that even though it's flooding and you're alone, it is class III, that there are no cataracts, nothing you can't handle or stop to scout. Of course a flip and sudden blow to the head or brain hemorrhage or stroke is always an option, but we don't go there unless it happens and then we go elsewhere.

One's first time paddling a creek has a wondrous quality. All good, wild running waterways, like their counterparts in art and in life, deserve repeated readings. I liked knowing this was the beginning of a long relationship with Jennings Creek and its tributaries. Yet I also felt a little sad that the mystery of its initial discovery, this virgin run, was passing with every breath and drop of rain.

It was still raining later that night, by the way. I remember sitting on the porch in the electric dark. Kirsten was on the phone, our daughter Sophie in bed. Six-week-old hens were scrambling for bugs attracted to their chicken wire motel by the warmth and shine of the heat lamp. A pumpkin, potted plants, the distant rumble of Interstate 81, and drip-sounds—gravel, gutter, metal trashcan lid. Not a bad place to unwind. But no paddler I know unwinds when the level in the rain gauge approaches the five-inch line. The mind cartwheels from one little adventure to another—rivers run and rivers not yet run. I was looking forward to plunging through the boulders of North Creek. I wanted to check out the creeks that run into the James just to the north of us, as well the creeks in nearby Craig, Rockbridge, Amherst, and Nelson counties.

I've been lucky in thirty-four years to know several rivers well. It all started as a kid growing up an easy bike ride to the Chattahoochee River in Atlanta. Then there was the Chattooga, where I guided rafts and paddled obsessively from eighteen to twenty-three. I came to know the Upper Cathance River near Topsham when we lived in Maine, and the Youghiogheny and Yellow Breeches when we lived in Pennsylvania, the

Moormans and Rivanna and James when we lived in Virginia the first time (in Crozet), and the Eno and Haw and New Hope Creek around Hillsborough in North Carolina. But by getting to know a river, I don't mean just paddling. I mean having a relationship with its tributaries and its woods and its people. I mean fishing, camping, hiking, loving, swimming, sleeping, hurting, eating, and growing in that watershed.

I already looked forward to giving certain rapids names as much as I did to leaving them totally anonymous. I was pleased to have Jennings Creek to myself, happy that it is not a mark on most paddlers' maps. Paddling in crowds is problematic, but paddling alone is not my first choice either. I hoped to find a river-running buddy, a local, to run Jennings along with me, its tributaries and several other creeks in the area. Paddling is not a spectator sport in the traditional sense. In order to watch the action, you have to be out there. I wanted someone to watch. And not just out of vanity and safety, I wanted someone to watch me. You learn things about a river or creek by watching someone else run it that you can't by paddling it alone, just as you learn about how you react to water when somebody's watching you.

There was also a vague sense that my daughter, Sophie, then seven, might share a passion for running rivers as well. Already she was cutting her teeth in Jennings Creek. In the weeks prior to the rain, we'd been exploring swimming and fishing holes and sliding rocks both on Jennings and North creeks, in places that looked very different today. We'd been gathering rocks, too, for structure in the garden and for delight. Not a shelf in the house was spared of greenstone, sandstone, granite, etc., their shapes sensuous and good.

So the water was high and the rain was even more inspired, and when I passed the inflow of Middle Creek, things began to feel a little crazy. Traffic gave way to The Ramones. Words were busting off my lip before I knew it was "Beat on the Brat." I remember one drop with a two-move approach—scram left, launch a slot, then scramble right— followed by a boil-licked flume of a runout, only the runout spit you into a bend that screamed through three boat-stopper hydraulics, the latter two of which stood like toothy, rabid grins on either side of a cement bridge.

Both North and Middle Creek had dumped their loads into Jennings now, and the water had cars stopped on the road, people checking the level to see how much till the bridge was under. Probably they were a little surprised to see a guy in a yellow helmet and red lifejacket wearing a big, blue Tupperware-like cigar under him, splashing through the waves. They probably couldn't tell or care that I am as cheap a paddling geek as you'll meet. I haven't bought a piece of gear in nearly a decade. My salvaged Wildwater LTD plastic rafter's paddle is nearly as unhip as the clunker canoeist helmet Curtis Roth gave me and even less cool than the long, big volume boat I scored used for two-hundred bucks back in the day.

I was a little more uncomfortable now than I like to feel. It was perfect. Things were happening fast, but probably not as fast as they seemed. Eddies were few and in the limbs. Now and then, out of the sycamore, hemlock, and ironwood, wood ducks shot out, vagrant lovelies, and sometimes a kingfisher or heron or two, and it was all vivid and vague and so beautiful.

I portaged the falls near the heart of Arcadia, a hamlet marked by an abandoned mercantile Baptist Church and stone monolith of an iron furnace, dilapidating and elegant with vines. Luckily, I looked back in time to see the barbed-wire cattle fence spanning the river below the last bridge before the James. I made it to the bank, which was gone, and grabbed a limb. I walked then, too. Portages are as good a way to see the river as any, especially when there are at least three No Trespassing signs in view.

As Jennings delivered me into the James, one of the Olivia Newton John songs from *Grease* was in my head. Gone was Traffic and The Ramones. I was at the end of the boogie water and everything was ooh, ooh, ooh. The James was over its bluffs, making the trees look like the necks of so many river monsters. I guessed at the fate of the pawpaws we'd bypassed in our foraging trip of a few days prior—catfish food perhaps. The water was moving slow and thick, and I was starting to relax as I came in sight of the bridge.

The rain seemed less intense until I stashed the boat in the cedars and started pedaling the bike up the road along the creek. It was hard to ride with your eyes open at all. But rain is rain and paddling is paddling and getting back to your truck is part of the deal. You see, the end of the rain brought Norma Friend, the woman from whom we bought the house, by our place a couple of evenings later.

"Did y'all have any water in your kitchen with the rain?" she asked. We told her the deal with the rain the day with the boxes everywhere, and Kirsten bringing the trashcan under the ceiling vent-turned-spout, and then gooing the roof.

"It's been weighing on me," she continued. "Weighing on my conscience. That real estate lady made me promise I wouldn't say anything about the leak." I looked at Kirsten then. Her face seemed to have spawned another sun.

"I want you all to take this," Norma said. "To fix the roof." She'd put her hand in Kirsten's and there was a hundred dollar bill in it and then in Kirsten's hand, followed by the requisite protests from each party. "No, we can't take that." "But you have to. I insist." And so on. I glanced at the rain gauge as the melee continued. It had crested near the five-and-a-half mark. I vowed not to empty it for another few days.

The Windfall

It was a Wednesday now, late in October. Kirsten came in to the kitchen, lovely and intent as ever. She had been at the barn. "I talked with Donnie yesterday," she said. "He wants to make apple butter this weekend."

I stopped fiddling with the coffee on the stove and looked out the window. The sun was nearly up. There was a hawk cruising a thermal over the near ridge. Early light on the hills shone like the root of all language.

"What do you think," she said. "You always liked apple butter."

I poured some coffee. "Not sure," I said.

A couple minutes passed, thick ones. I saw Sophie through the window. She was climbing the log wall of the barn. "He wants to do it here," Kirsten said.

I was running down a list in my head. There was a lot we wanted to do and equally much needed to be done that would feel good to do, especially once it was done.

"How much?" I asked. "How much butter does he want to make?"

"A good bit," Kirsten said.

We gathered on Thursday afternoon. We gathered blowdowns, plucked them from the ground. No experts on apples, we were surprised by how round the Staymans were. And their color inspired a haunted kind of thirst.

It was a windy day, October, cool air from the northwest, the third day of that wind and cold. There were bees, yellow jackets and honeybees. They moved sloppily, drunk on apple. They would have been more drunk were the air warmer. I was delighted with the bees, delighted with the whole frenetic, repetitive process.

We filled old spackle buckets, white and splotched and still attached to their handles. We knelt and squatted or else bent at the waist and snatched apple after, well, make your hand like you were a bear and had claws and were excited—that's how round they were, that's how they fit in your hand.

You take a Stayman and hold it close to your face and you're looking into a supernova at the speed of dark divided by light. Or else you're looking like a lunatic, staring close-up at an apple, of all things. But maybe you're looking at a cross section of blood the moment it knows the world outside the body. Like a Stayman couldn't decide between being green and blue but red was lobbying hard.

The Stayman apple is part of a story with subplots as kaleidoscopic as the fruit's color and taste. Apples, of course, are not native to America. They are believed to have originated in the forests of the Tien Shan mountain range, at the border of China, Kazakhstan, and Kyrgyszstan. By medieval times, apples were widespread in Europe, but even then they were viewed with suspicion, associated biblically with the Fall and thought to cause upset stomachs and ill humors.

I was thinking of none of this as we picked, at least not consciously. If you'd come along and said that each apple seed is a hive of genetic heritage and variety, that one seed can contain as many as eighty-five chromosomes, that almost every tree grown from seed is a new variety, and that its fruit may be nothing like its mother tree, I would have said, "Neat, give us a hand, and watch out for the bees." And if you'd continued telling me that Staymans are a variety of Winesap, that they were discovered in 1866, in Leavenworth, Kansas, by Dr. J. Stayman, and that they've been grafted and cultivated ever since for their mildly tart, spicy taste and muted red, striped, and mottled color, I would have thought, the wind has more to say about apples than you or Google ever will.

The trees, their canopies, were as wide as, if not wider than, they were tall. As we moved beneath them, it was soon very apparent that trees' shapes were as variable as the apples' hue patterns and variations of round. It had to do with sun and pruning, but more to do with something else, something elusive and true. Certain trees were easier to move beneath than others, in other words. Sophie, who was seven then, volunteered to work under trees with low branches. The bark, knobby and plated, was gray like a foggy window. And splotched with darker grays and blacks. Somebody had cut the grass recently, which made fetching the fallen fruit easier.

We worked like we were about to get caught, like the wind, blowing hard, was about to blow them, or us, all away. We reached and we grabbed and we squeezed, checking for soft spots. We bucketed two for every three. Working outside in a cold, hard wind fosters a kind of interiority that, when it rubs against what you're doing externally, physically, creates a pleasant, slightly electric friction and weariness. They were good apples, good trees. The ground under some trees was more populated with apples than others. Like a hailstorm. Like scree. Like apples in an orchard on a day of wind after a night and prior day and night of wind.

We took breaks. We turned over empty buckets and sat on them and couldn't even eat a whole apple, they were so much in our hands and eyes. We didn't know how many we had, but we knew we had a lot, so we gleaned even more. I felt greedy and ecstatic for a while, and then tired, grateful, happy. We filled buckets. We hauled buckets. Sometimes we lay in the grass and watched the clouds and breathed the apple air. And then we started gathering again.

It wasn't long, three or four hours, give or take, before we had the apples on the scale, one bucket at a time. The bill for three hundred and seventy-four pounds of apples, at eighteen cents a pound, ran close to seventy dollars. We settled up with the orchard keeper, who, with red and splotchy cheeks, resembled a Stayman herself. After a brief walk around the store, checking out the apple products and appley folk art, we hit the road, our old pickup less giddy with the apple weight than we were from filling it.

Where we live, between the Shenandoah and Roanoke valleys, near Interstate 81 and the town of Buchanan, Virginia, the James River leaves the Alleghenies at Purgatory Mountain, bends and flows north a ways before turning east again, joining spirits with the Maury River to cut through the Blue Ridge at Balcony Falls. It is a place of transition and confluences and very old mountains—there's a kind of ennobling erosion at work geologically, economically, and socially. In general, people do what they can to make ends meet, and they continue to prefer both the best and worst of the old ways over the new.

It is not a good place if you need yoga classes, iced mocha chai pumpkin pie lattes, high-speed internet, or the like. But if you favor woods and rivers, pastures and creeks, then you're in the right spot. There's a lot of National Forest, and the area is just far enough from both Roanoke and Lexington that its open country has not yet succumbed to those rank colonies of meadow mansions, nor to the seven-figure horse farms whose owners spend much of the year somewhere else. Our new friend Donnie Lewis, it turns out, was born in a house they tore down to build Interstate 81 in the '50s. His family then moved to a chunk of hillside further up a limestone drainage that drops—dramatically at times—to the James.

Though he's worked a ton of jobs, among them paving roads and building houses, fixing cars, selling firewood, and gathering hellgrammites, and even for a while cutting red oak shingles at the pioneer lifeway exhibit at Peaks of Otter—Donnie makes a living hauling junk nowadays. Junking, he calls it. He moves it in his truck, a '71 International, lifts it on the flatbed with a pump jack and boom or else his own hands and back and legs. Old woodstoves, trailers, farm equipment, lamps, magazines, beer cans—whatever people want rid of, old stuff or new, the new-but-cheap, built-to-break goods of the global economy—he moves it in his truck to the scrapyard in Montvale.

Some things he keeps. Like the 50-gallon copper kettle. "This was half in the ground when I found it on a junking job," he told us. "This was trash." It was Thursday. Donnie had brought the kettle from the machine shop in Natural Bridge. He'd seen our pile of apples and was excited as oil in a hot skillet. "You see how they patched it?" he asked, pointing to the kettle. But it was a statement.

We saw. His buddy at the shop had riveted copper sheets as patches where the rough spots had been. It was good, clean work. Donnie would settle for nothing less. "I hope it holds butter," he said.

"I like the legs," Sophie offered. They'd welded the kettle to a ring of steel and to that ring three steel legs. Tempered steel, black as the kettle would be after fifteen hours on the fire.

"This thing is old," Donnie mused. For a moment, I wondered about his father, whom I had never met. It was hard to tell who Donnie was talking to right then. "Real old," Donnie continued. The way he said it made you think he'd imagined being there, making the pot, hammering and shaping the copper. Imagined each stage of the process, from obtaining the copper to the design to the tools and how you'd hold the tools. The way a person thinks who, day or night, will cheerfully drop what he's doing to help you, who, each winter—gratefully, graciously—butchers several hogs, and each spring resurrects the riding mowers salvaged from junking and sells them, like he sells and gifts and barters the pork, for a fair price to neighbors and friends and friends of neighbors and friends.

"Yeah," Donnie continued. "It looks tarnished now, but wait till the butter comes out. The acids in the apple will have it shining like a new penny."

Kirsten laughed her wild, elegant laughter. "Look at the stir stick," she said.

Donnie said, "A trivy." It looked like a modernist's rendition of a praying mantis. I thought of Cracker Barrel restaurants along the highway, where such tools live on the wall as decorations, totems for travelers in highway dreamtime. "Called a trivy." It was new. There were still blade marks from the saw and dust on the salvaged pine. Donnie had made it over the last week, taken the design off a broken one salvaged from a shed on a junking job. I wanted to ask whose shed, but Donnie's quiet about his customers. He respects people too much and is too tidy, too thrifty, to give away information so private as to what a man or woman stores in basement, attic, shed, or barn. "You learn about people when you haul their junk," Donnie's said many times. "Things you wanted to know and also a lot you don't want to know."

The trivy was eight feet long and stout. A two-foot length with a groove cut out of the middle was fastened to the end that went in the pot. He called it the paddle, not because it resembled a paddle but because it paddled through the butter. "It doesn't smell like apples yet," Donnie said. "But after Saturday it'll never not smell like apples again," he continued. "No matter how much you wash it."

Five feet from the paddle end, there was a piece of wood that crossed the main shaft in the fashion of a lowercase "t." The stirrer held an end of this with one hand and the back of the shaft with the other hand. The design allowed for two folks to stir together, a feature conducive to the work's social nature. Both the paddle and handle were fastened with steel braces, ninety-degree braces from the same machine shop as patched the kettle. It was a large, imposing tool, yet there was a simplicity to the design that suggested it'd be efficient to work after warming up to it.

By eight Friday evening, after an hour of working the apples, there was an air of ferocious levity about the kitchen where we sat, four of us alternately peeling and slicing and every now and then sharpening knives. It helped to feel a bit of anger for getting into such an ordeal—I peeled faster that way. No matter how many different types of music the stereo played, none of it sounded good to me. Silence wasn't doing the trick either. The smell of Stayman, so delightful while picking, was almost oppressive. When we stood, if we stood, we waded between buckets and bags—whole apples, peeled skins, cut apples. It was a massacre of fruit, scalped and cored. I felt far too sober for such work. But maybe not. We each cut our fingers at least once. Among the various supplies garnered for our gig—spices, Mason Jars, lids, food—nobody thought to bring Band-Aids. Luckily we had duct tape; bloody apples wouldn't do.

We soon stopped worrying about peeling thin, about seeing the light through the peels. We weren't entirely wasteful either. The peels were some in our compost the next day and some in our chicken yard. I asked Donnie if he wanted to give some to his hogs.

"No."

"Why not?"

"It gives them the runs. Their feed runs right through them, defeats the purpose. The point's to fatten them up."

Time trickled to swipes of the blade. We peeled and cored and sliced. There were many pounds peeled and many, many pounds not peeled. I was too tired not to fret. It was perfect. I was glad my daughter was staying up past midnight, working with us. She's always looked up to Donnie, and not just because it's like he's stepped out of her Laura Ingalls Wilder books. Tonight he was outdoing the books. She was living her own chapter. We were in the project together, sure, but it was Donnie's show. We could have been doing it without him, maybe, but we wouldn't have been.

As with any repetitive handiwork, we grew more efficient to a point and then less so. By one in the morning, with a lot of apples still to peel, my learning curve dipped. I started throwing peels in the wrong bucket. Donnie's daughter and two friends had showed up past midnight and they'd provided a boost of energy, if not accuracy, for us all.

Evelyn and her pals left around 1:30. We peeled until 3 A.M. Kirsten's hands were fully purple now from a reaction with the apple acids. Hot water and soap didn't help. Donnie had mentioned a pal of his turning purple to the elbows on a previous buttering mission. Apparently Kirsten and this guy had similar chemistry.

If the rest of us weren't purple, we were sticky with juice. We were doused with apple essence. The whole kitchen reeked. The floor was sticky. Pants were sticky, arms and shirts, chairs and counters and tables. Even our laugh and talk and delirium was sticking together. Ants from a long way off must have caught a whiff; we'd never seen so many on our counters and floors.

"When was the last time you did this?" I asked Donnie at some point late, real late.

"Ten or twelve years back," he said.

"A good batch?"

"Didn't even get a pint jar of the stuff," said him. "Don't know how it tasted."

"What?"

He muttered something about a big party and moonshine and giving it all away. I thought, we're doing this with the right person.

A thin sliver of orange lay on the eastern ridges when we started the fire later that morning. The wind was still feisty, on and off, but mostly on. And from no particular direction. We'd humped the kettle to the fire, situated its three legs just so. We were set up thirty yards from the front porch, between the maples, one of which still had a fair number of yellow leaves, some rattling, others riding the wind. I'd split a heap of red oak and the pile was not too close by. There was a table for snacks and other equipment. We hauled the bins of shaved and cored and sliced apples and added a couple of pounds as well as some grape juice to the kettle, then started taking turns with the trivy.

It was all butter from there. We stirred. We chatted. We looked at the hills and the trees and the fields, at the crows and buzzards and hawks and dog and sun. We looked at each other, too, looked like fellow convicts guilty of innocent, perhaps noble crimes. Mostly we watched the apples and the paddle moving them around. You watched the smoke too. You watched it swirl and change and move. You rocked your hips as you worked the trivy, tried to be easy about it.

It was drowsy work. I stared from woods to barn to garden. There were still cherry tomatoes on the vines. Two weeks prior, Kirsten and Sophie had harvested a bushel of sweet potatoes. The beds had a burnished glow to them, deeply green, the way gardens look after a couple of light frosts, their last hurrah before the hard freezes to come. Drowsy work is indiscriminate in terms of where your thoughts go; staring down the handle of the trivy, at the kettle, the sliced Stayman turning mushy there, I thought of mosh pits I'd been a body among. I remembered a Ramones concert at Centerstage in Atlanta when I was a teenager, how when the hastily constructed barrier between floor and stage broke, the nail-studded two by fours inspired a near riot. Crawling up and out of the crowd on heads and shoulders, I'd lost one of my cherished checkerboard hi-top Vans. What other genetic information, memory-traces and whatnot, the apples and stirring sparked was no small amount, though it is lost to me now.

Each time the fresh apples softened such that the stirring—twice around and once across—grew easy, Donnie added more. We were taking ten-minute turns on the trivy—sometimes longer, sometimes shorter. It went on, this dance, the apples in charge, the fire, the smoke, the stirring.

The kettle blackened. We banked the fire. With the wind as it was, and even with the windbreaks we'd fashioned around the pit, the fire was tearing through the wood. There was smoke off the fire and smoke off the kettle. What else can be said? It went on like this. The day became a season. And though the process was at heart a similar sort of reduction, it differed from making our weekly stocks and broths; we had to be present now, active. There was no leaving these apples in the Crock-Pot for a couple of days.

By two in the afternoon, all the apples were in the kettle. By four, I knew our bodies would be butter before the apples. Mine already was. I looked at Donnie. Everything about him said there was no place he'd rather be. The man was a lot like his kettle, it seemed—copper-solid, 50 gallons of capacity.

New friends and neighbors had stopped by to help, starting in the afternoon. Some of them seemed to do it out of duty and appeared pensive, solemn, as though they were visiting a grave. I suppose there was a part of them mourning a process that used to be as regular as the falling of the leaves. The younger families were more jazzed by the scene. It was festive. There were kids running around. The wind, which would blow gusty all day and into the night, pushed hard on us all. Butch and Mare from down the road had turned out their horses on our pasture, and the filly mares were acting especially frisky with the wind, galloping now and then around the old, wizened catalpa. There was chitchat, music, gossip, stories. Near dusk, Donnie started tasting the butter with a wooden spoon. Our visitors had gone home by then. "We got a long while yet," he kept saying well into dark. "It's got to come down another couple inches."

Late that night, Donnie started adding sugar. Later than that, he added—carefully, mysteriously—drops of cinnamon and clove condensed in oil. Near the end, the butter only moved off the wooden spoon when you flicked it hard enough. It was as thick as we were tired and satisfied. Close to midnight, I looked at the fire from the table where we were ladling butter into Masons and screwing caps onto those jars. By the light of the shop-lamp's single bulb, I could see we'd worn a circle in the grass eight feet around the fire and pot. It was our orbit, our stirring orbit. We'd moved to avoid the smoke. We'd moved for another view. We'd moved because the apples moved and the motion boiled us too, cooked us down. A few months later, we'd be smearing the butter on a pork roast and feel that moving start up again. We'd feel it, too—the soil, the fire, the living—when handing pints and quarts to coworkers and folks in town. It would never really go away.

Cold Mist Burning

It was close to six in the morning on the last Saturday of duck season and my daughter was wailing. She stood by the chopping block, choking on tears, telling me her bunny was dying.

I looked at Sophie and was entranced by what seven years of life had made—the clarity in her eyes, the stoutness of her frame, the wavy hair and bed head. I normally didn't mind the polyester-stocking pajamas she wore, a gift from my mother, but now they looked frumpy to me, toxic.

"Where's Mama?" she asked, dodging my effort at a hug. Her syllables were pulpy with sobs. I heard the coffee boiling over, sizzling on the electric burner. There was a soft light starting out the window. The refrigerator hummed. Sophie was rounding the corner by the woodstove before I whispered loudly, "Still asleep."

The bunny had been having stomach problems for a week. Her belly gurgled every time you held her. It felt like something was percolating in there. We figured it would pass, that her stool would harden and stomach settle, but we didn't know. Soon we'd have a ragged, elaborate network of cages fluffy and desolate with meat rabbits, but at this point we raised chickens and ducks for eggs and kept a few sheep and goats and a mule; Bonnie, as Sophie named her, was our first rabbit, a pet. We weren't even sure if she was female.

My in-laws had found the bunny two weeks prior at a pet store in North Carolina, where we'd celebrated Christmas with them. They'd kept her a secret until late that morning, when Sophie thought all the gifts had been opened. She'd been immersed in making a picture with a new tin of pastels when they brought the bunny in her hutch from the basement, and then—I swear—my daughter's eyes were two planets very close to the sun.

Sophie was snuggling up to her mama as I rounded the corner. This was Sophie's way of waking her, and I didn't want to interfere—she needed her mama now. It mulched a bed in me to watch as Kirsten stirred and then awoke with prompt attentiveness to what our daughter was saying.

We took turns holding the sick bunny. She was a lump of softness in our arms, her fur milky-white with ocher splotches. The slow leak of time on winter Saturdays felt even slower that morning. The small animal didn't look afraid, but she didn't look confident either. Her eyes appeared more empty than glassy. After a half hour or so, I saw that my plans had changed, and I set to frying eggs while Sophie and Kirsten exchanged the task of cradling her by the woodstove. When I glanced over, they had her wrapped in a pink handkerchief and were fingering at her mouth, trying to insert chalky, BB-like tablets of a homeopathic. The bunny's nose twitched occasionally, but other than that there was no movement in the animal.

"Is she blinking?" I asked, remembering the fire needed another log.

"She doesn't blink," Sophie said. She had stopped crying for a minute or so. "I'm glad we got lots of pictures of her," she muttered before the sniffles led to more gasps and smeared cheeks.

I slipped past them, lifted and then dropped a chunk of locust through the stove's top door, which I held open with my right hand. A little smoke escaped and found its way to the dormer. Time passed. We ate eggs. Bonnie's heart kept beating, but the rest of her appeared close, if not already gone, to the other side. I felt less grief for the rabbit than for my daughter, who was losing her friend after only two weeks. Sophie is an only child and every animal we keep becomes a surrogate sibling. I thought of this as I washed the dishes, worked on another cup of coffee, glanced out the window. The clock on the old stove turned, all three numbers to read 8:00 The prior day's rain was still frozen on the deck boards, but it was looking mild for January where we live sandwiched between the Alleghenies and the Blue Ridge—something about the fog said so. Bumppo the rooster was making his usual ruckus. I doubted that the stout Barred Rock was telling me to be grateful for his hens, but the thought came to mind.

There were beagles baying in the cedars at Breedon's Bottom when I hauled the first of two loads of gear to the river. It was around nine-thirty. A heavy mist hung over the land. You couldn't see a hundred yards. As I shouldered the canoe past two trucks parked in the gravel lot of the public boat access, I caught a glimpse of four beagles, nose down, snaking through the cedar-pocked pasture. They were thirty feet over the embankment and their baying couldn't have sounded more mournful.

The last time I'd hunted that stretch of river, I fired once at the slowest of three wood ducks that jumped from the roots of the cutbank on river left. That place wasn't far from the bridge. It had been a long shot, but when you paddle alone and jumpshoot, most shots are long. To exchange paddle for the gun between the legs, and then to raise the weapon, aim, and fire, all before wood ducks manage a fair leap, is a matter of luck and vision as much as timing.

The canoe was half in the water and half on the rocks. All the gear rested in it but the gun, which was in my hands. I slid the shotgun from its sock, took three shells from my coat pocket, and pressed them into place. The gun—the Ford Ranger of shotguns, a Remington 1100 semiautomatic—was a hand-me-down from my father. The red-and-black striped gun sock oozed with the sharp reek of cleaning solvent. There must be the residue from as many of Dad's gun cleanings on the sock as my own, if not more.

When I was a kid, Dad and I still-hunted in swamps and flooded timberland. I only hunted with him from a canoe once. It was on the Etowah River north of our home in Atlanta. I remember missing a woodie we'd jumped; I'd fired too low. Dad smiled from his place in the stern when I looked back, shaking my head in frustration. My father didn't like getting advice, so he was careful about giving it. Whether he trusted the world, our fates in it, I'm not sure. He was not a religious man in any organized or public way, and he still isn't. Our plan that day was to walk the bank back to the Jeep, a '79 Quadra Trac. When the walk turned into a four-mile bushwhack through briars and tangles, we grunted and laughed and cursed our way through it, mouths straddling that border between grimace and smile.

Wood ducks are weird. You wouldn't think a bird cryptic whose plumage consists of nine or ten different colors, all bold and piebald. But the wood duck is hard to see. Some feathers are pigmented, others colored by structure, tricks of light and form, and their pattern mirrors some mirage of a winter dawn reflected and refracted from a mist and riffle-broken surface of water. The colors on that body resemble many other combinations of those elements as well.

First there's the head—iridescent green and purple, not unlike the martins that buzz over our garden in the spring. One could be reminded of the kingfisher by the wood duck's crest, similarly colored as the head, as well as by the shocking white line extending from the bill over the eye to the back of the crest. From its white throat there are white projections onto its face and neck that resemble the arms of some small human figure holding on for dear life. These white lines on the throat also bring to mind a second mouth, a grinning one, though birding-types call it a bridle or a bib.

Without the white streaks, the bird might lose some formality about its appearance, but not all of it. The bill is red with a thin yellow streak at the base and dark at the tip. The rest of its body is equally dazzling—the red-apple chest, white-striped and black-barred; the daffodil-colored sides, the steely luster of its black back, chromatic sheen of its tail, reddish-violet beneath, and the white belly.

With that red bill, the wood duck, foraging at the water's surface or else on land, ingests seeds, acorns, fruits, and bugs. I have never seen them feeding, however. When I see them, the wood ducks have usually noticed me and are flying away with a muted, gullish whistle that sounds a little like—"free-eek, free-eek." It isn't unusual to hear them before I see them. If it is winter and I am hunting, I do not think much of the plumage then. I think at what point in the movement of the gun's barrel towards the path of their flight do I pull the trigger—and is the safety off.

To see the duck at all requires close attention to the river's edges. On the James where I hunt them, the banks are rooty and cut and snagged with box elder, sycamore, stones, and vines. There is a skeletal, fence-like quality about the winter banks. Boulders and deadfall complicate the scene. The more littered the bank with wood and stone, the more closely I watch. Wood ducks like cover. They seem to me more wary than other waterfowl, save the grebe. One is not likely to see wood ducks tooling around city or suburban or even farm ponds the way mallards often do.

With the first few strokes of the paddle, I noticed a purple plastic sled washed by high water into a box elder on a cobble bar by the bridge piling. It looked to be in fair condition, and I made a mental note to fetch it later, when I returned for the truck. They were calling for snow in the coming days, and Sophie would be happy to try a new old sled, especially knowing it was a gift of the river.

My fingers felt like they'd been in a jar of snow all morning. I wore a pair of brown wool gloves, but they weren't doing the trick. It didn't help to dwell on it, so I dwelled on the bunny. In the last week or so, Bonnie had developed a way of popping a one-eighty as she hopped. The motion contained an energy both spastic and graceful, and it was always a delight to behold. Sophie, Kirsten, and I, we'd hoot and cackle and go and hold her a while and run our fingers across her head and over her ears and down her back each time she did it.

I hugged the left bank for a while and then the right and then I opted for the middle. The river was running at a medium level, the liquid too Scotch-dark for a waterway this far south—the result of runoff from the paper mill upstream. Rocks revealed themselves as dimples on the surface or as splashes and coils of foam. The canoe tracked with minimal effort of the paddle. I tried to watch with a balance of attention and aimlessness that works pretty well when I'm hunting or fishing or just paddling for the sake of being on the water in a small boat. But my field of vision was squiggly with migraine-like worms and flashes. It wasn't a migraine, it was the light. The late morning was deceptively bright with the low winter sun bleeding through the mist. You could see the particles of moisture. Every breath was a little sip. It smelled like the land was sweating and the river, too, though it was thirty-five degrees at most.

At once, I slapped the paddle across the gunwales and mounted gun to shoulder. I found the bead down the barrel and followed it across the tops of the trees, which appeared ghastly, leafless as they were in the mist. I practiced this motion several more times, and as I did so, a blue heron flopped awkwardly to flight. I took aim at it. I was ghost-shooting. I would not fire. But the motion was satisfying. I exchanged gun for paddle again and watched the heron as it rounded a bend downstream, the motion of its five-foot wingspan slow and sure.

I beached the canoe at the mouth of Renick Run, near Indian Rock. The ground was mealy with leaf-dank sand and gave way under my rubber boots. As I walked up the creek, I spun my arms around like propellers, one arm then the other, hoping to recover feeling in the fingers. I'd passed the creek's outlet many times in my outings, but I'd never stopped here. The creek was low, the water chalky in the way of limestone streams. I stood a while by a trail rutted with four-wheeler tracks, watching the flow splash through ledges and pool up at a bend below.

I imagined Kirsten and Sophie had dug a small hole near the concrete St. Francis statue by now. We liked Sophie's choice of a burial place for the two-week-old bunny. Watching the creek, I pictured them working there, mother and daughter, their motions earnest and careful, at the base of the maple, the wire fence and the pines beyond. Sophie was no stranger to solemn affairs. At two, she'd watched my father sprinkle her great-grandfather's ashes in the surf. I am almost certain she remembers that day better than I do.

My aim that morning was equally solemn: to take another life, the life of a very beautiful bird. My aim was to separate this bird from its mate, its offspring, its nest. But my intent was something else. I was after a feeling, a way of being alive that only a good hunt provides, kill or no kill. I was after, in essence, the way of the river and of all things. If I killed a duck or two this morning, I would feel immense gratitude and sadness and connection all at once, and much more. If I didn't kill a wood duck, I would feel a longing and satisfaction of equal mystery and immensity.

Kirsten, Sophie, and I would no doubt survive without duck in our diet. But we like good, slow food, food of our own raising or taking. If I took a duck, we would prepare it with all the care and reverence such a life and death and hunt deserved. We'd ingest the bird believing it would live on through us, our flesh as its flesh and its flesh as ours. Our relationship with the river and the land where we live deepens perhaps most tangibly when we eat. It happens with the deer, with the dove and grouse. And it is that way with the trout and chickens, mutton and rhubarb and fennel.

None of this piety saved me from the fact that Kirsten was frustrated right now. Frustrated that I left her alone with Sophie and the dead bunny and the burial. Frustrated that after a long week of classroom and office work, her husband was on the river again. I knew this. I had sensed it when I left. My wife buries little besides seeds and dead pets. She wanted more to be happening on the farm, and she was right in this—more firewood, more fence repair, more soil preparation, a hothouse for starting seeds. I felt bad that she was disappointed. I didn't like that Kirsten wasn't feeling good about her day or our progress at home. But I was telling myself that being a father and husband meant being a source of grief sometimes. Sometimes a lot of the time. And that being in love and being committed meant learning to accept this, that then and only then might such a fate be tempered.

It felt good to be back in the canoe. The day was milder, my hands warm, knees and arms less stiff. The mist had lifted to a place above the trees along the bank. I could make out the houses on the bluff below Indian Rock. Though I grew up a few states south of Virginia, it turns out the grandfather of one of my best high school buddies, Chan Dillon, was raised in one of those houses. Their family ran the limestone quarry there. I imagined sending Chan a telepathic greeting, telling him I was at his roots and they were looking okay with the mist fading and the promise of blue sky soon.

There's this way the river seems to move when the mist is moving over it and you're moving through it and on it and looking around with such attention you could nearly conjure a wood duck out of the ether—it goes back to the first drop of blood and extends forth to all subsequent life and motion. This way had me in its grasp, and I was liking it. It was a real pretty morning, in other words, and it was getting warmer, too.

I steered the canoe through the whitewater at the ledge of the old canal dam. I kept scanning the banks for wood ducks. Heaps of driftwood and fallen trees and hollowed bank drew my attention the way planets grab stargazers' eyes. There were two more stretches of water where I'd seen ducks on prior trips, and I remained hopeful as I approached the island below, where lay a promising log jam and good feeding water. I was hopeful for a sighting, if not a shot. This was my sixth trip that winter. If I dropped a wood duck, it would have been my first kill. I wanted that very much—the fresh, oily meat for dinner as much as the satisfaction of having made a kill.

There were no ducks, but that's like saying there was no chocolate cake waiting when Sophie and Kirsten met me at Solitude Farm to run me back to the truck. The first blue in the sky appeared about the time they showed up. It was sharp, crisp blue, the kind of sky that could erase you.

"Is Bonnie resting okay," I asked.

"She's good," Kirsten said. I felt a hard yearning as she scanned the ridges, thick brown hair brushing her shoulders. She seemed a little annoyed, but then she said something that cut along my every seam. "It feels like we're in a storybook."

"We buried her, Daddy," Sophie added, plainly. She was studying the knot—a trucker's hitch—with which I was tying the canoe to the rack. "We put a creek stone over her. The big purplish one." I remembered gathering that stone with her. Though we live just up Arcadia Road from the bridge over the river, there are several creeks only a little further down the road and they hold a bounty of good stone.

"I look forward to seeing it," I said with as much tenderness as I could muster. "Sophie," I continued, turning from the car and the boat and the rope, "I'm sorry we lost Bonnie today." She said nothing, turned and stared downstream.

Once the canoe was fastened, we moseyed around the field. The mountains were visible now, all of them, and they looked less like overlords than wise old ladies. Pine Ridge still bore the thinnest veil of mist. It was as though a photograph, an old Polaroid, was coming to resolution, and we were in it somewhere, at the edge—small, small figures.

We'd stopped near a turn in the fence when I caught my wife's attention. "Kirsten," I said, "Thanks for being here. I owe you." She said nothing and looked towards the ridge, where a buzzard was arcing in a thermal. My veins, for a moment, could have been drainage ditches. I suddenly remembered seeing an eagle near the old canal lock below Indian Rock. It had been fifty yards off, milky-hooded and unmistakably bald eagle. Kirsten remained silent. That was her response. She didn't look at me. Bonnie came to mind then, how I'd held her the prior day and watched as she munched a bit of carrot. I'd been surprised she could eat it so quickly and how sharp her teeth and how she hadn't nicked my fingers.

Kirsten and Sophie dropped me at the bridge to fetch the truck, a tough, little four-cylinder Mitsubishi that would be totaled in a month. Before heading home, I wandered down the hill to where two men stood by the same two trucks I'd passed earlier, while carrying the canoe. They were engaged in a task which had me curious. I'd stripped down to a wool shirt now—no more hat or gloves or flannel or vest or heavy coat— and I moved on the gravel, down the hill, with careful steps. Though it was warmer, everything about the landscape said the hardest of winter was yet to come.

The men were skinning rabbits. Satisfied, panting beagles stared at me from their small box in the bed of an old Dodge Ram. I decided, after a moment, not to reach my fingers through the bars of the box's door.

The men and I exchanged a curt greeting, a few words on our respective hunts. I had never hunted rabbit, and I asked them how it worked with the beagles, how far you followed them once they had a rabbit on their nose.

"The beagles circle them back to us," the one man said. He spoke with little expression and perhaps a little malice, as though I were poaching on something intimate, which I was.

"That's good," I said. The men, stout and weathered, looked to be in their late sixties. Something about their faces told me their families had lived in those parts a long time—something as indigenous as canned meat. "Did you train them to do it that way?" I wondered aloud.

"We don't really train them," the man running his knife under the rabbit's skin said. In his jeans and tucked-in camouflage flannel button-down and blaze orange ball cap, the fellow looked more formal than anyone I'd seen in a while. This struck me as a good sign. "Ain't that right, Purcell?"

"That's right," Purcell allowed. Purcell was dressed the same, except he wore a beige flannel and a camouflage ball cap. "That's right. It's bred into them. If they don't do it, then they ain't no use."

I remembered the sled then, the purple one I'd seen in the box elder, but I decided to return later with Sophie to fetch it. It'd be something to do. There was not a trace of mist anywhere over the land now, but there was a freshness in the air that made the trees seem more wise than they probably were.

I started to go, awkward about it, and as I did so, looking past the beagles crowded in their cage, I felt a surge of clarity. The day's strands, variously braided, seemed to make a rope now, which held me, kept me from a great fall. Something good, perhaps hope or simply life, felt as close and vivid and cryptic as all the wood ducks I'd seen and hadn't seen.

"Y'all have a good day," I said. The man with the blood-smeared knife nodded as he dropped a chunk of the rabbit into a Ziploc. Off to the side, the wind carried a trace of fur to a place in the barbed-wire fence—it was darker than Bonnie's had been.

A Saturday in January

We woke to temperatures in the fifties. A milky haze lacquered the horizon. There had been warm days off and on for much of that winter. The daffodils, a few inches high, were like little ears listening for spring. There was algae and scum in the bathtubs we use as waterers for the sheep and goats and ass. The smell of the land, an ill, unfertile reek, made a hard freeze desirable. Kirsten hadn't bothered to close the cold frame on the lettuce and the radishes overnight. Other plants—bachelor buttons and kale—had sent shoots. Something was off.

I started the day by unloading and stacking a truckload of locust. A t-shirt and long pants were plenty of clothing. The wood had been a stack of logs the prior afternoon, and orbiting from truck to stack and back, I could still feel the weight and impact of the maul and the sound of the chainsaw. Sophie and I had helped split the wood, a gift from the Nelson family, after we'd helped them run plastic tubing for their maple syrup operation in western Rockbridge County. For many hours, we scrambled on muddy slopes, stretching and hitching lengths of tubing to maples. At one site, there were more than a hundred and fifty taps. The tubing fed a half-inch main line, which fed a plastic tank at the bottom of the ridge. By the end of the day, each site appeared as though a bionic spider had spun a web. There was something medical and bewildering about the scene, like the woods had suffered an accident or were the subject of an experiment. Eating maple syrup would never be the same.

But the work was pleasant in a quiet and systematic way. We were on the flanks of House Mountain, under a canopy of hickory, sassafras, and maple. Rob had marked the maples with timber paint and color-coded each line. There was a good kind of attention required to figure out the run of the tubing, how it banked from tree to tree and at which side of the trunk did it bend. It seemed we were tying a very large shoe.

It is always refreshing to be with the Nelsons in the woods. To support their syrup business, Rob works as a forester, cruising timber. He moves across the land with the grace and agility of one for whom the outside likes having as much as he enjoys being there. It tempers my feelings about the big paper mill in Covington and about my own prolific use of paper to know Rob has a hand in its making.

I'd hunted deer with Rob a few times in the fall, when the weather was more wintry than now. We hunted on land near Jump Mountain, north of Rockbridge Baths in the Hays Creek area. As with the maple trees, Rob harvests and works up deer with devotion and rigor and generosity; to wit, along with the truckload of locust, Rob sent us home with a log of venison salami and a pint of maple syrup to supplement the four deer already in our freezers and the gallon of syrup we were going through more rapidly than seemed appropriate. I made a mental note as I stacked the heavy chunks of blond wood to bring Rob something he'd like and could use when we saw him next. At present, I had no idea what that would be.

I thought of all this as I ricked the wood on the front porch, off to the side of an older, drier mixed stack. The uniformity of the locust was vaguely burdensome but freed the mind. I prefer firewood with a mutt-ish quality. There are, I think, fourteen types of wood in our stacks now, and though you can't beat the BTU power of locust, there's something satisfying and more true to the nature of things about a woodpile with variety.

Kirsten was at work in the garden and Sophie was doing her chores at the barn. Over the Blue Ridge to the east, the sun was getting after it. A train squeaked and clacked down the hill on its course along the James. I thought of the conductor looking out on that stretch of river between Buchanan and the bridge at Arcadia, just down the road. I saw the places I was slowly coming to know, not as he saw them, of course, but as I'd seen them from the canoe and from swimming and fishing and camping at various spots along that stretch.

41

There were nuthatch and chickadee in great numbers, flitting from tree to tree, and the ass was heehawing for sweet-feed like a baby. I was ashamed for Charlie, the twenty-year-old jack adopted by prior owners of our place from BLM land in Nevada, but I was also enamored by his yearning.

It was shaping up to be one of those Saturdays when, with no one urgent project at hand, we'd weave between several small but necessary tasks, deciding among them according to interest as much as necessity. Such days are not unusual in January, and they are my favorite. There is, of course, a list of things to do, but none of it is life or death. There is a sort of whimsy involved. Tinkering may be the word for it, but really what's at the essence of such a day is an element of surprise. Surprise at what you are doing and surprise at what you have done. And the distinct sort of care such surprise lends, through its freshness, to your engagement with each task.

I knew, for instance, that I'd stack the wood and stack another heap split the prior weekend, dead and down gleaned from National Forest. I knew we'd change the water in the tubs and lay out plans for a greenhouse, plant a few fruit trees and mulch garden beds, watch a little college basketball, eat a good lunch, and visit with each other and the animals, but I also knew that a hundred other things would happen, including various wanderings and indulgences of mind and body and soul that such work tends to spawn.

Breakfast was late, French toast and sausage at the picnic table on the south-facing deck. I had finished unloading the truck by the time we ate. Eating the sausage reminded me that I needed to work a shed into shape so we could cure this year's hams in there. I filed that away while watching my daughter eat the last thick slice of toast cooked in eggs she'd harvested from the hen house the prior night—to express how satisfying that was would likely disgust you. We ate and we looked over the valley of the James, at Cove Mountain, the powerlines, vague outlines of clouds. The heat from the strengthening sun was not irritating enough to keep us all from licking our plates, like dogs.

Kirsten and I planted the fruit trees next. This was not as simple as it sounds. Planting a tree requires long-term vision, something I lack. We discussed the future effects of the trees' shade, as well as their placement in relation to one another. Apple trees need to be in proximity of one another in order to bear fruit. A lone apple will not produce. In the end, we planted the Winesap in the bed where last year we grew cherry tomatoes and the Fuji in a bed of perennials. It was satisfying to find rich, wormy soil where, when we'd moved to the land, there'd been a mobile home and wiregrass hell. Kirsten's decision for us to build, no dig, lasagna beds—layers of cardboard, manure, compost, and mulch—was paying off.

Such soil-building involves stages, and these stages vary from grower to grower. We first built a portable chicken house, four-by-eight, the size the beds would be. The chickens ate and scratched the grass and weeds, and they fertilized the ground with their waste. After dragging the chicken house to the next bed, we laid our moving boxes over the spot they'd primed. On top of the cardboard, we laid manure from local stables. We covered the manure with chipped trees dumped by a crew hired to trim trees and limbs from utility lines in the area. Last, we placed straw from old square bales from the barn. Once our compost cooked just right, we added that. Persistence and desire and a good shovel and wheelbarrow and back were all we really needed, in addition to the gumption to scavenge these materials.

As we planted trees and talked, Sophie was entertaining herself by playing with the barn kittens. When I looked that direction, she had rigged a length of baling twine over one log wall and was luring the kittens to pounce at its frayed end. I heard her cackling and giggling. Down the valley, someone was running a chainsaw. It sounded more like they were giving the tool a tune up than working with it. The machine growled and stopped repeatedly. I heard planes pass in the intervals. We were on our knees now, Kirsten and I, mixing soil and compost among the fruit tree's root ball and tamping it all down. "We'll plant comfrey in here for nitrogen fixing," Kirsten said. She was plugged in. "And bulbs to keep the voles out."

Donnie drove up as we finished. He would run the hog butchering later in the week and wanted to check in about that. When Donnie stops by, we all get to yapping, and then inevitably get sidetracked in various directions. Even Donnie sometimes leaves without doing what he came to do.

I found myself suddenly looking for the wrench to change the grinder pad and reorganizing half the tool shed in the process. I prefer controlled chaos over strict economy when it comes to order. Not being able to find the wrench where I'd hung it on a nail in a logical place was a delight to me. By the time I had the wire basket on the grinder to clean the watering tubs, Donnie had built a home of scrap boards for the barn kittens with Sophie. I was hungry for lunch. Kirsten mentioned a thirty-eight-egg egg salad made with relish from the summer cukes and generous mayo, so I dipped crackers in that heap of deep gold and watched Michigan State come back against Illinois in some Big Ten hoop action on the tube. Though it was NFL playoff season, the motion on the basketball court seemed more conducive to the way things were progressing that day. Run and shoot punctuated by passes, steals, fouls, free throws, time-outs. I decided, watching the action, that Rob and his family would get a dozen boiled duck eggs as a thank you for the firewood. But first I needed to change the oil in the truck. Dirty oil is wild stuff.

My Skateboard, the Hills, and Other Enthusiasms

I ride a forty-one-inch FlexDex Wingnut Pro Model skateboard. It measures eight and a half inches at its widest point. Royal blue stripes span the length of its base. As for graphics, there are no skull and crossbones or scantily clad, unnaturally shaped ladies anywhere on the board. Rather, the design reminds one of a sports shirt, a button down, the kind you see at T. J. Maxx on the discount rack.

The board has been gathering dust in the shed since we moved to these eighteen acres and got down and dirty doing the things we do. It is sad when one's enthusiasms take the back seat to one's other enthusiasms, but so it goes.

Skateboarding terrain is slim here in the country. Our place includes a gravel drive and borders a narrow road that winds steeply down to a bridge over the James River. Large pickups frequent the road at high speeds. Some drivers of these pickups think we're nuts for trying to farm this place. "I've lived here all my life," Stull Watts said. "I wouldn't think of farming." Stull runs a motel and Shell station at the end of the road, catering to the bleary warriors who filter off I-81. I didn't mention to Stull that I had my eye on skateboarding a stretch of the Blue Ridge Parkway, that horizontal scar near the crest of the ridge both Stull and I can see from the south and east-facing windows of our homes.

The wheels on my FlexDex Wingnut Pro Model are amber, translucent in the manner of congealed honey or Jolly Rancher. They are Kryptonics-brand wheels, seventy millimeters in diameter, and they spin on seven-inch steel trucks with eighth-of-an-inch risers. I bought the rig used at Play It Again Sports a couple of years back and have changed nothing about it. The board is slightly more worn than it already was—the grip-tape frayed, the tail carved like a prehistoric spear point, the wheels fluted with wear. The fiberglass board, as it is designed to do, bows perhaps more deeply under my two hundred pounds than it did under its prior rider.

When we were living in North Carolina last year, in the small, drowsily hip town of Hillsborough, there was a ride I liked to do. I'd roll down West Margaret Lane and slow at the four-way stop where Occoneechee crosses. Then I'd carve hard and snake down Occoneechee past Joe's house, past French's, past the house with the sign that says Old Depot House, and then I'd straighten to gather speed for the long flat that's Calvin Street. The vibrations through the soft wheels and bearings and steel trucks and through the fiberglass deck and then my shoes rattled my knees and every part of me.

Occoneechee Street was narrow and rough. I carved onside to backside in a tight, pumping motion that involved a pretzeling of torso and thrusting of the hips. Just as I initiated the turn—my Achilles stretched, the board arcing over the left or right wheels—I began to initiate the next turn. Offweight, onweight—I worked against gravity by working with it. The turns started with a swiveling of my head, and, quickly followed by that, almost simultaneously, I threw my arms and chest towards the new direction. The rest—the board, feet, wheels— followed, the whole affair a kind of coil and recoil and so on.

Carving back and forth across the slope provides a sensuous and heady rush. It is a base rhythm, two beats and regular—the bearings whine as you roll across, slightly downhill with the grade, and then they growl and groan with the heat of the turn, with its pressure, the downweighting flex of the board and the friction of the wheels. It isn't unusual to feel a stirring in the loins as you roll with it, knees bending with each carve, arms out, fingers loose, those of the uphill hand sometimes grazing the pavement.

On Occoneechee Street, it was best not to pause and let the hill do the work. Some might take the grade straight—the speedriders and idiots. I preferred to take it slow by working against it. For one thing, it felt good. For another thing, there was the gravel, acorns, construction debris—a carriage bolt, a shard of brick. When you saw these things and it was too late and you hit one, you were sometimes sure it would clear the space beneath the axle. The board stops if it doesn't, however, and you don't stop, not right away. Such is inertia.

Speed wobbles sent me to the pavement once when I was twelve. I went down hard and slid and was lucky. Some of us learn from our mistakes. Some of us test our learning. Though I could still walk home that day, I couldn't walk well. I remember cutting with little stealth through the yard of the divorced dad whose sons I babysat now and then, and thinking, "So this is what it's all about."

I'm a careful skater. I'd rather be careful than wear pads or a brain bucket. Also, I want the possibility of bodily harm to be as present as the growl of bearing and friction of wheel on pavement. I like the little wars in the head, how in the middle of linking several carves, the oaks and mockingbirds becoming a sentient blur, you suddenly picture your body raking the asphalt, the sound of it like slicing a fish with a dull blade, which is more an act of tearing.

So I kept an eye out. For vehicles, too, and for pedestrians and stray dogs. Occoneechee Street was my favorite warm up. It was sufficiently rough and sufficiently steep. No other road rattled me as it did. My knees tingled at first and then all my joints by the end of it. Maybe not everyone needs a good rattling now and then, but I like it.

Though the lower reaches of West Margaret Lane, closer to Main Street and the heart of Hillsborough, provided a longer, smoother ride, I preferred Occoneechee for its narrowness, for the way the trees— hackberry, maple, oak—lined it, and how the houses sat back from the road. Thoughtful architecture, of landscape, road, and building, is every bit as important to skateboarding as it is to other life matters. That stretch of Occoneechee Street was maybe a quarter mile, though I wished it were ten.

Riding a skateboard on the Blue Ridge Parkway might be illegal— I'm not sure. There are many rules in places like this. I know it is illegal to hunt here. You see, when I reached the end of the driveway this morning, I turned left. On Thursdays I usually hang a right and hop on the interstate en route to the office, but today—inertia again—my arms turned the wheel left. I crossed the James River and, very aware of the skateboard and fly rod and twelve-gauge all competing for my affections behind the truck seat, I followed Arcadia Road up Jennings Creek and then up McFalls Creek, where the road turns gravel as it winds up to T into the Blue Ridge Parkway.

So I'm wearing slacks and a button-down oxford under a quilted, upscale/downhome barn coat, a skullie, and deerskin work gloves. My hi-top Vans have droplets of roofing goo and paint and caulk on the toes, but I still look more like I'm headed to the skeet range than to a stealth downhill skateboard mission. This attire might come in handy if I have a run-in with the authorities, but I doubt it.

I left my truck at the trailhead for Flat Top Mountain, one of the Peaks of Otter, and have been walking, skateboard over shoulder, not on the trail but up the road. There is still snow in the shady parts of the shoulder. I head up an easy incline. It is several miles of steady grade to my destination on Apple Orchard Mountain.

Here, they built the parkway on the east side of the Blue Ridge's crest. I stare at the expanse of sky over Bedford County, which is mostly a foreign place to me. We live on the west side of the Blue Ridge, in northern Botetourt County, not too far from the Rockbridge County line. One day a buddy who works as a Forest Service law enforcement agent mentioned that rattlesnakes mosey onto the road on summer evenings to enjoy the last of the heat. Several cyclists had been struck, he told me. I told him I was looking forward to skateboarding up here. He said, with little expression, "You'd probably like being bit by a rattlesnake." I suppose a job like his gives insight into human nature.

There are some new pains in my thirty-four-year-old frame, and this bothers me as I walk. The mind, among other things, is fair aspirin, so I think of time in Hillsborough. I try to remember the house we were fixing up as we lived in it there, but that was mostly business and grunt work, satisfying enough when it was over, the job done. Sport is nice because you savor it eternally in the moment, and often it is as satisfying in eternity as it was in the moment. Getting a certain wall plumb after a bout of jerking and sledging may be nice, but it's a wall—sheetrock it, paint it, hang a picture, or don't.

One day a paving crew hit Nash Street, the road our lot bordered. Their signal car backed into a section of our fence. A couple of weeks prior, I'd nail-gunned nine hundred and seventy four pickets to the two-by fastened to the four-by posts set in concrete, so I was a little peeved when the foremen claimed innocence, even as I pointed to the tar on the busted pickets and on the tread marks in the grass.

But skating the new pavement of Nash, especially after the asphalt conglomerate of Occoneechee Street, was wild. It didn't feel real at first. It is never real, of course, any of it, but that's not the point, except most of the time. It was like silk, like being with a woman who shaves her legs with kerosene or something. Also, since Nash Street was wide, it was easier to ride than Occoneechee Street, as there was more room to turn and more room to check your speed. The traffic could be a problem, though, especially the bass-thumping SUVs and jacked-up pickups that accelerated when they spotted me.

I'm not a trick rider. I simply like the feel of carving turns, the wind in my face, and the friction of asphalt and rubber coming through wheel into my feet and up my legs. As a kid, I was a half-hearted skater, an occasional. I preferred the savagery and social clout of playing football. Not that skateboarding doesn't have its violence, but there was a skater scene and ethos that when I was kid in Atlanta in the '80s didn't suit me.

A hawk, a sharp-shinned, tucks and dives into the valley. It zings, not far above the canopy, like some dark shard of meteorite. The day is clear. I can't see the Atlantic two hundred miles away, but the thought crosses my mind, and the way it does that is almost as good as seeing the Atlantic. It is lovely to think of the ocean when you are walking with a skateboard on your shoulder along a road that stretches many miles uphill, a road built, as it happens elevationally, closer to the sun and further from the ocean than any other road for many miles.

Skateboarding, born of surfing and roller-skating, is as good a way as any to blow some time. I came to it after the roller-skating craze of the late '70s. In 1980, we held my ninth birthday party at a skate rink called Jellybeans on Roswell Road in Atlanta. I couple-skated with Mimi Thompson and did the hokey pokey and the limbo and probably played a few games of Pac Man in the alcove when the hot spots on my ankles turned to blisters. It was pleasant, but I remember having a sense that the place and scene were drying up. Maybe it was the music, shifting from bad '70s disco to bad '80s rock. Maybe it was the smell of pizza grease. Not long after this, I bought my first real skateboard, a Santa Cruz Jammer, at a shop called Skate Escape adjacent to Piedmont Park.

I am close to three thousand feet, and the surf is up. The waves are growing with every step. There is plenty of good grouse habitat along the road. Grouse season has been over now a week and in my ten outings this year, without a dog, I didn't flush a bird—not even a rabbit. Naturally, I'll see one now. Stoney Creek is audible, a distant espresso machine, and I'm beginning to see the light bouncing off the seams of its course. I swear some of the maples and oaks are blushing with early spring's red tide of buds.

I skated with a kid named Steve Roper when I was young. He was the most punk kid I knew. Rumor had it his father was Reagan's Georgia campaign manager. I liked Mr. Roper and felt bad for him, and fascinated when he ended up in jail for some kind of embezzlement crime. I saw Steve last when we were around twenty. He had a tattoo on the inside of his lower lip that read, when he flipped the flesh visible, "Fuck Off." He was taking steroids and hanging out at a gym and working as a bouncer at those lingerie places where girls model the latest fashions and you are encouraged, with the lotion they provide, to "Make yourself as comfortable as you like."

Anyway, when we were thirteen or so, Steve and I enjoyed riding the mostly empty parking decks on Sundays in Atlanta. It was easy to skate from my parent's house to Piedmont and Peachtree roads. At a mall and hotel complex called Tower Place, there were six or seven floors to the parking deck. You couldn't help but picture yourself funneling down a coil as you wound through the levels, smells of residual oil and exhaust oozing from the concrete, perhaps stirred to life by the heat of your wheels.

My connection with Atlanta was formed, in part, through skateboarding and other sporting activities—BMX, football, jogging, baseball, beer drinking under bridges, and making out with girls in the unfinished homes of the latest subdivision going up. A city is a made thing, and skateboarding requires the base material of any infrastructure—concrete or asphalt. I left Atlanta when I was eighteen, so I never experienced many facets of it, such as what happens in the high rises and what goes on in the model homes or townhouses when you move in and play that game called growing older, or whatever it is, in a city called Atlanta, with all of what makes Atlanta what it is coloring the fabric of your days.

I'm several miles from my truck and want to keep walking. In the last mile or so, I entered that zone that makes walking feel no less graceful, I suppose, than dying quickly in the midst of beauty. But after stretching for a few minutes, I step on the black, 80-grit grip tape that sticks to my board's deck, front foot then rear, and start to roll. The parkway has a bank to it where I start. When I turn east across the grade of the slope, to check my speed, I encounter another slope. It is hard to stay in control with this double downhill.

The grade, in other words, is not perpendicular to the path of the road. I'm starting to roll faster than I like to roll. I continue to glance both directions, checking for cars, any sort of traffic. The road is empty. I think, wishfully, there must not be a person for many miles. The Piedmont, east as far as I can see, looks unreal, like another sky, a lower sky. Fox grape, greenbrier. The roadside is a whir; near the edge of it, I run forward off of the board in order to regain control, shoes thumping on the soft ground. I hear the bearings go silent as the board follows me into the grass and stops.

Maybe it is vaguely secular of me to be skateboarding on the Blue Ridge Parkway. If a place has been paved, however, you might as well skate it. I don't take it as far as Ed Abbey, lusty crunchmeister, and justify tossing my garbage here by some logic that suggests since a stretch of ground has been asphalted it might as well be a dump. Somewhere along the way, upstanding guy that I am, I caught the germs of eco-correctness, and the thought comes to mind that I should be quieter, stiller, watching for endangered migratory warblers.

Well, screw it. I'm on my board again, linking one turn to another, and the motion is exquisite. I squat, or come as close as my joints allow to squatting, on both back and foreside turns. For a little while, the mass of rock, the compressed eons on which this road is built, feels like a wave. The whole Blue Ridge, the entire spine, seems to be traveling as a groundswell travels through the ocean. And I am a little speck, carving turns somewhere in the mosaic of that energy.

The parkway winds in and around the heads of various drainages. Two miles down, then another—fifty or sixty turns given to each one. There are icicles hanging off cliffs on the uphill side of the road, water dripping from them. No cars still, then one, an SUV, approaches from the north, behind me, really hauling. It is still a ways off. I wonder at the heat of the board's wheels as I round a curve and see three curves' worth of road down mountain. Four turkeys stand alert at the edge of the woods in the second curve. They scurry out of sight, appropriate omens, just as the SUV overtakes me. I'm able to wiggle tight turns in the other lane as it passes, and as it passes, I work hard to keep from blowing it a kiss. There is not a cloud in the sky.

Backstories

When Sophie was younger, she liked it when I read the lines on her hands. After a bedtime story, I'd run my index's fingernail gently along the grooves of her palm and invent fortunes. *You will make somebody smile tomorrow. A bird you've never seen will land near you soon. You will laugh in the rain. The rain will laugh as it falls on your toes.* And so on—positive and pleasant and quirky, these prophecies, laced with as much wonder as I could muster.

Sophie liked the touch, the tickly, relaxing feel of what was essentially a hand massage. I liked it too. I am not a palm reader by training, but my finger, tracing the geography of her palm, tingled with mysteries of blood, nerve, and form. I especially liked exploring the groove that runs from the hand's heel to the pad of the first knuckle. Palm readers call this "The Destiny Line." Sophie always relaxed deeply when I traced it. Looking back, I'm not sure how much the fortunes meant, since she rarely asks for me to read her lines these days. But the fortunes were not the point. What mattered was touch.

Our daughter is older now, and I have to admit that initiating the bedtime ritual can feel like a burden some nights. "Why doesn't she put herself to sleep?" a gruff voice in my head grumbles. "She's seven, for Christ's sake," it continues. "And you are so very important and have very many important things to do."

I come from the school of parenting where kids fend for themselves. You don't read to your kids at night. You don't spoil them with hugs. To the extent possible, you live as you did before kids except you shell out dough for babysitters and childcare and, in return, you have lovely photographs of your children in strategic places and something to complain or brag about when they screw up or excel.

That I don't subscribe to this form of parenting is easier said than lived. It takes discipline to resist the convenience mode. It is especially challenging when I am frazzled and tired. Having more time to wallow is not only compelling then, it is what I saw—or what I remember seeing— and experience for me is a grim master. Over the years, my daughter has sensed the little wars in me. They frighten her. I have sometimes wondered if a distant, peaceful parent is better for a child than a close one who is troubled. In the end, I don't believe you can substitute distance for intimacy, no matter how you rationalize it.

My wife's tradition is different, if not the opposite of mine. For Kirsten, it is as natural as breathing that we don't ask Sophie to go to sleep herself. For her, it is essential that our daughter count on this each day: that she will be accompanied to the brink of sleep or close to it by one of her parents. But there's more—another thing is consistent too: if Kirsten is home, she sings Sophie the same song at the conclusion of each story, no matter who tells it.

Nowanights, Sophie prefers when I tell a story on her back for bedtime. I enjoy this as well, often more than reading from a children's book. If I listen well with my hand, her back has many good stories to tell.

It plays like this. Sophie turns on her belly and lifts her pajama shirt. I lay the palm of my hand on the small of her back and press gently. We are silent. The breeze, if there is a breeze, fills a window. Maybe our dog is barking at a deer, protecting the garden. I squeeze a bit with my hand. The story has begun. It was there all along. I open my mouth, follow the lead.

Tonight it starts with *Twice upon a forever, in a land both far and near, there lived an old woodchopper named Susaneezer. Folks called her Eezer for short.* My fingers are making footsteps up Sophie's spine as I say this. She is still. We have dressed her three dolls in nightshirts and Katie, her old teddy, sleeps naked.

Now I trace the image of a face and then a body. *Eezer was a squat woman with a face like a cantaloupe. She was strong the way the spring sunlight is strong, in an inviting way. Her eyes were the color of the woods in early fall—dark green with hints of gold.* I am drawing eyes now on my child's back, from shoulder blade to shoulder blade, and gently. Pressure is everything, next to placement. How hard or not hard I press is like the tone of my voice, and where is like the words I choose. *They were unusual eyes*, I say while drawing them. *Her mother and grandfather had the same eyes.*

One day, clouds like noodles, but whiter, and the sky bluer, so blue, the story continues, *Eezer packed her saw on her burro, Sam, and headed into the forest.* My fingers are doing their best to press harder and with four legs in order to simulate a burro. Yes, my hand is a burro now; I trust this as I trust my daughter's back to tell the story from my fingers right out my mouth. I have to.

It so happens that tonight, so far, the story isn't too far from reality. We keep an old burro and heat with wood that Sophie helps spot and haul and stack. Most other nights, the story also contains elements from the life we live and especially from the life Sophie lives. I expect this is only natural, since we are working with bodies, stories rooted in bodies.

Near the crest of a wind-ravaged ridge, Eezer started sawing a log, I say, drawing the edge of my hand back and forth on Sophie's flesh. She giggles. *After she cut a length, she bent and hefted it.* While saying this, I grab a chunk of Sophie's flesh and lift. *Ouch*, Sophie mutters through the pillow. I do not fret, for deep down she is laughing. I feel the slight tremors of her giggling through my hand. *As Eezer lifted the log, she watched a butterfly drift on the breeze. Maybe it was a moth. Eezer wasn't sure.*

Then she harnessed the log to Sam, the burro. She was careful with the log and Sam. She didn't want to hurt the burro. My hand presses more deeply into Sophie's lower back as I tell this part. And stays pressed. Everybody knows the lower back is the best place to press deeply. *Then Eezer sawed another length*, I say, turning hand and sawing her back with its edge again. Softer this time is Sophie's light, convulsive laughter.

Once the second log was cut, the story continues, *Eezer moved it in place and fastened it to Sam.* It feels, as I press again my child's lower back, like she is becoming part of the mattress. She feels more relaxed than she did at the beginning of the story. Her trust in me or, rather, in this story is a little frightening. I try not to be distracted by this, but suddenly I'm wondering what tells the story most—the touch or the words, or at what intersections of voice and flesh. On Sophie's back I focus, on the story it is telling and touching me to touch and tell. I focus on Eezer and Sam, the Burro, and the warm world of my daughter's flesh, because if it is spoiling Sophie to do this, then it is spoiling me as well, and don't we all deserve to be spoiled.

Still pressing my daughter, the warm and tender place above her digestive organs, I continue. *But a strange thing happened once Eezer situated the second log. There was a voice.* My voice turns high and scratchy. With no forethought, I'm straining my throat to make the breath through the vocal chords go splintery. *"Hey, you," a little ring-necked snake said. It was crawling from under the rotted bark. "I don't appreciate you moving my home."* My index draws continuous S patterns soft and slithering on Sophie's back. My index draws them and then two or three fingers at once. A gentle, vaguely electric sensation runs from my hand up my arm, inspiring me to continue.

Eezer furrowed her eyebrows with anger. They were like caterpillars, I say, tracing them, giving them legs. *Her eyebrows were like caterpillars, thick and fuzzy and expressive. She looked at the sky, which had fewer clouds now. There was a buzzard turning on the breeze.*

"Hey, you woodchopper, put this log back down," I squeak suddenly, doing my best ring-necked snake voice. *"Leave us be."*

Eezer didn't budge. She placed her hands on her hips. She pivoted the toe of her old boot in the leaf-dank ground. "I cut this log and I intend to split and sell the chopped wood," I say in deep, matter-of-fact woodchopper voice.

"No you don't," wailed ring-necked. "I have a lot of friends. You better put me and this log back."

Needless to say, a battle-of-wills-type confrontation, with threats like what snake just said, might not be the most restful bedtime story for a child. But this is what the back's story is tonight. Maybe I should plan a bit when I'm channeling stories and it's late on a Sunday and I'm tired from a weekend in the domestic and undomestic wilds, but I don't. I go with what the back gives me—the first draft, the original draft, the only draft.

Just then, I continue, *there was a rattling sound.* As I say this, I tap Sophie's back as though making horse-galloping noises, but not; I tap faster, more frenetic, like somebody is dancing in place to real crazy music. And I scratch, too, real lightly. *Eezer looked down and saw not one, not two, not three—but six rattlesnakes coiled, their rattles humming.*

"See," ring-necked squeaked. "I have lots of friends. You better put this log back." Old Eezer knows about rattlers. All woodcutters do. If it was one rattler, she might remain stubborn about the wood. But six? Just then Eezer swiveled and noticed a fallen oak down the ridge. It looked to have come down the prior spring.

"I'll move on," Eezer said, looking back to ring-necked. She grimaced nervously. Her cheeks resembled a wild mushroom—chanterelle, lactarius. "I'll let you and your log be."

At once the rattling stopped. Eezer relaxed, almost cracked a smile. Then she unfastened the log from Sam and let it be.

"Thank you," said ring-necked.

"Okay," Eezer said, nodding. Then she trudged off, leading her burro, Sam, down the ridge, towards the big, storm-felled oak. She hoped it was a red oak, but she had a hunch it was a white oak, which when split she knew would spark some good memories in her nose.

Sophie isn't asleep. She is never asleep after these stories. She tends to fall asleep a little while after Kirsten sings to her. Sometimes I remain in bed when Kirsten sings the same old Shaker song she's sung night after night for almost eight years. Even when I don't remain and move back to being important and doing important things like the dishes or reading a magazine or catching up on some project, I listen for it:

"'Tis a gift to be simple,
'Tis a gift to be free,

'Tis a gift to come down
Where we ought to be,
And when we find ourselves
in a place just right,
we will be in the valley
of love and delight.

When true simplicity is gained,
To bow and to bend,
We will not be ashamed
To turn and to turn,
Will be our delight,
When by turning and turning
We come around right."

I like this song. Some nights, if I am lucky, the words trace a story through every part of me. There's nothing simple about our life, except that it will never be simple. This song helps me remember this. The way Kirsten sings it, the faith and doubt and beauty of that faith and doubt in her voice helps me be okay with this.

The Nature of the Take

Faced with a Saturday of cutting locust posts and digging post-holes, I muster before dawn to fish the creek down the road. It's balmy for early March in the Upper James region of Virginia. Loading rod, reel, and vest in the truck, I feel my forehead thickening as if with sweat. The birds have cranked up a notch. There's a deer, a yearling doe, at the far edge of pasture. Above the ridge, Purgatory Mountain lingers like a joke somebody's afraid to tell. March is crazy. I think of yesterday, how wet snow fell, melting within an hour of first flakes; it seems like long ago.

Once packed, I let the ewes, Bessie and Delilah, and the lamb, Pippi, out of their perhaps coyote-proof shed, open the chicken house, pour a little food for the barn cats and dogs, and take a handful of grain to Charlie, the old jackass. There is nothing sentimental about the affair; it is routine. I do it, and as I do it, steal glances at the ridge that delineates the western border of the North Creek drainage, a few miles east as the wind blows. But the wind is blowing now, as it often blows on warm days, from the southwest, carrying with it too much noise from Interstate 81. The daffodils along the gravel drive look close to opening; coasting down, truck in neutral to keep from waking anyone, I wager there'll be petals by afternoon.

Snooter is holding court with a few locals—Junebug, Tickweed, Boss Hog—when I stop for a twenty-six-cent refill at Stull's Shell Station. The fellows regard me with a little less suspicion than when we moved here seven months ago. Junebug even says, "What's going on?"

"Good," I respond, not entirely incorrectly. Then I overhear Snooter say they stocked North Creek yesterday evening, which starts a little war in my head. "Shit," I think, heading out. The sky is beginning to glow. A semi clips the rumble strip. Before hopping back in the truck, I pause, pinch a dip of tobacco to make the coffee taste better and maybe inspire a chemical truce in the mind.

There is no truce to be had. Even as I turn off Jennings Creek Road and start up North Creek, a part of me is thinking how nice it'd be to feel a hefty stocker or six, especially when I lug them to the kitchen for breakfast like a true hunter-gatherer. But the seventy-two, yes, seventy-two, trucks I count in the two-mile stretch of road along the creek are cause for easy surrender. I drive too fast past them and am able to breathe again when the asphalt gives way to gravel. There is not another vehicle for the next two-mile stretch of catch-and-release water. I park at road's end just as the sun is giving the sky an extreme makeover.

I can't tell you what sort of birds are audible while rigging rod and reel, but their noise sets off many flares. They remind me of the prior night, watching a bat do what bats do in crazy waves twenty feet above the wellhead, near where we'll be stringing a fence soon to keep chickens, rabbits, and whatever else out of the garden beds. We moved to this place with big plans last July, and I'm still learning how to be elegant about balancing a need to explore with a need to settle in. I expect to be sneaking off from farm chores twenty years from now, if we make it that long.

Where I park, North Creek is only three miles from its hemlock and laurel origins near the Blue Ridge Parkway. So it is a small stream, the kind that non-anglers aren't convinced holds fish worth the time or trouble. They might be right. But my two-weight, a sexy six-foot-six magic wand, feels made for such water the way such water is made for a March Saturday dazzling with towhee and spring beauties and spring azure, those moths that resemble scraps of blue tissue.

I fasten a #18 Adams to the tippet with the usual pre-arthritic fumbles, drooling purposefully on the clinch knot before cinching it tight. There is a short walk to the creek, just enough to get the blood moving in the legs. I stare at the water from a bluff above a plunge pool, which might as well be my innards, so revved am I by the air and the scene. There are better feelings, but few so striated with longing. The creek splats through a chute that drops seven feet into a pool the depth and color of which makes you think God might have had his eyeball lobbed out of his head. God must have many eyeballs is the logical next thought, because you have seen a few, you have pulled fish from them, and you have put fish back, and you have not done such things, too, and nothing was lost.

I sneak through the limbs, opting for an entry downstream. I will fish my way up to the confluence of Cornelius Creek and North Creek, a stretch of less than a mile but with six or seven distinct, very fishy-looking pools. If I am lucky, no other anglers will appear and I'll be home in a couple of hours, eager for breakfast and family time before trekking chainsaw to the tangled, west corner of our land. What lengths of locust we don't use for fence posts, we'll burn in the woodstove come winter.

It was a high summer night the first time I laid eyes on North Creek. I'd been traveling a thirty-mile radius around Roanoke looking for land, and was tired and needed a place to lay my sleeping bag. I find motel rooms exhausting, except maybe in winter when you have someplace to be in the morning that requires a shower and the droll state of mind that such affairs require. Though dark, I found a beach downstream of here, a beach where today there must be ten guys elbow to elbow, casting hooks with day-glow chemical goo stuck to them and catching fish still dazed from their truck ride just twelve hours ago.

I used to envy folks who baitfish for stocked trout. But I was wrong about the sense of community the activity provides. The crowds are rarely congenial. People jockey for position, tangle lines, exchange harsh words. When I tried my luck at it a couple of times, I grew as grumpy and competitive as the people around me. Trout fishing, for me, is not a group activity. Groups freak me out, and since I'm a teacher and work with a lot of groups, I go fishing to take a break from being freaked out. Two, at most three, people is enough; even then we fish alone, hopscotching pool to pool, pausing often and from a safe distance to watch each other in the heart of the dance.

That first night on North Creek I saw a sycamore tree with a trunk that so resembled petrified snow it nearly made the summer heat bearable. I stood with the dark all around me and the light that resides in it, ever more populous the longer you stand there. The stars were dissolving and reappearing behind fast-moving cumulous. There were thoughts of rattlesnakes as I squatted, cupped hands in the creek and then on my face. Soon enough, sensing rain, I set up a tent and then fell asleep on the mat outside it.

But it was the morning more than the night that set the hook in me about North Creek. Sometime before dawn, the clouds had dropped a little rain before pushing through, allowing the aftershock of crisp, cooler air. It was terrifyingly refreshing. We were living in the North Carolina Piedmont at the time, where summer days have that wet jockstrap feel about them for weeks. I could have been escorted there to North Creek on a community-service obligation that morning and still felt less than rancid. The decision to fish a while before breaking camp and looking for a place to move my family came quickly, as if it were in the plans. I'd landed a new job in the area; we had a little while yet, and I must have sensed the creek had some good advice about where to live and how to find it.

There was no activity in the pool by the beach where I'd slept. It was clear by the beer cans, salmon egg, and Powerbait jars that this was stocked-trout water. I doubted there'd be much of a rise but continued dropping an aged and frayed deer hair caddis in the thickwater of an eddy between flume and old log-bridge piling. Fingerling, or less than fingerling dace, spasmed at my fly now and then. The leaves on the sycamore and hazel and oaks had, that end of June, wearisome about them, even though the northwest wind, cool and dry as it was, made them shiver.

Two pools later, I hooked the rainbow that set at play a string of events that led to us making an offer on a place three miles from there. The creek ran for sixty yards between bends, in a staircase manner, the slottish falls two to four feet in elevation. I missed a good strike in the glare at the base of the first drop. It was clear that if there were any fish left after the last of the stocking sessions, they were holding in the coldest, most oxygenated lairs.

I was too frazzled from driving and thinking and not thinking about the move not to act a little foolishly after missing the strike. In other words, I fired another cast breathlessly, and slapped the entire leader down with a ruckus, spooking even the most jaded crayfish in those parts.

Upstream the creek turned out of sight. There was a butterfly bush at the outside of the bend, and from that point down to my station knee deep, old shoes on slippery freestone, there were more hemlocks and sycamore along with other hardwoods and shrubs and weeds in all manner of crowning, angular or else rounded and floppish with summer's crunch time. It wasn't a scene that brought trout to mind. Nothing, to be honest, came to mind except where was the nearest cold six-pack and why wasn't my wife here, jacuzzi-ing with me in one of these pools.

Woe is the angler whose thoughts go to family. There is little room for that when you're attracting a creature to swallow your bait, artificial or not. Fishing outings with wives and young children always have an element of the macabre about them. I don't care what Ranger Rick has to say.

There was a busted, flood-orphaned chunk of hemlock on the shelf that formed the next chute with its promising pool beneath. I crouched like some extra playing the enemy in a Vietnam War flick and false casted, drying the caddis before letting it fall on the boil between ledge and that place in a falls that resembles an industrial dough mixer.

The woods on both sides of North Creek ascend with the rise of ridges. The sun was shining on the west ridge, and that shine approached the creek the way light moves, imperceptibly, unless you study it. A fish rose. I set the hook with some blend of instinct and practice but mostly luck. Often when I fish, I run through my head how to respond to strikes. Sometimes I respond awkwardly, yorking the fly out of the water into a nest of tangles that impresses upon me the value of the mental picture, the see-it-in-your-head meditative visualization cornpone that is cornpone because it works. The trout ran downstream and deeply. There was nowhere else for it to go. To land and then release it didn't take long, but the sensation remains.

So it is March now, and I have the two-weight, and things feel fresh the way they do this time of year, when no matter what, you are going to catch as many fish as you miss, and maybe more, and there will be new spring flowers and birds and a fence to build and a chainsaw blade to sharpen, and nobody around for another couple of hours.

Later, working in the woods around our place, I'll sense how it is with fishing and chores. How to start a Saturday of chores with a little fishing transforms those chores into an extension of time fishing. And how fishing is as much a way to settle in to a place as it is an act of exploration, the way chopping wood is as much about exploring as settling. All devoted anglers have a life outside their passion for the sport, and it is often as passionately led. We know that getting on the water and wetting a line is not procrastination so much as a way to prime body and mind. Getting to the stream, rigging up, casting, resting, returning—the whole affair pulls some choke in me, allows the engines to start with greater ease. I love the way this works. I fish almost as much for this feeling as for the fish.

After missing a strike in the first pool, I rock-hop upstream, staying low, careful that my shadow doesn't spook any fish. The next pool is shallow, like a staging area for the flume and deep hole I just left. I drop a knee on the quartzite, check for limbs behind me, and then clockwork the two-weight, firing a cast upstream. There's a channel I like the looks of, green as summer hills in mist, eddies on either side of it. A hard, tinfoil-like glare crackles off the water. I don't see the Adams, but I strip in line as slowly as I believe the fly is drifting back downstream. Polarized sunglasses would help, but I prefer visual input to be natural. Fishing in light so bright the fly goes dark is exciting to me. On days when it is less exciting, perhaps a lingering migraine still sharpening its machete behind my eyes, I have to be more careful about position.

The channel offers nothing. After a half dozen presentations, I cross the boulder and step in the water, squatting a bit for stealth. The current surrounds my legs with gentle pressure. North Creek seems to be in no hurry to meet the Chesapeake. I don't blame it. The intimacy of this place is possessive—the soft hues of bedrock, moss-shawls, National Forest for miles in most directions.

My rod bends deeply, tight to a trout that must have struck at the upstream edge of a half-exposed rock. With the glare, I didn't see how the fly disappeared, but I was looking in the general direction and must have sensed it. The fish stays deep, as deep as it can stay, and my guess is brook trout. The rainbows up here tend to leap when hooked. At maybe seven inches, the brookie isn't small for North Creek. It thrills me to feel it sprint a couple of times. Before I bend to release the fish, it comes unhooked on its own and disappears with a fast, dazzling sequence of wiggles.

I sit down and feel a heavy, electric delight coursing through me. The creek seems at once louder and more muted, as though it were closer, inside me. I watch a small wave pulse crystal and milky, and have a hunch that the trees, adolescent locusts, will fall today just as they are notched. If they don't, so what.

Hair of the Dog

The expression originally referred to a method of treatment of a rabid dog bite by placing hair from the dog in the bite wound.

1

That was the fall Tika kept returning home with bones, flesh-and-hair-matted bones, large ones. It was November 1996, towards Thanksgiving. He wandered often and for long periods in those days. The nearest house was half a mile, and there were few cattle in that nook of Maine then, few sheep. He kept his treasures under the cedars at the edge of the driveway, in secret places. He doted over them, howled at them, and licked and rubbed on them as if they were his own. And then he ate them. After a time of this, Kirsten noticed he'd added a moose skull to his collection. A bull, antlered. It was cold then, rarely above freezing, so none of it stunk too bad. We asked the folks down the road if they had taken a moose that season. Yes, they had. But no trouble was Tika, they said, he was welcome to the discarded carcass.

2

His rear legs have been shakier than usual today. They quiver and twitch. Walking is the best medicine. Being Sunday, we spend time in the field, woods by the pond. Tika wanders, lifting his leg against the grass and eating grass and puking grass. Kirsten brushes him, and mats of his hair blow like dizzy cotton balls through the June fields and woods. Cream-colored blots hang in the alder and hawthorn along the shore.

3

Kirsten has spoken of Tika's time in Vermont, 1990 or so, before I knew either of them. How three piglets died from shock when he as a pup entered a pen to play chase. How two sheep became, through his curiosity, tangled in an electric fence. And how in high summer, on their walk from the farm where Kirsten worked to her cabin on the ridge, Tika would stop with her at the thickets and pull wild berries one by one from the stem with his teeth, little scratches on his snout.

4

When dogs yell and bark in the night, we sense the whereabouts of his wanderings. Mornings, briars hang in his nappy coat like evidence that's going to be dismissed. We think of shearing him, as it is warmer now, seventies some days, the sun out longer, his tongue, too, as he pants. The shears are elegant, one piece of metal looped at end, the blades sliding against each other when squeezed with a sound as delicate as it is sharp, a sound more soothing for me than for him.

5

Tika has a lion's mane of salt and pepper hue. And trousers, feathered tufts of silver brindling as bushy as his tail, which hangs and drags, rarely lifts at all anymore. So there is a certain nobility and goofiness. His coat extends even to his paws, hair protruding between his pads as though to keep the snow out when there is snow, and mud when there is mud. Like many coated animals, he takes great care and devotes hours each day to grooming himself, gnawing and licking with a tenderness and exactitude.

6

In our twenties, we worked with some wild kids. We took them on long backpacking and canoeing trips. On hikes or at camp, Tika stayed close to the kids who were in most turmoil. He just did. The kids loved him. He was distraction and solace, something to touch. Often they would make him howl. They would howl themselves until he riled up enough to begin himself. When he howled, the kids, Kirsten, and I always tried to harmonize. But one is hard fit to harmonize with a wailing so pure and instinctual. We might as well have been imitating the sound of the path of water at the falls on the Moose River as we portaged them, that trip when the pot of water nearing a boil on the camp stove tipped, scalding a girl's arm, that trip we saw a dozen moose, and a black bear swum across the river in front of our lead canoe, Tika's ears perked, head lifting from its resting place on the gunwale.

7

A black stripe runs off the corner of his eyes to the base of his ears, suggesting kinship to raccoon. He has large ears, perky and proportional to the size of his head. Brindle and translucent are his eyes, a kaleidoscopic cinnamon. They are loving, sad, stoic eyes, and they glow with the curious wisdom of emotionlessness. People think Tika is larger than his seventy pounds, but his hair creates this illusion. Wet, he looks like an overgrown water rat, with his thin chest and legs and haunches. He was never a fast dog, moving like some cross between a salamander and a cow, but he has jogged with us, a few too many miles at times. Or he trotted while we jogged.

8

Kirsten first named him Ferdinand after the bull in the children's story that prefers smelling buttercups to fighting. It didn't work. He was a rowdy pup, as if any aren't. Eventually, she settled on Tika, which means something like "correct, true, just." She'd heard the word often hanging out with some Maori people in New Zealand, and we've learned since that the same word or a word with a like sound has a similar meaning in Russian, Polish, and other languages. Though I call him by nicknames, the name Tika fits his demeanor best. He embodies the "true, just" meaning of the word, as though he operates on some level beneath waking but deeply wakeful.

9

That howl, that plaintive soulcry, not quite mournful, not quite joyous. Just music, a pure note held. Head up, lips stretched and throat, a high wail. He howls when he feels feisty, whenever he's been left alone and somebody returns or a visitor arrives—dog, person, cat, horse, cow. Sirens, wood through a planer, an orbital sander—these sounds make him howl. He howled a lot in '98, the year Sophie was born. Also, trains make him howl, steel on steel, the passenger train whistle more than the freight.

10

Tika lies in the entryway of the house where I'm running exterior trim. He lies on a bed of plywood, and he looks through the front door's rough opening as though it were his house. And maybe it is, at least for now. Seeing him, I'm reminded of when Henry and Mingus were kittens, and Tika would take their heads in his jaws and drag them from one end of the kitchen to the other. This was a while ago. We were staying in a big farmhouse in Maine and where caring for these cats and fixing up the place were part of the deal. Sometimes Tika would lie on his back and the kittens would swat at his nose and crawl up his chest and roost like a dove in his fuzz. He loved these cats. He probably wanted to eat them now and then. They were pretty cute and probably would have been tasty, but Kirsten was good about reminding Tika to be sweet. A few summers we got back to Maine and visited that place. Henry and Mingus are big now and crazy as any old barn cats. Tika and them, they are still friends. It takes a while at first: he perks his ears and bows up in hunter mode and the cats crouch and hiss. But soon enough they're sniffing each other, the cats rubbing against him, backs arched, tails whipping, as he lays there, the color of oats and chaff, opening his eyes or just dozing.

11

I started to tell you that Tika's father was a long-haired Shepherd, and his mother, a sled dog in New Hampshire, was half timber wolf and half Malamute, bred in Alaska. So he's independent, rarely coming when called, rarely nuzzling or asking for pets or scratches. He's a pack dog through and through, however, and he grows animated and joyous in crowds—dogs, people, or other animals. His favorite way to sleep is by resting his head on a foot, preferably a bare one.

12

Doing stuff with Tika this morning, walking from place to place, I'm aware of his simplicity, how he's so consistent as to seem too visible, too present. He reminds me of what a monk said to a guy who'd come to live in the monastery: he said to him, you are doing well—hardly anyone noticed you today. Friends have called Tika stoic, ancient. I watch him stop to sniff. He points with his ears, gazes for the owner of what musk—deer, rabbit, groundhog, fox. In his eyes that passion and warmth. He sniffs again, scratches at the grass and then holds his snout among it for a long while, as if there were a kind of music going on in his nose

13

At the beach once, Popham Beach in Maine, Tika lifted his leg on a small chair in which a lady sat, a perfect stranger. She wore a one-piece, red I think, and his warm urine through the mesh seatback must have been quite a shock. Maybe dogs won't change your life, but they will always make the holes more beautiful, put a little mend on you, mend your pace, too. Once, a mutt, some stray, lifted its leg on a friend's bag on a Carolina beach a few years back. She had driven to the coast to kill herself. She had a fillet knife in the bag and planned to swim out and slit her throat later that evening once the beach was less peopled. The plan was simple but years in the making—drugs, alcohol, abandonment, the typical despair. But the urine on her knife, on her bag—it screwed up her plans something glorious. Crazy thing is she's still a cat person.

14

It's Saturday, the first of July, summer in the air and in the people. Our daughter, Sophie, who is five, and I are in Lowe's. Another customer has her puppy in the shopping cart, a fuzzy golden retriever mutt. Sophie says that when Tika dies, she wants to get a puppy. A puppy would be great, I tell her, but Tika still has some living to do. Later in the day she tells me that a few people have said that Tika needs to be put to sleep. I'm washing Tika's crap out of the canoe when she says this. A dry day, clear, breezy. Dragonflies and skimmers make their rounds. Kirsten, Sophie, and I have been canoeing. Tika still loves to be with us in the boat. A green heron lights in an oak on the other side of the stream. Frogs whirr along the bank. Then there is ewing, a crying like a baby goat in the woods. A distressful sound, it nears. We look in the woods and see a fawn burst hopping from the trees. It is past the rock twenty feet off the bank when two dogs emerge barking on its trail. Kirsten runs after them, splashing through the creek. Tika, whom I grab then, starts to yowl and bark. He rarely barks nowadays. In five months, he will take his last breath. Kirsten disappears after the fawn and the dogs in the trees to the east. There is nothing in this world like a chase. We don't hear the barking or mewling anymore. I hold Tika. Sophie asks if the fawn is okay. I don't know, I tell her. We watch. Barking again, and the dogs dart for the woods from which they first emerged, a large doe on their heels. Tika barks again. I scratch him behind his ears. His skin is damp, scabrous. His hair tangles in my fingers. The wind takes it, and then the water.

Sandstone Is My Favorite Rock

What happened is, I leaned too far offside while paddling under Decapitation Rock in the first drop of a rapid called Towers. When I attempted to roll, my right shoulder dislocated the way shoulders do once they've been torn up a few times in the past. Many wasps seemed to be stinging it at once. Next thing I knew, I was out of the boat and standing here, my shoulder back in place and tender.

This is the Russell Fork of the Levisa Fork of the Big Sandy River—Russell Fork for short. There's a rock the size of a cement truck next to me. There are rocks everywhere. It's like a convention of sandstone. We're in Breaks Canyon, headed for the bottom. Daniel Boone is said to have named this place the Breaks when he ventured through here in 1767. That this is the deepest canyon east of the Mississippi and the heart of the Breaks Interstate (VA-KY) Park, one of only two interstate parks in the U.S., is not the first thing on my mind right now.

Steve Ruth sits downstream in a red kayak. He has found my paddle and is waving it, a blue canoe paddle. He holds it in his right hand, his own paddle in his hands too. He is forty feet below in a mess of boulders and water where I should be, had things gone as planned.

Steve is a friend of a friend and lives in Elkhorn City, a two-stoplight town at the foot of the Russell Fork gorge. He has run this stretch of river fifty times already this year and it is only May. I contacted Steve a couple of weeks ago in April and asked if he'd show me the lines through the gorge at a benign water level. I said I want to run El Horrendo. He said everybody wants to run El Horrendo until they see it. I thought maybe not everybody.

This trip began a good while before all of that. Sixteen years ago I was sitting on the bench of a five-seater composting outhouse at the rafting company where I'd come to live and work. I was alternately looking through the studs of an unfinished wall at a patch of jewelweed and the more general riot of fecundity that is the North Georgia mountains in high summer, and also flipping through an old issue of River Runner magazine. There was a picture of a rapid called El Horrendo on a river called the Russell Fork. Photographs rarely do justice to landscapes, and this was not an Ansel Adams, but even so, the rapid appeared as thick and seductive and full of velocity as its name.

The word became a localized bit of slang among our river rat pack, a group of raft guides who, when we weren't on the river guiding, spent as much time on the river as possible. El Horrendo was an exclamation one attached to the kind of bad news that is more complaint than tragedy. Saying it was a gentle way to tell the complainer to quit whining. Now and then you heard somebody pluralize the word, especially when the news was especially pitiful. But the plural version wasn't effective. Los Horrendos sounded like a bad restaurant, a recipe for food poisoning.

I have several favorite names for rapids on rivers and creeks in the Appalachians. Big Splat, Recyclotron, Marginal Monster, Super Soc Em Dog, Gorilla, Lost Paddle, Jawbone, and Swiss Cheese—these are names that embody a particular rapid's power as well as the rowdy blend of skill and play that running it—and the sport in general—inspires.

When you run a rapid that has a juicy name, there's a sense of acquiring the name yourself or at least its potency. But when the rapid flips you and you end up, for whatever reason, unable to roll and having to swim from your boat, in that case the name acquires even more power.

A rapid does not have to be especially difficult to earn a juicy name. Some rapids inspire hyperbole not because they are difficult but due to their vertical, heavy-duty-adrenaline factor. Since you spend most of the run in the air on these kinds of rapids, if you hit it right at the top, at the launching place, then that's enough. More intricate, technically difficult rapids sometimes have understated names. That they were born on the tongues of loggers and locals rather than weekend warriors often accounts for this. Consider The Narrows, Entrance, Woodall Shoals.

When I first encountered it, El Horrendo seemed unique for its slangy ethnicity. Unlike many names for rapids, there were no allusions to animals or power tools or pop culture either. No Tablesaw here. None of the cinematic charm of Bambi Meets Godzilla either. El Horrendo was exotic. Every time I heard the word, I vowed not to let it remain an abstraction.

Around 1:30 this morning, I found a site at the Breaks campground and didn't bother to set up a tent. When I stay in developed campgrounds, I feel compelled to first walk around and spy on my neighbors, see where they're from, the way they set up their camps, their gear—it's as though I'm not getting my money's worth otherwise. So I did that and then laid out my mummy on a pad and tarp and scooted in and tried to sleep. A generator hummed on a nearby RV. Winged things buzzed around my face and ears. I didn't really sleep but I rested some, cocooned in that space between delight and anxiety I always feel when morning holds a new river in store. That I was missing my wife and daughter and our home and having doubts about my mettle as a middle-aged, very part-time whitewater paddler silted the experience even muddier.

On the surface, this is sandstone country, coal country below that. There are cliffs on either side of the river that span to a height of two hundred feet. It is another thousand feet to the top of the gorge. Towers is the first of several big rapids. Towers as a name is unimpressive. But say it in its entirety, Towers Falls, and the name changes considerably. As a rule, any word for a rapid followed by "Falls" suggests drama. There's still another drop, or falls, in Towers to run, but I'm carrying around it. My shoulder will not let me roll up if I flip again, and the river is undercut down there and everywhere else too, meaning there are caves and sieves under boulders where the water goes. At least one paddler has died at four of the six big drops in this gorge, usually by being pinned by the water in a cave or sieve. You better stay in your boat, in other words, you better roll fast if you flip.

When I first saw El Horrendo in the magazine those years ago, the fact that the rapid existed on the border of Virginia and Kentucky made it even more compelling. I'd never seen that neck of the woods. I pictured the John Sayles movie *Matewan*, which I admired and which was set nearby. It didn't surprise me that such a river cut a gorge in those parts, nor that people were paddling it, but part of me still believed then you had to go to Colorado or somewhere "out West" to run real whitewater.

A few years later, while rowing a baggage raft for a commercial trip through the Grand Canyon and then running rivers and creeks in Idaho and Alaska, I learned there was an abundance of good whitewater out West, much of it larger in volume and more dramatic and scary and cold than what the Appalachians hold. I also learned that both places have everything that people who love paddling whitewater need. Running rivers, like any pursuit, is a matter of taste. It is not so much a sport as a vehicle for getting closer to the nature of moving water and rivers and drainages and rain. I prefer the intimacy of Eastern waters, the dense growth on the banks, rhododendron, mountain laurel, dog hobble. The spiders and salamanders. I was raised fishing and camping in such places, so my experience with these watersheds feels deeper than in other regions. The smell of the dank soil. Which wildflowers prefer calcium-rich soil over more granitic soil. The stories of people making lives there. How the rapids, too, differ according to geology.

Though raising and growing one's food is a more intimate and responsible vehicle for getting close to the natural order of things, I haven't outgrown my flings with the rivers and streams and woods surrounding our place. The fishing, paddling, guiding, and romping around in the woods that I've done all my life led me to embrace my wife's desire to farm or homestead or whatever you call what we do, which is more of a marriage with place. Life at home with Kirsten and Sophie and our land and animals, buildings and fences, is always showing me better ways to be a husband. The lessons in patience, tolerance, endurance, and care are endless. I am a slow learner, one who grows through dreams and remorse as much as through experience, and I am easily overwhelmed by rewards and dependent on escapes into the wilds of woods and words to settle down. Someday, I trust, this will change. For these first couple of years, I have given myself permission to explore the country beyond our fences. There is self-indulgence but there is necessity, too. I am not unlike a dog laying his scent beyond the borders of our place, hopefully bringing some good discoveries home.

Back in the boat after carrying Towers' last drop, paddle again in my possession, I follow Steve towards the next big rapid. The chutes and ledges are more nonstop and technical than any water I've paddled since I first blew out my shoulder four years ago. I'm not entertaining the idea that I'm too old and banged up and sleep deprived to paddle this gorge; maybe I am, but there's such an odor of honeysuckle and mud and sun and water in the air. Riversounds conjure a montage of memory traces from the six years of my late teens, early twenties, when I put as many miles on the river as on my truck. It feels delicious to carve through boat-sized slots and ride out on planks of ledge to avoid horseshoe pourovers, to drop edgeways into foam piles, watching Steve disappear with a left angle over a horizon line, every moment a new vista, the cliffs high above and the trees thick with May green, perfumey with blossom.

"This is Fist," Steve says. We're bouncing around in a pulsing eddy like pieces of debris. "Fist of God. You can hop out over there and watch my line." Steve appears as straightforward and careful as you'd expect somebody to be with over a thousand runs through this gorge. People often think that a long time paddling makes you more risky and reckless, but the opposite is true. With experience comes wisdom. I know that Steve has helped pull several bodies out of this river, injured or otherwise.

Steve paddles with left angle into the first drop of Fist, a twenty-foot slide, and the current rockets him into an eddy, where he carves with the elegance of an athlete at the height of his game, paddle braced ninety degrees with the upstream flow of the backwater. He has a little grin on his face and it brings one to mine. A dozen tiger swallowtails erupt from where they were feeding on the silted, damp boulder next to him. I have the sudden conviction that sandstone is my favorite rock.

Fist of God, I say to myself, liking the sound of it. I glance upstream at what appears to be some giant's mad game of marbles— boulders and boulders and more boulders, a steep slope of them where the river's supposed to be, no water in sight, the gorge nearly vertical on either side, trench-like. Earlier, Steve mentioned that the gorge deepens by the day and that he's noticed rocks have moved each time he comes down here. Looking back, I see him paddle hard with an upstream angle and ferry to the river-right side of the final tongue, avoiding a large hydraulic and just below it a sieve between mammoth boulders. I decide to run it, tell myself do not swim, do not screw this up.

Being on a new river brings the old ones to mind. The key to a fulfilling run, if not a safe one, is a mix of desire, awareness, will, and luck. You try to grasp a river's essential nature, as you would anything you cared about getting to know. You summon everything you have and hope to have. You do this by feel and by study. Easy breathing helps too, which for me is a matter of singing. Today, the brain's shuffling through a mix of Rolling Stones, The New Pornographers, and Lynard Skynard, sometimes all at once. "I see a red door and I want to Tuesday's gone with the laws we changed them o hell what'll be revealed today Sweet Virginia sit beside me my only son." The muddy blues of the Stones and Skynard must be in some way kin to the way the water pitches my boat here in the Russell Fork, but who knows. And maybe Neko Case's smoky, half pissed, half whiney alto, along with the bouncy melodies of The New Pornographers, has less to do with the river than with the way I drive this big Tupperware-like boat through it.

Fist of God is merciful. My run is clean, undramatic, a blast. I ferry in front of the sieve with some trepidation and then meet up with Steve in a swirly eddy. He points at a plaque on the boulder that forms the cave. It is a memorial. I look at the dates and do the math. The guy was forty-three years old. "He was one of the best," says Steve with no sentimentality. "Knows this river better than anyone." Steve's tense shift strikes me as unintentional and true, like the man is here, his voice in the sound of the river, the trees' fresh green.

When we're moving—dancing really—through the class III and IV boogie water between the big drops, I watch the water just ahead of me, glancing now and then at Steve as he disappears over a horizon line. I try to watch his head and does it jerk left, right. Do his eyes grow large? I look for any clues he might share as to the nature of this steep, pounding clutter of river. I've always like technical whitewater best, rivers and creeks with an abundance of exposed rock and gradient, not too much—the Chattooga, the Watauga, the Chauga, the Tellico, the Upper Yough, Big Sandy Creek; and the Russell Fork is as busy and steep as any of them.

I paddle a decked canoe and paddle on the right, so left to right moves are safest for me. Because of the damaged shoulder, I'm keeping my paddle close by holding my elbow in. I try to finesse the moves as much as I can with hips and use of current. Though I feel more comfortable, having had a clean run at Fist, it is apparent that as soon as I'm off the river, my shoulder's going to be very sore and that a good night's sleep is still a couple days off.

"What do you do for work?" Steve asks. I tell him and he says nothing, as though there isn't time now to be interested or work itself is uninteresting. "Watch me close in here," he says. "This rapid feeds into Triple Drop."

I like the understated names—Maze, Triple Drop. They are concrete, lack the figurative charge of Fist of God or El Horrendo and will probably be more challenging than both of them. When I first injured my shoulder some years ago, I stayed out of heavy whitewater for several months. It was May then. Some nights, feverish with spring and the sound of falling rain, visions of creeks pulsing and bankful, I would imagine rivers and rapids and names of rivers and rapids, and write about running them in the voices of fictional paddlers. Like many meaningful things, it was a waste of time, but the act made for a good way to go paddling without being able to do so in real time. I was free to explore various characters and the characters of the rivers and creeks they were paddling, explore them in the same way one runs a river for the first time, discovering its personality and voice with imagination and some abandon.

Steve and I continue to snake through a maze of crazy currents and several four- to six-foot ledges. In the final eddy above Triple Drop, my mouth goes dry. I wonder if Steve would mind if we stopped a while and I took a nap. Instead, I enter the first drop two boat lengths behind him. I don't want to be too close to him nor too far. The joy of paddling resides in the finest lines, the quest for placement, angle. Speed is rarely necessary. The river takes care of that. Too much speed prohibits the quick adjustments, the degrees of motion and finesse that one comes to love so well.

I join Steve below the drop in the eddy on river left and let my heart rate subside. So far, so good. But looking over my shoulder at the chasm of the next two drops, I'm dismayed. It seems wrong that water could do that, fall and break that way, and not turn to flame. These drops appear much more challenging than the first one, the consequences severe. There's little to no room for error. I climb from boat to boulder and stand there feeling as though the water in my body has harmonized with the river. It is terrifying, and I love it. The water has no particular rhythm. It is too chaotic to even be chaotic and therefore has a pattern, indescribable, yet a pattern nonetheless.

Steve peels out of the eddy and enters the maw. He makes it. He makes the next moves too. He makes them almost look easy. To be watching a paddler so at home on a river is a great privilege. His motion, like that of any skillful boater, resembles a bat bug-surfing the dusk air. It is a dance at once freaky and graceful, a mix of bob and rock, both controlled and beyond control, brilliant. The trick to it is letting the river have its way with you. The key to it is knowing the river's ways and being on the side of its easiest, gentlest ways, even when there seem to be none.

I haul my boat over the boulders and then cram back into it and stretch and snap the neoprene skirt around the cockpit rim. We are in a small pool below Triple Drop, before the next rapid. Steve, drifting, seems overly nonchalant. My eyes follow his to a beach and mossy, weedy grotto scene on the river left side of the river.

"Stay close to the left bank here," he says suddenly. "At higher water this one's easier; we'd just drop through a cave."

I see from his eyes that he's serious.

This rapid, nameless, yanks my shoulder as I have to brace hard dropping sideways in a hole. I curse but stay upright. Steve says nothing. I wonder if he thinks I'm faking the pain. Below, in a small and swift pool, Steve looks at me and then downstream. "El Horrendo," he says. I smile. He doesn't. "Start left and get far right. He points with his paddle blade, sun crackling off the water dropping from it. "You want to ride the plank left to right and take the meat two feet off the right bank. Stay out of that hole on the left." Then he adds, like an afterthought, "You can scout it over there."

I pull over at the dry part of the boulder that forms the first entrance drop of El Horrendo. It'd be nice to follow Steve, just run the rapid blind, but that pleasure feels like a version of insanity today. As I peel from the kneeling position in the C-1 to watch Steve's line, I admit that I'm off balance from lack of sleep and recent challenges at work and at home. For a moment, my ankles have just enough feeling to support me. For the last ten years, each time I do this, I vow to get out of decked canoeing and into kayaking so I don't have to kneel. It never happens. I suppose I like to kneel, the vision it affords and the pain, the power you get out of the torso, even the worshipful quality of it. And I'm used to it. I've been doing it this way almost twenty years.

No matter how easy Steve makes it look, I don't like the left to right look of El Horrendo's entrance move. My shoulder is throbbing worse, like somebody's hacking at it with a dull hatchet. Any cross forward stroke hurts a good deal now, and such a move would require several of those strokes performed with precision and strength. Steve peels from the final staging eddy. As the big drop takes him, he resembles a leaf some kid has thrown into a flooded drainage ditch. I mean he disappears in a maw of foam and roar. Then reappears, upright and beaming.

I drag the boat over the ledge and put in at that final eddy above the second drop. As the boat bounces around in that rowdy backwater, tremors begin in my sternum. Eddies have that effect, especially above large drops. The way they allow you to stay in one place when so much energy is moving downstream provides a feeling of having escaped time. The sensation is thrilling. I look over my shoulder, see the horizon line, and visualize being in my boat in the proper place with the proper stroke, angle, trajectory. As I do this, a gorge begins to erode in my chest. I think this is ridiculous. I think you're too old for this. I think shut up brain. I think God grant me the serenity have you ever seen a she-gator protect her young there is no place I'd rather be.

I'm not where I'm supposed to be. Instead of two feet, I'm six feet off the bank when I hit the drop, the water so aerated it feels not like I'm flying but like I'm on some planet where there's no taking off, no gravity either.

For a moment, a moment beneath and more stretched out than most, the sound of the river conjures an entirely different spectrum of color. No reds or yellows or greens, but a world just as colorful and with no terms of reference. Maybe that's what El Horrendo means, in translation, if not at its root—color blind.

"You were lucky," Steve says once I make the eddy. Something in his voice suggests relief, something else regret. The guy is a hard read. I like him.

"Are there trails out of here?" I ask.

"No. We're going into Foreplay now. It leads into Climax. Don't screw this up. Climax is nasty at this level. We'll walk it."

I'm so jazzed from El Horrendo that Foreplay is a blur, then gone. As we walk Climax, Steve takes a minute to point out ways to run the rapid at various river levels. Though it is hard to hear him over the sound of the water, his passion is palpable. He resembles a docent who, in giving a museum tour, has led us to his favorite piece.

The gorge opens to a more gentle aspect not far below Climax. We are back in our boats again. The river seems less angry but no less wild. The rapids are calmer, now, quieter. I start to remember how it is to feel relaxed. You can actually hear the birds now. They are adamant with their voices.

I paddle up alongside Steve and thank him for showing me through the gorge. "No problem," he says. "I like sharing this river with people." Suddenly he looks up, and I do the same. There is a buzzard two hundred feet above us. It is carving a tight orbit near the same spire of sandstone I saw at the put-in.

We don't say anything for a long while. There is the sound of our paddle blades entering and exiting and reentering the water. There is the sound of the river and there are other sounds further off.

At the take-out, Steve offers me a beer.

The Buffler Trout

That week was more like reconnaissance, a mapping out of waters that from reading and hearsay were growing a little too mythical in the mind. Even the place names—South Fork of the Holston, Mossy Creek, Buffalo Creek, Roaring Run—had begun to strut through my ears like some mantra more sinister than pleasant

It was the end of May. Kirsten and Sophie were out of town until the following Saturday. The semester had ended where I teach, and some more time on the water was in order. Each morning, I let the hens out of their house. They were ravenous about the honeysuckle that dwarfed the fence with its vines and the air with sweet reek. I watered and fed them and did the same for the sheep, ducks, ass, dogs, and cat. And I fed and milked the goats, too. No animal had coffee but me. It was going on three weeks without rain, so I spent a strange hour hosing the garden, at once entranced by the shower coming from the nozzle and worrying the contents of our rain barrels and well. There were snow peas now, and on the third day, I ran eight heads of buttercrunch and romaine as well as some bunches of chard to the Lexington Farmer's Market and Donna Janeczo, who was running the booth for our grower's guild.

"You have errands to run?" Donna asked.

"Oh, yes," I replied earnestly.

Ten minutes later I was eating the first of two venison, mayo, and lettuce sandwiches I'd packed after watering. It was nine in the morning. I was driving a county road, looking for the special regulations stretch of Buffalo Creek, up near Effinger, Virginia. For a moment I shuddered at the recognition that our freezer was down to only twelve packages of last winter's venison, but then it hit me—it was Wednesday and I was going fishing, as I had the day before and the day before and would for the following two days. What could be wrong with my life?

The morning was hot. A creamy haze saturated the hayfields, the barns and farmhouses, and the mountains beyond. You sensed the entire state of Virginia would be a fire hazard by afternoon. The trees still had a youthful luster to their green, however, which was encouraging, as the air was very much August air, and you half expected to see August's weary, washed-out foliage.

I'd heard of big browns in Buffalo Creek. I'd heard, too, that it had been heavily poached, the special regulations stretch, by bait fisherman, and I'd also heard that locals called it Buffler, the area and the creek. I'd crossed the stream a hundred times downstream on trips from our small farm up Route 11 to Lexington. It had been on my mind to fish it for some time.

It was as good a time as any. The day before, I'd fished the South Fork of the Holston with Morgan Wilson. I always learn a lot when I'm on the water with Morgan, and those few hours on the Holston proved no exception to this. I mean the kind of learning that defies description, the kind that comes from close observation, trial and error, and that quality of yearning anglers know well. Morgan and I had a good day. We took turns working a two-mile stretch of that swift, cold river, each of us releasing more than twenty fish, several over eighteen inches, all of them healthy, wild.

The road ran along Buffalo Creek, but the special regulations stretch didn't appear marked. The air smelled like heat and fresh-cut hay. In places, box elder and sycamore and multiflora rose and much else made a tangle, nearly a tunnel of the creek; in other places it ran sun-flecked through pasture, the grass nipple high on the undercut banks. The water had that milky aspect of limestone chalk streams. I'd be reminded of it on Friday, the last day of my trout binge, when I'd fish Roaring Run's primeval, snaky gorge as a string of thunderstorms blew through the area.

I stopped at a gravel wayside to check things out. After negotiating two deer carcasses and several Styrofoam bait canisters, I came upon a shadow-struck pool fretted with current and with the slithering of a sizeable water snake as it coursed from a boulder to a lair in a root clump half in the water and half on the bank. The place looked fishy despite itself.

I drove on slowly in the troutmobile, an '89 Jetta, wishing we'd replaced the AC compressor when it had died the prior fall. The confluence of North and South Fork of Buffalo was my aim, and though it wasn't clear where that was, things were starting to look familiar the way they do when you've awakened from a dream that's as freaky as it is vague.

I remembered that Eben and his mother, Penny Hulme, lived nearby. One night in the wintertime, very late and snowy, I'd picked up Sophie, who was no longer feeling good about spending the night at her pal Eben's house. I think she was distraught about not waking to her morning goat-milking routine. Here was their road now. There was their house, a car in the driveway. I turned.

Penny is a caterer, and though busy prepping a gig slated for that afternoon, she visited with me as she worked. Eben, who was eight, took a break from riding his bike and snooped, flushed and eager, in the doorway.

"They catch big fish right out there," Penny said. I looked across the road from the house. The creek was fifteen feet wide. An axle was lodged half in the mud on the far bank. Eben, who had disappeared, returned with a photo of a two-foot rainbow the neighbor caught in the pool below the bridge I'd crossed to access their house.

"Prince nymph," Eben said, as if uttering a dirty, glorious secret.

I said to Eben, "Why don't you show me the creek." Never mind the special regulations, I thought. I didn't feel like bothering the landowner for permission anyway.

Eben grabbed his rod and tackle box, and we paraded through a field not yet hayed and then around a clump of nettles before entering the creek. I don't like to fish downstream, but that appeared the most favorable option now.

I bit off the bass plug from Eben's line and fastened a Mepps Spinner. He seemed distracted as I explained the knot I was tying. We were standing in swift water to our knees, and the coolness felt very fine.

It was hard not to remember the time I'd stuck a Mepps lure, barb deep, in my eyelid. We lived in Memphis then. I was seven. My father and his pal Michael Murphy had towed me along to fish a farm pond in Arkansas. They were in a canoe, casting poppers for panfish, when they heard screams from where they'd left me on the bank. I'd been yanking on a snag when the lure freed and shot back, one hook of the treble lodging in my eyelid. I must have thought I was blinded.

"I know that knot," Eben said in such a way that suggested he did not. He took the rod then and snagged a deadfall on his first cast, which relieved my outing, indeed my whole day, of some pressure I'd felt since deciding to fish the prior night. Kids are gifted that way, blasting our expectations to hell, or other heavens. Eben relished the opportunity to unsnag the line, as the water was to his waist there. It was clear he was more into hacking around in the creek than fishing, which was slowly becoming okay by me.

I had a #16 Royal Wulff on 6X leader. Fingerling dace struck it on nearly every cast. The following day, on Mossy Creek, I'd land two twenty-plus-inch browns on that two weight, bending it dangerously, thrillingly, to the cork. For now, the dace, when I was both fortunate and unfortunate enough to hook one, only slightly flexed the rod.

We stalked pool to pool downstream. Chunks of limestone made for decent cover from which to drift the Wulff or for Eben to troll his spinner in the current. The rocks, slipperier than prayer, looked like the old bones of some large, extinct mammal.

There were subtle rises here and there; it seemed from their slight, smoochy quality that the fish, whether dace or trout, were taking emergers.

I stuck with the Wulff, which is a good all-around attractor, suitable for the one-size-fits-all demeanor that the heat of the day demanded. With each landing, Eben was eager to unhook and release the dace, which pleased me as much as him. Though it may be easier to tolerate a one-hundred-degree day in August than ninety-five and muggy in May, I thought, as Eben freed another dace, heat only intensifies the pleasure of standing waist deep in running water, casting for trout.

We approached a promising looking pool. Eben had first cast rights all day. He snagged on a rock and I convinced him to leave it there while I drifted a few times over the run. I stripped some line and roll casted, reminded of how much good music is contained in the ticking of a reel. I then wiggled the rod tip to pay out the line. What clearly was a trout, a rainbow, attacked the Wulff. I lifted the rod and set the hook.

The fish wasn't big, but it was big enough to bend my two weight deeply, especially when it ran edgeways with the current where it plunged through a sluice. I landed the nine-inch rainbow and gave Eben the pleasure. As he groped the fish, I saw the bold colors—the lateral rays of pink, the bluish nebulas—and had a hunch it was born in those waters. Eben dropped the stunned fish as soon as the hook freed, and it lay still a moment before swimming into a box canyon in the rocks. I tickled the trout's tail, spooking it into deeper water.

We unfastened his snag and marched sloppily over the slippery stone for the next pool. There was a bend in the creek now. The water piled up on the outside of the bend, with some of it running under the roots of a walnut. It seemed unusual that a walnut tree would grow so close to a creek, but the habitat patterns of trees, especially in the South, is about as consistent as the rest of life there.

I saw it at once. A fish, a powerful fish, was slurping emergers not an inch from the root. I saw it without even looking, it seemed, as though I'd been seeing it all day and for weeks, maybe, and knew it would be there. The surface disturbances were ginger enough to suggest a fish of some proportion, age, and wisdom. I did not give Eben the first cast.

It was a tricky move, landing the fly in the lane of water heading to the spot. That there weren't dace snapping at the Wulff seemed like a good sign. Brown trout like dace real well.

Eben was getting impatient. He had his eyes on scavenging some kind of rusted power line apparatus in the cobble on the inside of the bend, but I told him to hold his horses, that we'd move on soon. There wasn't enough room under the walnut's branches to roll cast, so I was taking the fly between index and thumb and slingshotting it the way Russell Kelly showed me some years back on Deep Creek in the Smokies. The results were mixed, but not so mixed as to have spooked the fish I hoped.

If there'd been clouds in the sky that day, one would have covered the sun now; I had the fly where I wanted it. The hackle lay on the water just right. The line was on a good drift. I half expected a bee to sting me or some other minor disaster to occur. When the Wulff was an inch from the roots, the fish rose. I lifted the rod tip and stood up from a kneeling position. The weight of a strong, large fish shot through rod, hand, arm, and then the whole body. I felt the hook, too, as it set, the two weight noodling fiercely, and felt the fish as it bent, turning, flexing away from me. Whatever Buffalo there was in Buffler Creek went stampeding between my sternum and spine just then. You know the feeling.

I have to mention the two weight's origins. All gear, even the soggiest sock, can take on a totemic significance for the angler who gives a hoot about the craft. My six-and-a-half footer came to my possession through an act rich with context. Five years before this day, I traveled to Atlanta one weekend to help my father move into an apartment. His marriage to my mother was ending after twenty-nine years. I was separated from my wife and daughter at the time, and we were trying to work on things. Everybody was having a tough go of it.

There was something fun about gathering toilet paper, silverware, trash cans, and other staples with Dad, and it wasn't just that he was paying for it. I think it had to do with the fact that Dad and I were making the most of a situation that was bad but wasn't as bad it might have sounded, even to us.

There in the Target, outfitting his apartment, we talked, as Dad and I often do, of fishing and hunting trips. I was living west of Charlottesville at the time and fishing, whenever I could, for brook trout on the North Fork of the Moormans. I had a six weight he'd given me, the same one I'd slammed in the passenger door in 1979 after a day fishing the Chestatee north of our home in Atlanta. Instead of an eight-six, the rod became a seven-footer then. I'd been meaning to replace the four lost ferrules for many years, but I'd been meaning to do a lot of things.

In the kitchen aisle, Dad and I exchanged curt musings on our endeavors with water and fish and birds and gear. Neither of us is at a loss for words, yet we might be taken as the reticent types in matters not involving the outdoors. "How about a pot and pan, Dad," I suggested.

"Sure," he said, laughing. When you're in Target, the miles of merchandise ties more than your tongue in blood knots.

But it was after Target, you see, driving back to the apartment, when Dad steered into a strip mall. Atlanta was teeming, surreal as a bloated tick—exhaust, glass, concrete. There was an Orvis store next to a frame shop. We parked in front, entered. "Happy Birthday," he said. "We're getting you a brook trout rod."

The fish was gone. I glared at the walnut tree as though it were responsible. Then I checked it all again—the line dead, the rod straight as a builder's level—making sure I hadn't entered another dimension or something. The line was slack, yes, and wrinkled the way line wrinkles when it remembers the force that snapped it. I moaned feelingly.

"What happened," Eben asked. He was tearing a jewelweed plant from the sand.

"I hooked a big fish," I whispered. "It broke the line."

"Look," said Eben as he yanked another jewelweed from the sand.

"That stuff is good for poison ivy," I said, not thinking about it. "Crush up the leaves and rub them on it." I didn't know it then, but the instant the trout broke the line set the hook of angling even deeper in that namelessness where obsession resides. What could I have done differently, was what I was thinking at the time. A softer set? A release of tension once I felt the hook set?

Though that moment a fish strikes and you set the hook is not one in which you are particularly cognizant, I was slightly comforted by a feeling the muscles and mind might have their shit together the next time I dead drifted a #16 Wulff on a 6X towards a large trout holding under the roots of a tree on a bend. Eben had recovered a chunk of metal from the cobble bar, and his face contorted with excitement at the discovery. Pleased by this, I reeled the line into my spool and scanned the bank for a place where we could access the road without having to crawl through briars and weeds so large and dense it seemed they could eat you.

"It's good having a caterer for a Mom," Eben said as he slapped fresh chicken salad, egg salad, and pasta salad on his plate and then mine. We'd had a hot walk up the road back to their house, but my sweat eased off as we sat on the front porch eating a late lunch. Penny and Eben talked about the flood of the prior fall. As they spoke, I remembered there was a clump of daylilies about to blossom along the road where that big trout now lay with my Wulff in its lip. Had it won? That was a ridiculous question, but I asked it anyway. Had it earned my leaving it be was more like it.

There were dried cranberries in the chicken salad, and we savored their zest with each bite. The three of us ate and as we ate and chatted and looked out on the field and the trees and the creek, a pair of cedar waxwings lit in a box elder limb that stretched over the stream, just below the bridge. I took them as a sign to return, and soon. It was that kind of day.

Going to Natural Bridge

It was spider season. The orb weavers were all over. To duck and edge through the limbs was to wear them, hairnet of webs, armnets. The sticky stuff covered my clothes. Every step demolished hours of work, who knows how many meals. But it was a kind of light, too, the way of any embrace, a kind of motivation.

The woods felt the way woods feel in Virginia in August—crowded and unattainable yet welcoming, maybe too welcoming. At a fork, I chose the central game trail, the path that traversed the middle of the slope. The high one might deposit me on a cliff, the low in overhead stickweed, chiggers.

Across the road from where I'd parked, the deer had crossed from the field to the woods enough to make a little trail, quick entry. If anybody noticed, they couldn't see me now. The truck was another matter. It sat on the grassy shoulder a hundred yards from the bridge and Bed and Breakfast; being a quarter century old, people would likely assume the old Dodge was broken down.

The day had started the usual summer way. After book work and animal chores and breakfast, we chose, from several ongoing projects, a session with tape measure, pencil, Skilsaw, etc., as we fitted and hung rafters for a shed roof, a dry place for firewood. It was a cool morning for August, but we needed rain, needed it bad. I was antsy. The drought and the fact that classes started soon weren't the only thing.

There was this trip I'd been meaning to take. On the map, it looked to be a mile or so from the bridge on Red Mill Road down Cedar Creek to the famed rock, or water formation—Natural Bridge. We'd driven over the chasm a hundred times on Route 11 (built on the bridge's spine), each time wondering and talking about what was beneath. We'd passed the billboards and attractions—the gift shop with its massive parking lot, the wax museum, the caverns, the haunted mansion, the zoo.

And, too, we'd seen the paintings by Frederic Church, Jervis McEntee, and others, and we'd read histories of the place, sensing how the importance of Natural Bridge in the past compared to its status now said something about all of us, and about time and time's more physical side—erosion. I'd even compiled a list of quotes about the bridge from an exhibit at UVA's Alderman Library. I liked how the voices and takes on the spectacle served as a kind of topographic map, evoking nature and culture's shifty terrain. Among the list was the following from *The New York Times*, May 14, 1899:

> After entering the grounds of the Natural Bridge property, the descent by a path is very steep and jagged, to the level of the stream which flows beneath the arch. President McKinley took the lead and progressed so briskly over the stones and slippery places that he soon was far in advance of the remainder of the party. Directly beneath the road of rock were assembled about fifty girls, pupils at the Hollins Seminary, near Roanoke, VA, who were there on an excursion. The President stopped for a few moments as he reached them, and each was introduced and shook his hand.
>
> A curious freak of nature directly in the centre of the dome was called to the President's attention. This was a distinct impression of an eagle with outstretched wings, such as is on silver dollars, made by moss and rock stained by the action of water. Mr. McKinley was greatly impressed by the scenery, and so expressed himself several times. The ascent to the level of the roadway was hard work, but it did not appear to affect the President, except that he became somewhat heated.

And this from *Moby Dick:*

> But soon the fore part of him slowly rose from the water; for an instant his whole marbleized body formed a high arch, like Virginia's Natural Bridge, and warningly waving his bannered flukes in the air, the grand god revealed himself, sounded, and went out of sight.

And this, one of my favorites, from a postcard with a fuzzy color image of Natural Bridge, postmarked 7 P.M., 18 July 1910, Buena Vista, Va.

> Hello! Gladys:—
> I am having a *delightful* time. Miss you all so much. What have you been doing? Have you seen Katie lately? Guess I will come home Friday.
> Lovingly,
> Alice Bell

But, you see, we hadn't visited. We'd been living less than ten miles from Natural Bridge for nearly a year. It seemed a deficiency. To be physically ignorant of the local watershed feels as dangerous to me as not knowing the creosote level in the stovepipe—things can catch fire.

After lunch—Kirsten's pesto goat cheese and roasted red pepper on Sophie's cornbread—I tried to enlist some accomplices. I wanted to hike in from upstream.

"You go first," Sophie said after a pause.

They were headed out for chicken and goat feed, always a decent, ceremonial affair, even if we'd been emptying the feed sacks as quickly as they were raising the prices on grain.

"Come on, y'all," I said. "I'll pack some snacks, water. We'll go when you get back." Our animals erupted in one of those cacophonous medleys right then. Nellie, her Nubian ears flopping as she trotted down the hill on the far side of the pasture, wailed so mournfully it seemed she'd disrupted a hornet nest. The pigs grunted. A rooster called. The dogs, guarding the livestock, barked at an airplane. "Join me on this one," I added.

Kirsten flashed her big brown ones at me from the driver's seat, right eyebrow raised. "Don't get shot," she said.

The creek felt close when I happened upon an old limestone foundation. There were no piles of junk, just a sheet of metal roofing, rusty and nearly covered with growth. The stonework was careful, the joints tight, dry, mortarless. At the edge of the homesite, thirty feet from the hearth, the ground dropped. There was a cliff. Cedar Creek slumbered below, a mosaic of shadow and shine. Limbs and leaves made the view a kind of basketry. There were many places here.

I sat at the edge. A damselfly landed on a box elder leaf. The bugnoise swelled and receded. A blue heron stood in the creek; it was the same color as the rocks where they were wet from higher flows. The creek had dropped a couple of inches; the air, sticky and ripe, seemed to hold that excess water on its breath. Descending a small gulch to the bank, I wondered if there'd been a storm in the drainage overnight. There hadn't been rain at our place.

Cedar Creek ran a chalky green, just like Cedar Bluff and Purgatory Creek, the two west slope tributaries of the James near us. There was something medicinal looking about it. Horsetail grew on the banks, tubular and segmented, and I remembered a phase when we were drinking a delicious, nutty tea made from horsetail we'd harvested along North Creek.

While the cliffs were limestone, the rock underfoot felt metamorphic, the creek bed blocky with river-wide ledges—a strange, winding staircase. A lot of the stone was gently blue even with the thin layer of silt. The gradient was steady with shallow pools between the drops, the footing not nearly as slippery as it is in the streams we usually haunt. Here and there was evidence of prior industry—a steel rod, stonework. The evidence suggested the former presence of a mill. Purple lobelia, a spiky, gaudy flower, was in bloom, its square stem and thick, orchidy blossoms making the kind of sense that blurs other kinds of sense.

Meanwhile, the cliffs remained consistent on the right bank. It was comforting to have so much rock not just underfoot but overhead. Something about the stone, its form and bulk, suggested a great deal of weight and compression, a prior ocean. I was reminded of a layer cake.

So I walked down the creek in old running shoes and socks and some light nylon pants. There was little graceful about the affair. If I felt like an intruder, I felt as much like a piece of driftwood. It was thrilling, calming, silly. I'd worn a button-down shirt in case I ran into anyone who cared that I was trespassing. Somewhere along the way, I realized that my pants, these geeky nylon numbers, still smelled like the Lexington Goodwill.

It was strange to hear the sound of running water with the gurgles and splashes of my own wading among it. Truthfully, I'm not sure what I heard. My head was still hazy, but I was excited, too, and smiling. Even in the shady places, the water felt steely and astringent, like a faceful of spider web.

Downstream, the creek bent to the south. The cliffs stood on the left bank there—softer looking outcrops, doughy and loafish, less outcrops than rock exposed by water digging in. Cavities and caves in the stone gave the place an anatomical look. You could see faces in that stone, bodies. The walls of the gorge were steeper now, taller. Leaves fell—redbud, basswood. The Joe-Pye Weed stood six feet in height, top clusters leaning over as if tired of so much blooming. It all seemed too private. Because it was. Things were just right.

I had been walking an hour. I had been stopping as much as walking. There was so much to see. But there were fewer pools now. The rocks in the bed were wormier, striated. They were softer. They were more broken than upstream. The walking wasn't as simple with the congestion. I must have dropped a hundred feet of elevation. Very few trees lay fallen in the creek, though there were many hemlocks standing dead along the banks—they would come down soon.

There seemed to be voices. I stayed by the edges, trying to blend in with the limbs and leaves and rocks on the banks. If I had come a couple of miles, more or less, I had come further than that in wonder and paranoia. The highway across the field from where I'd left the truck was no longer audible. The moss and lichen might as well have been screaming. There was another horizon line downstream; I couldn't see the creek below it, not even in the distance.

Soon, too soon, from the brink, I watched the water pour a long way into a small pool. It is hard for me in such situations not to imagine falling or just stepping off the drop. The pool at the bottom was the deepest water I'd seen on Cedar Creek; below it, another slide dropped fifty more feet into a larger and wider pool. I couldn't see over the cliff that jutted off the left bank, but I had a hunch that something was there.

I was getting close to my destination, that being a decision as much as a place, so went with care down the left side, putting hands and feet on only the driest rocks. It wasn't a dangerous descent, but it felt that way.

Near the base of the first slide, I could peer around the cliff and see downstream. Full sun glared off the water. The gorge was less constricted. There were smaller horizon lines in the distance, wrinkles in the shine.

A rock wall stood on the left bank. It ended in a round, turret-like overlook. Inside the boundaries of the wall was the paved path the paying folks use—it had to be.

The water fell. The water pooled. There were so many crazy ferns. After sitting a while, I scrambled back up to the lip of the first drop and then up from there, up a crevice on the steep bank, arborvitae and cedar and oaks and shrubs. It was a high way. The rocks were slick and crumbly. I've always liked it when going downstream requires going uphill.

There was a path, larger than a game path, and I followed it over the nose of the ridge. The cliff was to my right and over it a very long drop to the creek. I was descending slowly along the contour of the cliff's top lip. The edge was closer the further I went; a slip would mean the kind of drama nobody needs.

And then there was a roof, oak shingle—a tired, lovely roof—on a little gazebo near the edge of the cliff. It was vacant, but you could taste the ghosts, the place empty with the fullness of the past. I entered softly, tested what remained of the floor. The shingles, it was clear from underneath, were cut nailed to old tongue-and-groove oak. There were initials carved all over the plank benches and cedar posts. Many of the initials had dates—'54, '37, '21, '76, and so on, each decade from the last century.

The bench was comfortable, the air cool, the birds and clouds more everywhere for not being visible. Eventually, I decided against turning back. The path went on. Natural Bridge couldn't be far.

A man snapped pictures from the stone wall-enclosed path. He wore a knit shirt, shorts, eye jewelry of a digital camera. I told my eager, anxious self this man has paid his admission fee—thirteen dollars. He can take as many pictures as he wants.

There was nobody coming up the path beyond him, a long straightaway of pavement and stone wall. You could see a couple of hundred yards before sycamores obscured the way.

The man turned and headed downstream. Once he seemed beyond hearing my feet on the crushed stone, I scrambled to the paved path, leaving the gazebo behind. A steep and root-tangled descent, I slid down the last pitch.

A sign said you were looking at Lace Falls. It said other things about the place, things you'd expect a sign like that to say. But the quote at the bottom of the sign seemed to apply more to Natural Bridge than to Lace Falls. The words were Reverend Andrew Reed's from 1835: "Really, it is so sublime—so strong and yet so elegant—springing from earth and bathing its head in heaven!"

I felt the lean exuberance of a thief now. A kind of patriotic despair coursed through all of it; I was elated, though it was a muted, pathetic elation. Nobody was coming up the paved path. I couldn't see any cameras in the trees. No surveillance equipment appeared rigged to the stone wall. One can never be sure.

My pants had zippers above the knees. I sat on the stone wall and messed with the zippers. Very soon the pants were shorts. Unless you looked at my black shoes and black socks and saw they were wet, you couldn't tell I'd been wading through the creek.

Everything was swell, the paved path easy going. Even the creek seemed to have surrendered. There were more sycamores, big trees. People passed, headed to Lace Falls. We exchanged greetings, nods.

At the re-created Monacan Indian village less than a mile from Lace Falls, a large bearded redhead in skin clothing was talking about brain tanning deer hides. In the adjacent roundhouse, also shingled with dried cattail bundles, a black-haired lady spoke of native culinary arts. A woman among the tourists resembled a feature in a cliff I'd passed upstream—she was beautiful and chasing a kid who was doing some overtired pow pow routine. I lingered a while, quieted by everything, especially the cattails.

Later, past Saltpetre Cave, where—according to the sign—they'd fetched bat guano to make gunpowder during the Civil War and the War of 1812, a man and woman stood off the paved path, staring at the ground. They wore matching purple t-shirts with the words Natural Bridge on them, no other graphics.

I approached and saw the water snake as well; I mean, it looked like a copperhead, so I figured it was a water snake. Copperheads don't even look real they are so beautiful and spooky. It has something to do with their eyes, the source of the copper and that sinister, stunning shine. And it has something to do with oak limbs, which copperheads resemble the way a good myth resembles the first time you fell in love.

"Pygmy rattler," the man said.

I looked at the snake again. I wanted to believe the man, but this still looked like a water snake. "I don't see a rattle," I said. The man looked at the woman as if I were an idiot. There are worse ways to look.

"Pygmies don't have rattles," the guy said.

I moved closer to the snake. This was a beautiful snake, the same kind we swim with at North Creek, or who swims with us. I was surprised I hadn't seen one upstream.

"They can strike the length of their bodies," he said, voice steady. You could tell he wanted me to get bit. I squatted. The animal wasn't coiled. It was small, head like a fingertip.

"I didn't know pygmy rattlers lived in the mountains," I said.

"Sure," said him. I wondered what the woman thought. Her face was as hard to read as the snake's.

"A pretty snake," I said.

"Sure," he said. Clearly, he knew I was a trespasser.

It was around the bend, Natural Bridge, tremendous and silent. The sun beaming through, the long shadows. What can be said? I sat on a bench—there were lots of wooden park benches at the edge of the paved path—and looked at all that rock and at all that air and light where once there had been rock. It reminded me of going to feed the chickens and finding two of them dead, victim of possums.

I don't know what it was. It was wild. It was numbing. It was like trying to read a book where the pages are a kind of food and only by eating them with the proper care are the words revealed. The landform felt so significant as to feel insignificant—maybe it was the other way around. Eventually, I fell asleep.

Later, I had a run-in. If I'd awakened from a historically accurate dream, vintage 1834, in which I was being lowered in a hexagonal iron cage by windlass and steel cable from the top of the bridge while an attendant stroked something eerie and elegant on the violin, I don't remember it. I remember a man in uniform—forest green pants, beige shirt—asking me for a ticket.

I had come to the end of the paved path where there was a paved road and a café, Natural Bridge behind me, upstream. I said I didn't have a ticket. The man looked at me. He looked like a guy I'd seen fishing on the James the prior week. I looked at the menu above the order window—the beer and sandwiches were way overpriced. The man didn't seem to notice my wet shoes. I wiped at some squibs of soiled spider web still gummed on my arm hair and looked dumb. He didn't look smart, but he looked like he knew. I didn't know where to go. A bus arrived, and when he turned and helped people board it, I followed some other people past the bus.

It took five minutes to ascend the steps, which were concrete and rose at an easy grade along a tufa stream postcardy with small falls and pools, mosses and grasses, shade and light and big, old arborvitae trees. You had to enter the gift shop then. It was quite a gift shop. There were books and magnets and toys and clothes and snacks and things. It seemed there were as many square feet of floor space in the gift shop as on the rock face that framed the great absence where water had done its work. Three miles of hot blacktop lay between this place and my truck at Red Mill, but I wasn't thinking about that. I was walking around the gift shop, wet socks making wet sounds in my wet running shoes. The air conditioner felt sublime.

2006–2007

Small Waves

Catching small waves, like catching small trout or raising food on a small scale, involves a spectrum of intricacies. It's true that you can't beat the gut-wrenching pleasures of surfing larger, more powerful waves. But we know that. We know all about big, groundswell waves and the adrenaline surges they inspire. They announce themselves just fine. Look at any surf magazine. You catch the drift. You know the fear, risk, reward, how they plunger you through.

With small surf, or windchop, you have to be accurate to the point of dainty. There's no muscling your position. It is a matter of degree: inches and quarters instead of feet. You tend to focus on other aspects of the sport when you ride small waves. Maybe focus is not the word but wander. The mind wonders. There's no danger that demands you stay constantly alert. You're either alert or you're not. You're in the ocean, so you're attentive, no doubt. And there are many variables outside of the waves, outside of riding them. Studying the color of water could occupy a person for many lifetimes, not to mention the sand, sky, birds, and all their juxtapositions. That one can ride such small waves at all, that there is power enough, has a lot to do with that—the ocean's multiplicity, its allness.

We arrived at the Carolina coast yesterday evening. Friends are staying on our homestead, tending to things. After they walked through the morning and evening chores with us and got a handle on milking the goats, we left them our home and a list of things to do, people to call in case of problems, and so on. It is a long list, involving feed and water instructions for chickens, ducks, rabbits, pigs, sheep, dogs, cats (barn and house), and goats. The tasks, mostly, are simple. And if they are numerous, they are small.

Nathan and his wife and their kids will walk from place to place with old buckets and coffee cans full of water and feed, and they will return with the cans empty, maybe a couple of dozen eggs in the bucket where the water was. They will follow paths and go through gates, open and close the latches. There don't have to fire up the old Farmall or even use any electricity, assuming they use the rain barrels for water and not the well with its electric pump. No, that is a lie; there's electricity involved in washing the milking pail and icing down the milk and cleaning the gallon jars and washing your hands.

It is mid-August. My cousin Alex has work obligations and is absent for this year's family beach gathering. I'd hoped to visit and surf with him, just as I'd hoped for a tropical storm to be kicking up some kind of swell, but when we arrived the wind was blowing hard onshore, from the east, and the waves were sloppy and small and beautiful. People played in them. Pelicans cruised like another horizon, hardly beating their wings, as if on patrol. It quiets me in a thrilling way to see pelicans. Their beaks alone conjure some Paleolithic instincts. I mean, it feels strange to even be wearing a bathing suit. I like especially watching the big, hard-skulled birds sway and tilt as they coast along the coast, wings and bodies rolling with wind. Sometimes you sense that they've caught a jolt of breeze created by a wave breaking or the wind eddying in the wave's trough.

Since I surf once or twice a year nowadays, I take what waves I can get. It is not so much about the waves anymore as the chase and the waiting. The last time I lived near the coast was in Maine. I had the luxury then to wait for a good swell to ride. Nowadays, it is hit or miss. Recently, at my oldest pal Harrison's wedding in Savannah, I hit. The morning after the rehearsal dinner, I drove to Tybee Island, discovered a good swell, found a surf shop, and rented a board. An hour later, I was riding away a long, strange night in waist-to-chest waves, mute with glee.

This morning I paddled out early. This was my morning chore: to feed from the ocean's bounty, to take care of nobody but my own selfish desires. The sun was not yet high enough to force a squint. But that fat star was larger and more orange that it would appear all day. The water juiced it, pulp and all. The waves were tiny. I was logging, as they say, riding an old longboard that weighs forty pounds now with water damage and fiberglass repair. The tide was coming in all morning. The wind was slight, allowing the waves to approach and roll glassy and long. Their forms varied as the beach disappeared. For a while, the waves closed out and rose and crested in one long curtain, as opposed to peeling left and right. They began to peel again not long after this, when it seemed the tide had covered a sandbar.

As I did my thing out there, I thought of the trim I'd run on a kitchen remodel the prior week—one-by-two spruce to cover gaps where beadboard panels met, roofline to gable, in our old, far-from-square house. It had taken a half day to shift gears from the rougher work of furring pine log rafters with two-by strips. Even rougher had been the tear out at the beginning. I removed one ceiling to find it had been floated down from an older one, above which were enough desiccated rats, mud-dauber nests, insulation, and dust to fill five contractor-grade trash bags. Running the trim involved sanding and then pre-drilling the small pieces so as not to split them. It was slow, delicate work, and I messed up many times, fewer once changing the music from Arcade Fire to early Dolly Parton and replacing the framing blade on the saw with a trim blade.

Small waves can't eat you the way large waves can, but they are fussier. You have to want a small wave. You have to work to catch it and work to stay on it. One is always ready to bail in big surf, especially when the wave closes out. It is different with ankle-biter waves. You pump the board in order to stay on the wave. Sometimes you squat and paddle with your hands. Other times you walk toward the nose, moving weight forward to aid with momentum. I don't only ride them for their resemblance to large waves and the memories and hopes that likeness conjures, no, I ride small waves because the process is squirrelly and I like to scramble.

The fog was thick our last morning at home. Everywhere—even the tomatoes—smelled and tasted like the river, the James, like its rocks and its mud and its fish and bugs and foam and tributaries. There were so many strands of moisture in beads on the spider webs it seemed strange that the silk didn't fall apart or fray. The sunflowers, planted early and past their prime, no longer needed walkers—they were just falling over. The damp couldn't stop beginning. The mind wandered. The bugs hardly flew, as if their wings were too heavy with moisture. Maybe the spiders waited for the sun to mop their walkways—it was hard to say.

We were inside the fog, though later, when we were feeding ourselves at the picnic table, we watched the fog disperse—was it mist then?—and rise over Purgatory Mountain and The Knob and Cove Mountain and Diamond Hill. Inside it now, we carried water and food to the various animals, the systems as entwined as our relations—a couple of cracked chicken eggs each for the dogs, some whey from goat cheese for the hogs, goat bedding for the garden beds, driveway weeds— plantain and dandelion—for the rabbits, canning scraps for the chickens and ducks. The morning was a watercolor, a duck dive, Eskimo roll. We all said thank you somehow. We waddled but it was as much a kind of swimming. The ducks seemed especially happy in the pond of that morning.

The bird and bug song seemed to come from the air itself, some tweeter in the density. Now Sophie emerged, drifting from the barn with milk pail heavy. Kirsten's bedhead bobbed above the tickseed sunflowers and above the beans on their bamboo tripods—she was giving water to the pigs. I was dumping chicken hearts in the dog bowls. Every chore, every detail and pause between, was a wave, and we, while wrinkles on its face, were waves, too—we built on the approaches. And at the fences and cages we broke, rolled. Back to the house or across the pasture, we rolled, fed as much as feeding.

Another benefit to riding small surf is there are no crowds. You don't have to jockey for position or even think about there being another surfer on the wave. Of course, the mind can get crowded. Especially when the wind blows onshore, the scene reminds me of the mixed CDs my friends Peter Relic and Rob Hull make. Whether it is the sixth listen or the first, you're going to hear something different each time, in the order of songs and the stories they tell through lyrics and melodies and how they segue, have quarrels, arguments, whispers, brawls.

There are times when a good wave approaches up or down the beach and I do not stroke to catch a piece of its shoulder but sit quietly on the board and watch it grow steeper. I anticipate the form of its breaking, whether hollow or mushy, peeling or windowshading all at once like the final curtain on some performance about moon and gravity and time and wind and depth. The imagination has room to roam then. It is as though the mind catches the wave, but more like the wave catches the mind, and they join, roll towards land together. I watch the wave as if I were no larger than the pelicans or even the plover, and surf it as in a dream or in the muscle memory of having ridden waves of similar character only six or seven times the size, perhaps in the North, in Maine, but not always there.

I love waking to a sore belly the morning after surfing for the first time that year. The flesh on the ribs chafed. How the ankles then, stiff, lend to my steps a wobble. It is as though rust has formed and yet the feeling is less of weakness than strength. Even the muscles of the face are fatigued from the squinting. Perhaps I hold mouth and jaw in tense positions when I ride a wave. Certainly when paddling for a wave I grimace; I must, such is my desire to ride it. I am a greedy surfer most days. Yet lazy too, greed being laziness on steroids. Position is the key to endurance. Good placement means less work, three or four strokes before standing instead of twenty. I like when it is clear from the take off which way I will ride the shoulder. I angle the board in that direction and avoid the trouble of a bottom turn. Small waves hardly require a bottom turn. The face is not large enough to merit a drop. You are at the bottom from the start, or close enough to the bottom.

Morning and evening chores and the tasks we do throughout the day deepen the pleasure and the nourishment of our meals. We walk a half a mile or more each morning on paths we know well, orbits of food, extensions of the kitchen. We veer, too, and wander. Even in sour moods, it is hard not to honor the origins of what you eat. Indeed, our days are a continuous food preparation. We don't just go to the source for our food, or close to it, the true source being always hidden, we also have a hand in the clarity and the health of these sources. The buckets are a sensual kind of heavy, the fences a kind of weaving as well as safety. The way you slap a fifty-pound sack of feed on your shoulder, the way it rests there, balances on its own even as you walk rough ground, can be a pretty wild massage.

Of course, we check in with the animals. We touch them and talk with them and watch them; there are always several entertainments at once anywhere you look. Most of the animals, of course, care more about the food than we care about them, and this is lovely for the ways we try and don't try to feel otherwise and feel, always, more in tune to the mysteries of the world and our inconsequence.

One of the deepest pleasures of surfing is walking into the water with your surfboard. Call it the approach. It is not comparable to entering some great event, because surfing is private and inconsequential and better than great. Even though there are often no spectators, it always feels as if there are many. I am vain, so of course I believe all the beachgoers are watching me. They aren't. And if they are, they're likely saying, "Look at that fool with the antique board. There aren't even any waves."

Once I crossed the dunes at Scarborough Beach in Maine in November. Tika, our old malamute/long-haired shepherd, was at my heels. There was a lovely swell. You could hear the waves peeling hollow and strong from the parking lot a half mile away. The wind was just right, offshore and not too cold. As we crossed the peak of the dunes, we saw not twenty feet away a snowy owl perched on a "No Lifeguard on Duty" sign. The owl ratcheted its downy, shocking face and put holes in my bones with eyes at once fierce and tender. Tika, rather ambivalent to feathered life, went sniffing along the plants at margin of beach and dune, laying his scent until it seemed his bladder couldn't have held another drop. I hadn't seen a snowy owl before that time. I haven't seen one since, only that one almost every day.

Twice I've paddled into a break from a boat anchored just outside it. This is a thrilling entrance, as you have no visual of what the waves are doing. Paddling from beach to surf lets you study and surmise the nature of a break, but from a boat you have only a sparse idea. You might see a slight turning and folding of the water's horizon as the waves break. The first time I surfed off a boat was at Otter Cove in Acadia National Park. A lobsterman, surfer friend from Little Cranberry Island took us through seas running fifteen feet in a twenty-foot lobster boat he built himself. It was September, the day fluffy and mild, bold counterpoint to the wild, raucous ocean. Waves churned at all the ledges and minor islands between Little Cranberry and Otter Cove. The hurricane, a big one stalled off Hatteras, sung its heavy rock and roll. Spray was everywhere. We'd learn later that evening of a tourist washed by a rogue swell from the rocks at Otter Cliffs. We were much luckier. We rode head-high wave after head-high wave, each one spilling into a channel for an easy paddle back out.

The daily chores keep us close to the seasons and the weather and the way weather and season manifest in the animals and their habitats. We watch the rain and lack of rain, and we see it in the color of the grass in the pasture and leaves on the trees and composition of the soil. We take note of the animals' waste for signs of illness, parasites, and worms. A hen's comb tells you a lot about her health as well as the color of her egg's yolk. You look in and at the eyes and around the eyes, especially with goats. Every day there are surprises and changes, not all of them welcome. One evening last summer, Kirsten counted our flock of meat birds out back the barn and found ten missing. We'd noticed foxes a few times at the far end of the big field. We moved Beau, the male Great Pyrenees we'd recently adopted, from guarding the sheep to guarding the birds in the yard. There were two weeks before they moved to the freezer. His and Stella's puppies, now three months old and annoying as hell to old Tika, held their own with the sheep and the lambs. No more meat birds disappeared.

The other time I surfed from a boat was at Bomba's off Tortola in the Virgin Islands. Kirsten and I were honeymooning at St. Johns. This was ten years ago. On a trip to town, we discovered a surf shop. The owner mentioned a good swell. With Kirsten's blessing, I asked if I could join him and borrow a board. At four the next morning, he handed me an old seven-foot single fin with no nose. The tip was broken, blunted, and he hadn't even bothered to duct tape it. We zipped and bounced in a small Boston Whaler across the rough channel to Tortola in the dark. Dawn found us anchored offshore and rocking steady and hard. My host lit a spliff and offered me a toke as we paddled into the break. No thanks, I said, sufficiently paranoid. The swells were running thick and large. He pointed to a colorful shack at the edge of the beach. It was small with the distance. He said they served magic-mushroom omelets there. I nodded feelingly, too nervous about the waves and the borrowed board to know what was what.

Now it is dawn and there has been a thunderstorm overnight. I see lightning offshore. I see pulses of light as orange as they are red. There is the paler shine of a shrimp boat. The waves are still small. The moment I step from boardwalk to sand the rain drenches me. I hope all is well with Nathan and his family and the farm. Through the bottom of my feet it is raining on my head. A quiet kind of thunder and the patterns of its sound in the way the wind and the waves and rain have sculpted the sand.

There are plover. There are gulls and pelicans, sandpipers and osprey and egrets, terns and crows. I watch them feed, wild birds, their patterns of chase and scurry. Footprints and beakprints in sand. At a distance, silhouetted against the sun oranging the sky behind a line of storm clouds, there are more birds flying—who cares what their names are—buttoning up the sky or perhaps more accurately unbuttoning it, taking off its nightclothes. It seems they are waves, too, breaking, reforming, gathering food—it seems they know all the moves.

Chicken Midwife Girl

My daughter raises chickens, laying hens, keeps fifty or so, as well as a good number of ducks and guinea hens. There are twenty-two birds in her flock in the yard off the back west eave of the barn. They are two-year-old hens, a mix of Barred Rock, Buffs, Rhode Island Reds, and Aracauna. She ordered them based on appearance and laying capability from the McMurray & McMurray catalog not long after her seventh birthday. There are a variety of bantam mutts out there, too, semi-wild and just as full as the purebreds of that curious nobility of manner and plumage that chickens possess.

In her other flock, there are thirty young hens, heritage breeds, and two roosters. Also living there are ten ducks—five Indian Runners and five Buffs. She keeps this raucous, lively community in spaces defined by a portable electric mesh fence/chicken tractor combo that we just moved to a new spot where, after they fertilize the ground and we move them again, we hope to plant some fruit trees before long. This year, for her eighth birthday, Sophie asked for this: a portable electric fence with a solar charger. I have to admit this perplexed me.

"What about a softball mitt?" I asked.

"No, thanks," she said.

"A dress."

"No."

"A doll."

"No."

I saw it in her eyes then, in the wild mulch of her pupils, iris. She wanted a fence for her hens, portable and easy to move, so as to keep them in fresh grass and bugs, and to let them fertilize a wider area of ground. The moment shone simple and dazzling. I thought of Delia, our fuzziest barn kitten, pouncing on a grasshopper, chowing it. I thought of the fifty or so migrating monarchs that had been drifting like song in and out of the tithonia for the last several days.

It wasn't the first time I'd seen this spark, but rarely had it felt so palpable, so voluptuous and primal. Something, right then, about the link between my daughter and her hens haunted and delighted and eluded me. I didn't understand it, didn't need to understand it. I tried to bathe in it, like one bathes in what the river says when it breaks over rocks: with no comprehension and utter belief.

Kids, by their nature, resist definition. To say you have to raise them to understand them is not saying it right, nor is it true. Even once you know that a big part of raising them is letting them raise you, it is hard to talk about the matter without sounding maudlin. Growing vegetables and raising animals is the same way; you're better off pouring your friend a glass of fresh goat milk than telling him what it's like to milk a goat morning and night for months on end. Your pal who also milks a goat may as well have a glass, too, because her experience and how she thinks and talks about it will likely be different than your own. Smile and give them both a bouquet and they'll know the deal, your deal, with growing flowers. But serve early spring collards, steamed in gobs of butter, with trimmings of last winter's salt-cured ham drizzled over it hot—and they might know the meaning of life.

I was thinking these thoughts, if thoughts, the other afternoon as we zipped in our four-cylinder down I-81. Traffic was the usual hallucinogenic mix, more tractor-trailers than SUVs and compacts combined. We were twenty miles from our home, headed south and about to descend the long hill into Buffalo Creek Valley, in Rockbridge County. A beautiful place, even at seventy miles per hour.

We were almost back in the right lane when my daughter burst into tears as a semi passed us, its trailer loaded with cages, too many birds to a cage, some of the chickens dead. It was a crowded moment. I don't know what you call what I did. I didn't think about the dead and dying birds. Nothing came to mind about the recent Avian Flu policy at my workplace or the level of the gas gauge or the hard-working guy driving the semi or the how the semi, with its crowded, wind-tortured birds, served as a banner flaunting tax breaks for agribusiness. Things felt, suddenly, very tender. I was quiet. I watched the road. I let her cry it out.

This isn't about highways or driving. This is about my daughter and her chickens and how she and her chickens turn over all my fields, and it isn't really a story. It's about Permaculture, too, but that's a big, ungainly word, defined better in practice than in words. I wish I could be more clear about all this, but sometimes it's our nature to be clear by being impressionistic. So the wind blows. If whatever we don't know about living on this earth we don't know even more wonderfully each day, then things are going okay.

People who know Sophie know her as a sturdy, sensible eight-year-old who looks a bit like Shirley Temple in the pastoral mode. Her hair is dirty blond and less curly than it used to be, and some days she wears a cloth head covering to keep it all in. She is a good-natured, sensitive kid with a sense of the absurd that seems even more well-honed by the fact she swore off wearing anything but dresses, preferably homemade ones, at the ripe age of eight.

I don't have any other children, except for the several in me that vie for the spotlight most days. Sophie is more mature and interesting than any of these rascals. Truly, this girl has a joyfulness and vigor that very few people in my experience can match; among them, her mother and an old friend, Patrick, a chef and Tai Chi master, also do not seem to be of this world and yet more deeply of it than is probably legal in many circles.

So it isn't all proud daddy to say that Sophie is our most constant guide when it comes to the wild waters of family that we, like so many others, navigate. The girl bears a grace that's both innate and cultivated. She knows instinctually, in people and places, when things are amiss and degraded beyond the hurt general to our century. But it isn't all instinct.

That Sophie attended a two-week Permaculture design course with Kirsten for the opportunity to camp and be with new people and then participated in all the lectures and projects, earning a certificate, gave her confidence and helped shape her intuition towards a more fluent sense of the land as a living system. Even now she loves discovering new guidebooks and cookbooks and people for inspiration and know-how. When she's not learning from her chickens or goats or whatever else— playing with friends or jumping on the trampoline or doing schoolwork or reading or doing the thousand other things a young girl does—she's often dipping into the latest issue of *Backyard Poultry* or *Countryside: The Magazine for Modern Homesteaders* for new discoveries.

There are eggs, of course, daily, beautiful eggs, and what dozens we don't eat or barter, Sophie sells. She sells to a co-op, she sells to all sorts of people, and she keeps her earnings in a quart Mason from which she draws to buy feed, feed made with the best stuff she can find. Finding feed that isn't made of crap, by the way, is one of the kid's latest projects; naturally, she'd prefer that we just grew and ground it ourselves.

Recently we arranged a deal where we trade eggs for bread from a local baker. I hope he grows as excited for the thick, sunset-orange yolks as we for his La Miche and multigrain, sourdough, and rye, all made from the finest unbleached flour. Taking eggs to Alex is as satisfying as bringing the bread home for Kirsten and Sophie. He opens each pack, less to inspect them than to ingest the sensuality of their color and form, as subtly different from day to day, egg to egg, as the weather and changes in air pressure, the timbre and density of the garden and woods.

This all reminds me of the time I needed Sophie's help with something and found her in the chicken house. It was cold. She was bundled in parka, facemask, hat, and mittens. The ground was frozen. I stood by the door and saw her squatting to pet a chicken in a laying box. "What are you up to?" I asked.

"Rosie's laying," she whispered.

I watched Sophie and the hen a while. The one eye of the hen I could see seemed to be looking both through and at the things there were to see—waterer, feeder, roosts, laying boxes, shafts of light, shadows, hay. Sophie continued to rub her hand down the chicken's head and over her back. It was quiet in there. I remembered a poem by Baron Wormser, a fine Maine writer. I hadn't thought of it in a while.

A Quiet Life

What a person desires in life
is a properly boiled egg.
This isn't as easy as it seems.
There must be gas and a stove,
the gas requires pipelines, mastodon drills,
banks that dispense the lozenge of capital.
There must be a pot, the product of mines
and furnaces and factories,
of dim early mornings and night-owl shifts,
of women in kerchiefs and men with
sweat-soaked hair.
Then water, the stuff of clouds and skies
and God knows what causes it to happen.
There seems always too much or too little
of it and more pipelines, meters, pumping
stations, towers, tanks.
And salt—a miracle of the first order,
the ace in any argument for God.
Only God could have imagined from
nothingness the pang of salt.
Political peace too. It should be quiet
when one eats an egg. No political hoodlums
knocking down doors, no lieutenants who are
ticked off at their scheming girlfriends and
take it out on you, no dictators
posing as tribunes.
It should be quiet, so quiet you can hear
the chicken, a creature usually mocked as a type
of fool, a cluck chained to the chore of her body.

117

Listen, she is there, pecking at a bit of grain
that came from nowhere.

The poem, which I love for many reasons, I loved even more for what it now so glaringly left out—any consideration of the person who keeps the chickens and how the chickens are kept. Sophie looked up. Her face reminded me of nothing but her face. "I do this a lot, Daddy," she said, breath visible in the cold. "I like to play chicken midwife." The quiet grew very broad just then.

Later, I thought about the title of Wormser's poem and how gently it prepares readers for the reckoning with quiet the poem dramatizes. "This isn't as easy as it seems," the poems says of boiling an egg before it blasts in a complexly instructional tone into a braided litany of the industrial and spiritual realities underpinning the manufacture of, well, energy. Wonderfully, the poem works through all this, this astute and mouthy mental-politico-mystical-social realm, to its physical, image-based ending—chicken and grain—that enacts a quiet all the more quiet and palpable for the struggle, the shifts of mind and thought and perspective it has entertained and endured.

There is very little quiet about Sophie's life with her chickens. There is so much quiet about her life with her chickens. I don't know which sentence contains more truth. They are both true, the way saying despair can be more quiet than joy is not untrue. I know this much: Sophie, Kirsten, and I, we all get fired up about the eggs. I can't help but to sing badly and loudly sometimes when I'm cooking them or holding them or Skilsawing an old fence board to build another nesting box. Once—this must have been in a dream—I witnessed Kirsten and her mother standing over a loaded skillet, describing the color of the yolks. Fire, Kirsten said. Turk's cap lily, said her mom. This went on. Pumpkin, one said. Tangerine, said the other. Autumn, I say now, trumpet vine, gravity, brook trout, roe.

Quiet or not, Sophie's time with her chickens can get wild. She has been pecked in the eye by a broody hen, crapped upon, spurred by Dinosaur, a feisty old Brahma rooster that later she helped me pluck and gut before she sliced the onions for to enrich the broth of its stock. She has found chickens in various states of disrepair—victims of opossum and fox and hawk. She has shined the light as I shot at an unlucky opossum returning, perhaps, to again rip the head off a chicken without having the decency to eat it.

And Sophie has boiled eggs, painted faces and flowers and butterflies on eggs, hid and hunted eggs, and dropped eggs on her way back from the barn. She has fed cracked eggs to our hogs, our dog, the barn kittens, the housecat, and the chickens themselves. Most every day she feeds the shells to the garden via the compost and to the delight of many through the flowers and vegetables raised in soil made rich by that compost.

There was a day in August. Sophie was in the chicken yard. The air was hot and dusty and still. I had taken a break from gutter repair to see what she was doing. The girl was up to something—I could see it in her face, sweaty and red, as she dipped an old coffee can in the barrel that collects rain from the roof. A storm cloud cauliflowered over Purgatory Mountain, just to our west. Bugs hummed. Chickens strutted. I could sense my kid's awareness of these things in the easy, intent way she carried the full coffee can, stepping between birds, to an old wooden crate she'd stood bottom-side up.

There was a handleless frying pan on the crate. I recognized the pan from some cobwebbed nook of haydust and woodscrap that are indigenous to our old log barn. Sophie poured a bit of water over the layer mash in it. There was a stick leaning on the crate, and she took it and looked around a minute, pausing to watch Rambo the bantam rooster chase Abner the big rooster in a comedy of manners as much as scale. Eleven and a half thousand other things were happening and not happening. A hen clucked. The fence hid in weeds and grasses. I had a sudden hunch, not entirely whimsical, that I was present at the origins of Noh theatre, the Japanese form that embodies transience and quiet elegance, where the stage is simple and actors never rehearse together.

Sophie lurched then. The commotion, among the other commotion, was sudden, strange, inevitable, like an old take on a new idea. "Be patient, Greyledge," the child clipped as she shooed a big Barred Rock away from the pan of mush she was stirring with the stick. Greyledge twirred. I smiled. Sophie grinned, resumed her stirring. Why do chickens always look so endearing and ridiculous, I wanted to ask, but my daughter was in a groove. I wouldn't bother her with Chicken Appreciation 101. No need to consider, out loud, the way a chicken's head pistons on its neck, the chest puffed out, the strange boots of their legs, what it must be like to have wings, very beautiful wings, and yet spend so much time on the ground.

Sophie kept at it. She picked some honeysuckle leaves from where a plant grew along the fence. They were dust-covered, leathery. As she ripped the leaves into fine pieces, she hummed a song I didn't recognize, a sort of hymn. I fell into rhythm with it. Her voice was natural and wonderfully unpolished; in it somewhere I heard all the chickens on highways and in restaurants, barns and kitchens, warehouses and backyards. I wondered if there were more of these birds at any given moment than humans on our continent. It was a weird moment, spreading its paint somehow on all to come. What she was really singing for, I don't know, but it probably had something to do with the day and the life and the birds and the gift she would soon offer them, a layer mash cake with an icing of shredded honeysuckle leaves. Whatever it was, I was glad to hear it. The chickens, they seemed to like it too.

Among the Tributaries

1

The Moormans River begins as two forks draining the east slope of the Virginia Blue Ridge in Western Albemarle County. It dashes, steeply at times, to the Sugar Hollow Reservoir and then runs into the Piedmont, merging with the Mechums River to form the Rivanna's South Fork. On its way to the James River, the Rivanna flows east and south of Charlottesville, gathering tributaries as people do experiences, though with a quieter sort of grace.

I paddled the Moormans River often in the years '99 to '02 when we lived around Charlottesville. It remains a mystery. In many ways, I paddle it still. The Moormans, as all rivers I have known and loved, touches me every time I am in my boat, and often when I am not in my boat but in the presence of moving water—something as simple as crossing a bridge.

2

Kirsten did not join us on the James yesterday. She had some reading to do, gardening, phone calls. She hoped to catch a nap. I was in the stern of a canoe. My father, who was visiting a couple of days, worked the bow. Sophie paddled from her seat on a cooler in the middle of the boat.

We put in down the road at Arcadia Bridge. There was not another vehicle in the parking area. The water was low, the air cool and crisp for early July. We took our time, drifted a lot. The river's sluggish, summer flow and the nearly chilly air was a bracing combination. Sophie kept a tally of wildlife we saw in a little journal with Tasha Tudor art on it. There were many painted turtles sunning on logs. Green herons screaked and bounced and hunkered and flew. The kingfishers seemed to have learned to sing from the raccoons and were trying to outdo them, doing a fine job of it. If there were no otter or mink at first, there was an eagle—it was in the distance flying away, but we saw the white head, the wingspan, the myth.

3

The Moormans is dammed close to its source. Sugar Hollow Reservoir, which catches the North and South Forks of the Moormans, is part of the Charlottesville water supply. Running a dam-controlled river was not new, but for most of my paddling days I've made a habit of exploring free-flowing rivers. I like the predictability of unfettered waterways; if it rains they rise, and if it doesn't rain they fall. Aquatic life, with all its dazzling ambiguity and particularity, goes on. Dammed rivers are only predictable to the degree that there is a human, or several of them, in charge of the water supply. Fish, bugs, snakes, birds—they manage, or else they don't.

But the Moormans was pretty close. It was seven miles from our house in Crozet. I could do the run solo and jog back to my truck on a lovely gravel road, do the whole deal, get my fix, door to door in two and a half to three hours. I need a local stream to paddle the way others need church or bars.

Six-in-the-morning runs were not uncommon. More frequently, I ran the river at dusk, many times taking out in the dark. Depending on the time of day, river levels, and the company of other paddlers, I ran the Moormans from the dam at Sugar Hollow to Millington Road, or from the Doyles River just above its confluence with the Moormans to Millington, and sometimes from Millington to Free Union Road.

4

The last time my father and I paddled a canoe was near his home in Lowcountry South Carolina. We put in on Penney Creek and ran into the Edisto River. I remember it well. The Edisto felt wide open after the tunnel of foliage that was Penney Creek. Our rhythm was steady, patient, quiet, and it seeped through us like the terrain. I took a stroke and a half for each of Dad's strokes. It gave the canoe a nice flow, with a subtle punch to it, like an extra clove of garlic in your favorite stew.

A warbler with yellow markings lit in a bay tree. Along the waterline blossomed white flowers like morning glory but with fleshy spears darting off each sepal's node. Dad remarked that it looked like the flowers were waiting to close up on something, as if carnivorous.

It must have been ten-thirty in the morning. We'd come three miles or so and would turn back soon. For some reason, I thought to the way Dad had regarded my truck when I arrived at his and his wife Donna's home the previous day. To its hail-dimpled body, balding front tires, cracked windshield, the wires like a colorful pasta where the radio used to be, he gave a look of perplexity and respect, as though to acknowledge that if you're going to drive a piece of crap, yours is top of the line.

5

It didn't take long to fall in love with the rocks on the Moormans, the sloping ledges in the river's bed, and with the bluffs and cliffs, the outcrops. Dull pinks and purples, the metamorphic stone there deepened in color when wet and in the light. Also the meanders, the slow bends, and lazy pools were crazy; they seemed to liquefy what's commonly known as time.

Not two decades before we moved to Albemarle County a flood retuned the Moormans. Localized rain in the North Fork, north of Sugar Hollow, swelled the river high into the trees, tearing them loose, roots and all. The massive flow shoved boulders to new resting places. Evidence of that maelstrom remained. Each time I paddled the Moormans, I noticed debris and changes in the bed resulting from the flood. Rejuvenation was visible as well—limb growth extended over the river, fresh shoots, moss.

Where the flood originated, in the Moormans' northern headwaters, was a great place to explore. The upper part of the North Fork (and the South Fork) cut through National Forest. In the winter, because it received more light, Kirsten, Sophie, and I favored poking around the North Fork, which, being flood-gutted, was reminiscent of Western creeks—logjams everywhere, cutbanks riddled with erosion. The South Fork, its trailhead accessible from the same parking lot as the North, was dense and shadowed. Hemlocks, poplar, hickory, and oak formed a magical, multi-tiered roof. Hot summer Sundays when the Moormans, due to the dam, lay stagnant, we'd hike the South Fork, reveling in the shade and swimming in the frigid waters of a waterfall locals called—as many swimming holes are called—Blue Hole.

6

I watched my father casting a black smallmouth fly from the bow. We weren't far below the bridge on Arcadia Road. He worked the shoreline on the west bank and placed the fly with skill and care under the box elder limbs. Fish struck, but they were small fish and they couldn't seem to fit their mouths around the fly. Dad was tuned in. You could sense his body getting more comfortable in the canoe on the water. He often would let the fly fall—it fell gently, naturally—and then he'd look around a moment or two at the surrounding fields and woods and ridges before he stripped in excess line. There were a few clouds, high-pressure clouds, something minimal and wrought about them, not the least promise of rain.

Sophie watched him, too. She sat on our lunch cooler in the middle of the boat. She helped me paddle, keep the boat in a good place for Dad to cast—not too close to the bank, not too far. We wanted to give him access to the shadows. At low flows, the fish see further, are more easily spooked. They are also more susceptible to raptors and larger fish, muskie and such. They stay under cover.

7

I get a deeper pleasure paddling a river when I know its headwaters. I suspect it's like drinking a wine, the grapes of which you've had a hand in raising and gathering. It's not ownership I'm after, just care, patience, nuance—a well-rounded sense of time, gravity, gradient, flow.

The first time I paddled the Moormans I was unaccompanied, and for much of my time on it, I boated alone. In those days, the organization required to make plans with another paddler was often beyond me. While Kirsten made our rental beautiful with friends and food and kids and decent living, all the while hoping—gracefully—for a home to call our own, some land, a garden, perennials, I was in graduate school, teaching, working, and a new father and husband, all of which felt manageable because there was a good woman, a good kid, and a good river nearby.

8

My sleeping bag and pad lie on a fallen maple's branches. They appear to be drying quickly in the March sun. Camp is a muddy place between two small creeks that drain a swamp feeding Devil's Gut. Roughly ten miles long and never more than a stone's throw wide, Devil's Gut cuts a swampy island in the Roanoke River between Williamston and Jamesville, North Carolina, not far from Albemarle Sound but plenty far from the Roanoke's headwaters near Blacksburg, Virginia.

The river continues to drop. Where I stand now, casting into Devil's Gut, I spotted crayfish last evening. The eyes of those spidery nocturnals turned an electric cobalt in the flashlight's beam. A pair of anhinga fly eastward, circling once over camp before resuming their course. Their heads appear narrower than a hawk's or those of other raptors, and they are white and black, a kind of cookies and cream underwing.

Turtles, river birch, sycamore, holly, mistletoe, Spanish moss—early March in the Mid-South Coastal Plain bears so much promise, of mysteries revealed and withheld: strange footings and shifts of mind and seeing. As I pack up to seek camp in a deeper neck of the swamp I feel a visceral yearning. It settles me in unsettled expectation, a kind of joyous anxiety.

I paddle for a few hours—fish, drift, look. Sardines and an apple for lunch. Another mink chugs near the bank. Shad splash, driven to spawn—the South's version of salmon. Heron, wood ducks, an occasional owl hoot. Now a fisherman in a small boat slows to pass. We exchange pleasantries, a few words on our luck.

I find a cut off Devil's Gut and paddle up to where it narrows in the trees. I snake through the maze of cypress and tupelo, through channels sometimes no wider than the boat. I love how the canoe floats the gear and me in just three inches of water. There are voices; the water here is a busy tongue. It swirls through and around the tupelos' buttressed trunks, around the cypress, the knees of the cypress and the countless logs and sticks hung among the crowd. Schools of shad break the surface. I stand in the canoe to watch them, grayish and sleek, many scarred white from run-ins with predators. I catch a few on a chartreuse shad dart and hold them briefly, amazed by their phosphorescent backs, their big eyes and strength.

After some time I tie off. This dense forest has water running through it for miles. Each trunk is a tripartite of color bars—heavy, Rothkoesque hues of brown, grey, green. So water and wood leave their marks, a history of flow and of mossgrowth and mossdeath and much else. The sun glimmers on the eddy lines and boils. It is warm and bright for a while, and then the clouds take over and I don a wool cap. It is afternoon. Some slumber among the chorus of swill and rip. Like water, a satisfying fatigue runs through me. Like water and the fish in the water. Leaps of minnow, leaps of mind: my boat and paddle know me better than my legs. Soon I untie, land on a hummock and step shakily onto the soft ground, roots, and moss. Here I will set up camp again; there is just enough dry ground.

9

Dad and Sophie were swimming in the riffles below the island at Solitude Farm. Was this yesterday? This was yesterday. I could see their heads and their shoulders. The river seemed to be more a function of the summer sun than of water. Everything was brilliant and severe. Undulant, too. My dad and daughter appeared more turtle than human. Really, we could have been small spiders on the petal of a sunflower, waiting for prey. I watched them while I casted a day-glo yellow popper for smallmouth upstream. If there was something melancholy about those moments, there was something equally tender. A strange compilation of feelings swirled through me; indeed, my roles as father and son felt more defined than they had in the past. There were many other rivers, all of varying gradient, color, season. They had wonderful names, but their voices were more wonderful and haunting.

Later, we were in the canoe, headed downstream. Sophie wanted to fish, but there wasn't room for her to cast safely. I was paranoid that she'd hook Dad in the cheek, maybe pierce his ear. We didn't need any of that. After a while, Sophie elected to swim next to the boat. Kirsten's lifejacket, which she wore, was still a little large for her, but she floated well and safely and she giggled and splashed and seemed to be deeply— or shallowly—at home.

10

Twenty miles downstream the Black River meets the Cape Fear. Carlton Henry, who runs a machine shop across the road from the slow river, told me he's never seen a gator on the stretch I'm paddling. I wouldn't expect to see one in February, but it is very warm. I love it. I love any weather. It could be dumping cold rain. As long as you're outside.

Carlton said there's plenty of gator below the bridge. I'm a good distance above the Hwy 702 bridge, where, thanks to Carlton, my truck is parked under a big oak. I've settled into a good groove, alternately drifting and then paddling a while. The geriatric cypresses stand along the banks. They look more painted than real. They have the chiseled outline of cirrus on those days when the clouds seem to be shavings of metal and it isn't windy on earth but you sense it is blowing like hell way up there.

I came here to be among the bald cypress that in 1986 they carbon dated to nearly two thousand years old. I came to stand in the canoe and watch the sun turn to freckles where the current puckers at the trunks and knees. I came to see the river run over pale sand but mostly darkness. And see mistletoe and Spanish beard thicken the canopy. The birds are tough to see in the dizzying growth, but you can hear them making a fuss by the dozens. It is February. Last night a deer, snorting and kicking, woke me. Beaver slaps woke me. Everything else was a night song and so was being awake. The ground served as a sleeping pad. I came here less to sleep than to rest.

I think back a few days to when my daughter and I were walking along New Hope Creek, near our home in Hillsborough. We'd encountered several good pieces of driftwood exposed by recent high water. Sophie, in six-year-old splendor, asked me what is driftwood. I said it is wood that has spent a long time in water. It is often bits of root, I told her. She kept walking along, thinking, apparently, of something that happened somewhere else, another time.

The river's channel narrows. It is dense and wooded the way swamps are. I follow a path marked with flagging tape. The tape was orange at a previous time. It is the color of banana pulp now, and the channel it marks winds a mazy course through, under, and around the ancient cypress. The current plunks and tinkles as it strains through the roots and knees and clogs of sticks and nuts and leaves.

I feel dirty following the flagging tape. I tend to ignore the rules once I've learned them. Half the time my thoughts are as dark as any Unabomber; I'm certainly not unique in having them or in letting them drift on by.

Look, my daughter and I are going to open a driftwood museum. You are invited to the opening. We have a good collection now. The Black has lent me a knee, old and broken and polished by years of tannins and flows.

I paddle off the channel, go not five minutes away from the flagging tape before I'm tangled in a dead end of trees and knees. This is why I'm here. To get stuck, to turn around and retrace my path. This is what I'm doing here.

11

According to Dad's guidebook, there was supposed to be a plantation on the Edisto's right bank. But there was no bank. There were miles of arrowroot and sedge, blossoms, leaves, stalks, and mud. Blackbirds squarked their watery-voiced mewlings and rose and fell on the horizon like blackorange waves on a strange water. Here and there a cypress tree stood stately and soft-edged. You had the impression there were many more cypress at an earlier time.

Solid ground was far beyond the swamp; a line of trees said so—live oaks and Spanish beard, all of it hazy and hard to see with the distance and the auras of heat. It was an expansive place, the Edisto, but I preferred Penney Creek for its smallness, its intimacy and shade.

There was an alligator in our path now, about nine feet of its body visible, though it seemed to rise and show more of its scaly back and sinister eyes as we approached. I pried my paddle off the stern and kept us a couple of boat lengths away from the animal. "What does it mean when a gator shows more of its body," Dad asked, drawing with his paddle as though to pull closer. It wasn't a question that needed an answer, but as I countered his stroke with another pry, I said, "I think it wants petted."

12

My boat of choice for the Moormans was a chunky, late-model Buick of a decked canoe, the Dagger Cascade, though when the water was high I sometimes paddled a sleeker design—a vintage New Wave Acrobat C-1, expedition lay-up. Both boats were well used, purchased third hand. I can't imagine running the Moormans or any river in a new boat. When Kirsten and I made the trip, not often enough, we paddled a decade-old Dagger Legend tandem canoe, its hull soft, even with the Kevlar patches.

My solitary trips on the river were one day supplemented with a fresh and needed camaraderie. It began when the mailman brought our delivery past the box and up the driveway to the door. Over his shoulder as he approached I noticed that he had a kayak on the roof of his Subaru, the kind of postal-service edition Subaru with the steering wheel mounted on the right. He was curious about the Chattooga Conservancy newsletter in our bundle. For what seemed like a while that day we talked rivers and boats, and when it rained hard next we ended up running the Moormans together.

Ted's mail route took him over the river at Millington where there is a spray-painted gauge on the river left bridge piling. It was lucky for me to have made a connection with Ted. Because it is dammed, a heavy rain does not mean the Moormans will run. It takes a combination of flow from its major tributary, the Doyles River (where we put in often), and water over the dam. The level of the reservoir was hard to tabulate without actually seeing it. Sometimes wind in the right direction would push water over the dam, giving the Moormans a necessary flow. And then a drencher, two inches of rain, would do nothing except to the Doyles, and that wouldn't be enough. But I could always check with Ted about the river volume; sometimes he left a note on the mailbox if the river was up and he was having a paddle after work.

13

The air was heavier than it had been my first day on the Smith. Smoke from the cook fire hovered in the sycamore branches. Rain felt imminent. I sipped coffee and watched the water. It looked like many scales on a long, long snake, each scale different in its blooming and bubbling and coursing, its froth, ripple, and pile. The river had dropped another inch or so overnight, as though the snake had exhaled or digested some meal.

My canoe lay hull up in the sand. I inspected the new scrapes on the new patches I'd epoxied to it the prior week. Fiberglass, Kevlar, and epoxy are strange, useful things, a kind of chemical paper mache. The boat, a tandem canoe designed for whitewater, retained its graceful lines despite the wear and tear and patchwork.

I looked at the fire. I looked at the water and then at the canoe and then back at the fire. I wanted to make another fire. Maybe four or five more fires, each one a point in some pattern I'd have little to do with. It always feels good to gather wood and set it ablaze. It feels like a part of me—now glowing, now smoke—is turning to ash.

The coffee proved plenty of breakfast. My stomach swelled with the promise of new rocks, new rapids, and pools and other sights. I love being on a river for the first time. There is something necessary and deliberate and completely absurd about the whole affair. It reminds me of religion, but mostly it reminds me of travel.

A ruby-throated hummingbird fed from the fire pink at the edge of the beach that was camp. Fire pink is a red flower. It resembles a paintbrush, a frayed one. The hummingbird, no larger than a large moth, hovered and dipped and licked and flew. As if priming the brushes for their next strokes, the bird visited several of the flowers before disappearing in the woods.

I was fishing now. A sandpiper rocked and twirped on a wet stone bankward as I flicked a spinner from my place on a boulder midstream. The little bird pecked its beak into the moss on the stone at water's edge. A mayfly rose like a bit of ash. Oak fronds tangled in my lure. I cleaned it, cast again. There was a great basswood growing over the river. It had such a dense and orderly canopy compared with the wobbly oaks and arthritic sycamore. Maybe it was the tree, the distraction of it, but suddenly I hooked the bugger that'd been playing with my lure. It fought bullish and torpid, less like a trout than something with larger girth and scales. It turned out to be a redeye bass, its eyes brilliant, redder than blood, almost unnatural. I wondered what colors it saw through those eyes.

14

Over time, with attention, desire, and luck, I learned to guess with fair accuracy whether the Moormans was running. It became a part of me, the river, as if a mood, another limb. I could check my rain gauge as well as the level on Lickinghole Creek, a small stream near the house, and have a good sense of the Moormans' character.

Zero on the gauge at Millington meant the river was run-able, but barely. Not until one foot did it get a little juice. Nine feet was the highest I ran it. In addition to Ted, I met other local paddlers. I ran the Moormans several times with Josh, a bartender at a restaurant where I waited tables for a while; Dave, a post-doc in ecology at University of Virginia; a friend Blake; Jonathon, the son of a builder for whom I worked; random boaters I met at the put-in; Kirsten; and out-of-town river-rat friends who, when visiting, were lucky enough to catch it running.

15

Once, driving to visit my father, canoe on the roof, I stopped to paddle on the Lumber River. I found the river off 15-501 with no trouble. This was my first time in the Sandhills, an area of remnant dunes from the ocean that made its shore there during the Miocene Era. The roads in the region were straight and flat and well marked; they cut through a curious, shabbily elegant mix of golf course communities, modular homes, run down historic farmhouses, pinewoods, and farmland. A small fraction of the once vast longleaf pine forest survives in that region, but from the road it was mostly golf courses. A hand-painted sign preceding a farm stand along one of the byways read: Okra, Tomatoes, Golf Balls.

Arriving at the bridge, I was shaky with a late-night and road fever. It took paddling a mile downstream to an impassable multi-blowdown limb situation and then turning and attaining a few miles upstream, before the grime, mental and physical, of highway travel began to rub off. I almost felt solid again, as if my feet were on the ground.

So I drifted. The river drew the boat in the slow orbit of an eddy. A dragonfly with a blue-tipped tail landed on my arm. If its feet had contained ink, then they'd have made dots on my hair and maybe on my skin. Shadows from the bay tree, the cypress, tupelo, and maple lay as black lines and blobs on the chocolate water. Heron prints in the mudbar said the river was low.

16

It was time for Dad and me to head back and we did that. The tide was rising. There was more water now and just as much land. I saw that the couple was still fishing at the mouth of Penney Creek. We stayed close to the rushes on the opposite side of the boat from which they cast. "You didn't leave your truck at Penney Creek, did you?" the man asked, his voice a white dye in the dark paint of the river's quiet. He hardly looked up from his line.

"We did," Dad said from the front of our canoe. Dad sounded too cheerful, confident, but such is the habit of a salesman, especially a successful one. If I inherited any of Dad's charm, it ricochets between a suspicious stoicism and a gushy, overly self-aware shield of vulnerability.

The guy was bearded and dressed in hunter green. He took another jerk on his baitcaster, shifted his rump in the padded chair, and shook his head. "I wouldn't leave my truck there for all the money in the world," he exclaimed.

Another alligator surfaced then, near where the lobelia bloomed, a red tower of petals and stalk. "Nobody will mess with my truck," I said. "It's a beater."

"They might not want your truck," the man said. "But they might want your battery and crankcase." As he spoke, I noticed the lady in the bow had a sloppy tattoo on her leg. I couldn't tell what picture the ink made. Dad paddled a little harder then. He pulled the paddle way past his hips. I'd been wanting to tell him that he was wasting energy doing it that way and slowing us, that the stroke ends at your hips and beyond that you're driving the boat down instead of forward. But I kept my mouth shut. Dad didn't need to hear that. The physics of paddling has no place on a hot morning in the Lowcountry. Ours was a short, makeshift expedition, my favorite kind.

No more words were exchanged. It was an awkward encounter and we didn't discuss it. Dad and I both felt the man was playing with us. All the money in the world—he just sounded too dramatic to be sincere. Also, in the two times we'd approached and passed the anchored boat, we'd noticed that a lot of fish were tailing at the confluence of Penney Creek with the Edisto, and that the guy and the woman were not catching a thing. I can't remember if Dad or I commented on this. Anyway, it seemed likely that the guy was adding a little excitement to his slow morning by giving us a scare.

17

It would seem natural to begin at the dam and recall the various stretches of the Moormans in order, but such a run is not true to my experience of the place, to its essence or the essences it evokes in me. When I paddled the Moormans the first time, I started four miles below the dam and a mile up the free-flowing Doyles River. From then on, my explorations were as piecemeal as memory.

I think now of the three roads over the Moormans, not the bridges but the driveways, cement slabs that when we paddled at high water made waves and ledges. I think of the demi-gorge where in a stretch of a half-mile I could slip my boat in and out of nearly forty eddies. I remember the coffee Dave poured from his thermos while we scouted a ledge when the snow had melted from a foot to a couple of inches and it was raining and witchy with fog, and the river was high, nearly cresting—hot coffee with cream. I remember balancing stones with Kirsten and Sophie at the cliffs above Millington one hot summer day, the river a mere trickle.

I think of swimming with our dog after a roofing job in August, and one time, when paddling with Jonathan Ball, his first run down the upper stretch, I turned, and while eddying out to watch him approach a tricky ledge, I witnessed two deer leap from the bank and land a foot in front of Jonathan in the river, and then leap again—whose eyes wider I do not know.

I think of starflower, fire pink, and Mayapple on the banks. Kingfishers, a light like divinity and a dark sometimes malevolent, sometimes soft. Sunrise and the backlit waves, the sweetness of pawpaw fruit in October. Geese and mist, and a smell in the air over the water like mint chutney. I remember stashing my boat in the creosote drip under Millington Bridge so as to jog back to my truck—gravel under feet, then under tire. And I think of seeing the discarded satellite dish first on the Doyles, then just above the bridge at Millington, then gone, washed further downstream.

18

A canoe, which is a vehicle, is a kind of ground, the way a tree is a river or a flower a winged thing with a song of color, aroma, and shape. Or maybe all those bright green dragonflies were doing something to the mind, something like the heat and being on the road does, something weird and fine.

Cider bugs were as a breeze on the Lumber, riffling it as the swarm darted, group-wise, in one direction and then another, pausing and dispersing now and then, but never too far. They are called water boatmen in most insect books, but I have always called them cider bugs, for they smell more like apple cider than apple cider when you hold one. They exert a pheromone when threatened, one that is more unappetizing to their predators than to me.

As the boat and I continued to slowly spin and I took a stroke now and then to keep from washing out of the eddy, I thought back to the put-in, a trashy cut in the woods on the Scotland County side of the bridge. As I'd unloaded there, I met a local guy smoking a cigarette in his Toyota sedan, a lowrider with serious rims and a fresh wash to make the jet-black paint job shine. He said that he lived just over the bridge, but he didn't know the Lumber was a good place to explore. He left his bass-heavy music going in the car as he stepped out, a short, curious fellow with braids, a fellow thirty-something. His name was Robert. I opened my *Guide to Paddling Eastern North Carolina* to the Lumber River description and handed it to him. He seemed positively startled by how far the river flowed and the fact that people paddled its many sections to see the swamps and wildlife, not to mention the water itself.

I invited Robert to join me, but he had to be at work soon; he said he was a cook at the Red Lobster in Southern Pines. I wished he could have been with me just upstream of the bridge a little while ago, when I encountered two barred owls. The owls were on a branch over the river, but as I approached they lit for a place just over the bank. We stared at one another for a while. Good air ran in all the little holes that seeing them was putting in me. I made a couple of hooty noises, but they didn't respond.

19

The prior day, getting on the Smith River, I'd had another of those encounters that make you want to kiss life hard on its ripe, cracked ones. After stashing my boat and gear under the bridge, I stopped at a small engine repair shop to ask for a ride from the take-out at Philpott Lake back to the bridge. A nice lady, a friend of the repairman, graciously offered, and I followed her on a shortcut to the take-out. On the return trip, in her small import, she pointed to an old, elegant house I'd noticed earlier. She said it had been the home of a renowned moonshiner. "He was the big man in Franklin County," she told me. "During prohibition, he supplied the politicians and ran his liquor to D.C. in hearses or ambulances, the floors rigged so the bottles rode concealed." After another turn or two on the road, as we drove by a cemetery, she took another drag off her Merit Menthol and said, "That tall one there, that's him."

I released the bass with a hunch that the water was too warm there to support a healthy trout population. It was fine. I fish for wonder more than fish. I waded downstream from camp, working a few more pools, watching the water curl over ledges and boil from under mammoth boulders. Amber sand, green depths, and dark, moss-laced cobble marked the bottom. The surface was all furrow and curl, light-streaked and bubbly in places and smooth in others. It was late April, and on the banks the wild azalea was in bloom, also flame azalea, spiderwort, fire pink, starflower, to name the most obvious. Leaves shone with newness, all the leaves save the evergreen of pine needles and the rhododendron's thick lances. I caught a bluegill and a few more oak fronds, and I found an inner tube and a plastic trash can among the flotsam on a boulder. There were the remains of a suckerfish on a rock, in the form of big scales and bones and bird shit. The osprey I'd seen several times that day perhaps had made a meal there recently, if not just a few minutes ago.

It was time to paddle now. The canoe looked like a ragged workbench or banquet table on the beach, which both saddened and thrilled me. I loaded it and headed downstream. Short pools punctuated the rips. The rapids were nothing drastic, but they were lively enough to lead me into a quiet, rhythmic state of attention and steering. Less than a mile from camp, floating down the river, submerged in its music, the gospel I trust most, I encountered a steep drop—a small sluice. Scouting the rapid by foot, I found a crushed copper kettle in the sand, its rim and handle of wrought iron and in good shape. It was clearly a relic of the bootlegging days. Spots of brightness shone amongst the general tarnish and slice and wrinkle of the crushed copper basin, as though some clinging things, lichen or egg sacs or shellfish, had cleaned those places in their time there. I wanted to put the kettle in my boat and haul it with me, but that seemed wrong.

20

I don't know if they were crickets, grasshoppers, katydids, cicadas, or what, but the bugs were noisy as we sat on our lifejackets eating egg salad sandwiches with slices of striped Romas from the garden. Sophie explained to her grandpa how she'd made the mayonnaise that went into the egg salad, and then she explained how she'd made the egg salad. As she spoke, two men in a plastic johnboat called a Crawdad hung up in the rocks as they came through the rapid below the island. We eyed them with curiosity and amusement, much like we watched the wood ducks.

When they unhung their boat, the men paused and fished just off the bank from where we were eating. They asked if we lived around there. I told them we did, that we lived near the Shell Station on Arcadia Road. They said they lived at the county line, that they had the garage on Route 11 where they built and worked on race cars. There wasn't much said after that. We exchanged good days and they headed downstream. They were hung up on rocks again when we passed them a little while later, not far from where we'd eaten.

21

Dad and I were lucky to have wind back here on Penney Creek, for it was dense with growth and hot. The purple blossoms of the arrowroot stood as numerous as the shots of light ringing across the breeze-rippled water. There must have been a strong blow on the ocean. A few horseflies pestered, but nothing too bad. Later, I'd find the top of my legs deeply sunburned, but for now I was looking for more alligators or any other surprises that might emerge around the many bends and walls of arrowroot and sedge.

Heron, hawk, turtle, baby alligators, big gators, warblers, kingfisher, murky, cinnamon-colored water, and an old sailboat stuck in the mud were other things we encountered. We saw a lot more, too, such as when the alligators would grunt in the rushes and I'd see indefinable things in my mind, as doubtless Dad did, too.

To be honest, I was pretty anxious. I tend to be a worrisome fellow, and now the fisherman's statement about the put-in had given my fret a focus. I worried less for my truck, though, than of screwing up a trip with dad. Dad is in good shape, but as he ages, his strict weekend routines—newspaper, bike ride, sit-down lunch, tennis or golf, nightly news—are even more important to him. He often jibes himself for them, but he knows they are as essential to his health as a woodpecker is to the life of a pine. For Dad to be on the river, I figured, was an outing he'd tolerate for a few hours since his son was visiting. It would not be good for a few hours to become a day involving a messy situation, such as a stolen or bandited truck.

22

I had left the eddy and was traveling downstream. It was good to be going with the current again. Sometimes the Lumber, a dark river, took on an emerald sheen. It was like a film continually developing, as though the sunlight burning through the foliage made the river appear more green than golden and then more orange than green, more blue than orange.

I was almost back to the bridge; the sound of retreads on asphalt told me so. I knew that Robert wouldn't still be smoking in his car, but I hoped so, so we could chat some more. What it's like to live around there, the different seasons and people, had me curious. Suddenly a warbler with a black head and an orange color like an oriole, no, a pair of them, darted into and out of a tupelo limb. In a week or so, I'd check my book and decide with no great certainty that they were Blackburnian warblers migrating north. For now I tried hard to see them up there, small wonders on an immensity of green.

23

Kirsten, Sophie, and I moved from Crozet several hours south of the Moormans. The water we paddled for the next few years flowed to the Cape Fear, Neuse, Roanoke, and Tar rivers. One rainy time just before Christmas, Kirsten and I were able to paddle New Hope Creek through Duke Forest. A lively Piedmont creek, New Hope is as similar to and different from the Moormans as falling in love is from being in love. Twice, Kirsten and I spooked a kingfisher from its perch in ironwood branches. Nostalgia, or some abiding groundedness, rose in us each time we saw it fly downstream, its path watery, free flowing. It seemed as if all the waterways we'd known and hadn't known opened their mouths then, and there was voice, a little voice. I hear it still.

24

Sophie's tally—Arcadia to Alpine Farms, four miles—seven wood ducks, thirteen turtles, two blue heron, three kingfisher, five green herons, four blue-winged teal, eight smallmouth, one bald eagle.

25

After a smooth run over the drop, I continued down the Smith with the sweet little buzz you feel after running a rapid. I wondered further on the fate of the copper kettle, which led me to think again of the woman I'd met the prior morning and of our drive and her stories about the local scene. In addition to the moonshiner story, she'd pointed out a famous gospel singer's house just over the next ridge, before we descended to the bridge. I'd had a hunch earlier that there was music going on at that place, due to the traveling bus in the driveway, a real nice one, luxurious—glittery paint job, tinted windows. She began to tell a story about the family and their kindness, but well before finishing, she stopped her car in the road by the bridge. I thanked her and offered payment for her gas and time, but she shooed me off and said, "Have a good trip."

I stared up from the canoe and the river. It looked to be a thirty-minute to hour hump by foot to the ridge at any point. The gorge was deep enough and the slope dense enough with growth as to make the river feel very remote. It was soothing to sense this. Whatever pain life deals me seems far away when I get in the woods and stay a little while, long enough or frequently enough to let the place erode me. As I continued downstream, it seemed that most of the activity on the banks was of bugs and beaver. Deer prints sometimes pocked the sand, and there were coon tracks in the silt and crayfish shells picked clean. Every now and then there were bullet casings on a rock—.357 mostly—and these were near a place where four-wheeler tracks emerged from the woods to the riverside. Trash was commonplace, but there wasn't enough to make the place feel trashed; it wore the trash as many Blue Ridge Mountain rivers do, as though people lived upstream.

Perhaps a snake is an imperfect metaphor for a river, I thought a couple of miles downstream. I had beached the canoe and was scrambling up a side creek. The creek curled and pinballed from one eroded ledge to another. The bed of the creek was one rock, carved and pocked and scoured by years of flow. I hopped from foot to foot on the slippery, sloping monolith, as if the place were teaching me a spirited dance. The banks, steep and cliffy, teemed with jack-in-the-pulpit, mountain laurel, witch hazel, yellowroot, oak.

A river cannot be a snake because a river has legs. Each tributary is a leg, and they, too, have legs. Save a grossly deformed millipede, I could think of no insect with such limbs. No mammal either. It drizzled now, and a vague mist seemed to ooze from everything. Moss resembled melted wax from some green candle. Somewhere my truck sat in a parking lot full of larger trucks and trailers by Philpott Lake. Maybe the only metaphor for a river is time, I thought. I was in the canoe again. Or maybe it is rain. I was taking forward strokes, wrist-twisting them at the finish so the boat stayed straight. I was watching the water. I was watching the rain and paddling and seeing snakes, nests of pale and dark living snakes, and I was seeing other things, too—too much to know, too many to name.

Corn Stalk, Night Hawk, Dove

There's little to be said for dove hunting. You shoot at and mostly miss small, beautiful birds. Birds known for a call that's as sorrowful and miraculous as their noble life pattern and buff lavender color. The best season is the early season when the air is hot and dry and any guy in his right mind is in the shade, better yet in a mountain stream, getting in touch with his inner salamander. On average—who computes these numbers?—hunters kill three birds for every twenty-five shots. This means bruised shoulders, bruised egos, money, and resources down the drain. People shoot across the field and BBs rain down on your ridiculous camo ballcap.

You also need twelve birds to feed three people, so that's a lot of shells. And then there are the hunters with their theories and dramas and excuses. The guy who raps waxsodic on the beauty of the dust as he loads his $1200 dollar Browning in a flashy four-by-four can't help but make me wonder whether he's here because A) his wife was tired of him cutting the grass, B) he's tired of his wife asking when are you going to cut the grass, C) he's a hunter-gatherer at heart and this is one step in the path to his true nature, D) all of the above, and more, or E) none of the above, and more.

I like to hunt dove. On opening day a couple of weeks ago, I blasted two boxes of shells without killing a bird. I flinched each time I pulled the trigger. I didn't follow through the shots. It was excellent. I made all sorts of excuses, not the least of which was the six hours I'd spent chain-sawing that morning. In all, the feelings of failure and shame were exhilarating, a kind of internal tantrum that primed me for a blitzkrieg wood-splitting session the next morning.

The field I hunt belongs to Preston Wickline. He runs a dairy operation and raises corn for silage on an expansive acreage. There's a big, T-shaped field he lets people hunt once it's cut. The killing's best when there are twenty folks spread along the edges to bounce the birds back and forth. There are usually birds, but there are rarely more than five or ten people, which suits me. I prefer the hunting to the killing.

But the killing is important because I like to eat the dove's dark meat. I have an innate inclination for that taste, something that goes back to the womb and maybe farther, to the ideal of peace, which the dove represents. Ideals are messy, as Mencken said, but there's nothing messy about the dove's rich, fruity essence. When I turn them over a fire and then eat them, I don't feel every place the bird roosted or every sound made by its throat and wings, but such thoughts come to mind.

I went back to Wickline's last weekend. I wanted to feel a different kind of excellence than opening day. I wanted dinner. In the throes of wants, I am at home.

It was about four in the afternoon, hazy and hot, when I set up in the field. I sat at the tip of an uncut point, on the stool, over and under on my legs. Ragweed surrounded me. The dirt was uncultivated in that small thicket, a chalky hardpan, ants the only visible movement on it.

Everything was just right. There was no breeze. Ten feet off, a black fuzzy caterpillar moved among the shin-high corn trunks like a bushy eyebrow looking for a face. Actually, it was a Woolly Bear caterpillar looking for a place to curl up for the winter. They say you can predict the winter by the thickness of their fuzz. I don't like predicting weather, especially for a whole season. Winters are rough and lovely no matter how severe or mild they are.

Blue Ridge to the east, Alleghenies to the west—the ranges appeared unattainable, like green clouds you'd pass through, dust instead of dampness on what exposed skin. It was beautiful, but we needed rain. The water situation was more desperate than anyone would admit, as though saying it—we were in a drought—would confirm the obvious: there was nothing anyone could do, there was nothing anyone couldn't do.

I kept looking up, around, shifting often to keep from cricking the neck. There was shooting at the far end of the field. I saw the dove. They were high but not out of range. They kept flying. They flew west to east. They had come over the tree line and now they crossed the field. At the far tree line they turned and darted over the canopy, some settling in the standing dead, others disappearing out of sight.

It went on like this: more shots, more dove in the distance, small against the dirty blue. I sat on a folding camo stool, though the cricket and katydid noise made it feel like floating. There were lines and lines of corn trunks, some ancient script, spidery roots, weeds in between. If I could have read that script, I might have known which noise was made by the cricket and which by the katydid. It went on. I watched the field, but mostly I watched the sky, annoyed by the visor on my cap but needing it, too—for shade, for to hide the whites of my eyes should dove approach.

Sometimes the birds came my way. They came by chance. I had no decoys. When they came, I chose one dove and when it was within forty yards, I stood, positioned, fired. The sun grew more orange all the time. I thought of many things. I thought of nothing. Now shots erupted again. I found the birds, not so high this time and thus harder to see, Purgatory Mountain behind them, dark like them. The flock banked hard and broke up with the shots. A few set a course in my direction.

My fingers flexed in position on the gun. I tried to be still. There was a butterfly not ten feet away. There had been butterflies and dragonflies on and off all afternoon, and I always mistook them for birds at first glance. Each butterfly I'd seen, including this one, was headed south. My thumb slid to the safety. I inhaled. Two dove lay dead under the stool. I'd fired eight shells, been hunting an hour and a half or so. I exhaled, inhaled again.

The breathing didn't keep my friend Morgan's voice at bay. "Dove do what dove do," he'd said opening day as I whimpered about being a lousy wing shot. "They make a fool of you." I grew more tense. Breathed more rapidly. It was perfect.

A pair of dove looked to pass on my left. They were veering and carving as though on some bobsled track. I saw the gray underwing. They were seventy yards off, sixty. I figured they were headed to the creek behind me, down the hill, the one along the road.

At forty yards I stood, drew gun to shoulder and squeezed a shot out the top barrel. The lead bird fluttered, dipped. My finger moved to the front trigger. I swung the barrel, eyed down the bead. Squeezed again, the barrel stopping, not far enough, not loose enough, shoulders flinching.

When I do something, I want to do it well. I have a hard time when hunting knowing how to miss well. The birds disappeared in the sun's glare. I watched the edge of all that shine, down to the southwest, where a big cedar stood like the definition of uptight. Soon the dove were visible again, headed away as fast and as wing-busy as they'd approached.

That was that. Crows cackled. Time did what time does, as the dove had done and I had done. I felt like a bowl of ice cubes on the counter in a hot kitchen. I felt like scrap metal at the edge of a tired farmer's tired fields. Things were good. An hour passed, maybe longer. There were more shots fired by the unknown party across the field, a few shots by me.

I watched nighthawks, a moth, an airplane, swallows, crows, blackbirds, distant traffic, distant dove. I fired at a dove over my shoulder. I watched the tree line. I rearranged the spent shells in the dust. There was milkweed down. There were stray feathers, deer tracks in the dirt, a few gauzy, feeble clouds. Everything was catching my eye. I thought of Wickline's dairy cows, all of them run down from the drought, their production slow, he'd told me, when I asked permission to hunt again this year.

Soon I dropped another bird. Fetching it, I found it hobbling, wounded. One hard jerk and only the head was in my grip. I looked in those eyes and felt the calm center of the world's grace and horror. I thought of the milk that dove, both male and female, make for their young. There was no white on my fingers, just a smear of blood. As I fetched the body, warm and still and soft, from the dirt, a cold front of regret collided with pleasure's low pressure, making some wild internal weather.

Later, when the sun was nearly balanced on the long ridge on the west edge of the valley, a body crested the higher point of land at field's middle. I had been glancing at the dove under the stool, having a romantic moment, thinking what the barn cats would taste when they gobbled the dove guts and chewed on those weird orange claws.

He was a large man and he walked slowly along the tree line to the east and north. He carried his gun as though stalking, expecting a bird. I could not yet make out the features of his face, but his silhouette suggested that he carried a single shot.

When he was a hundred yards away, a bird, a solo bird, fluttered from the ground between us, and the man fired. It was strange how fast the lead sprayed me; though it wasn't painful, my world grew very small and very hot. The bird shifted direction and flew between us again. "Low bird," I yelled as he pointed at it. He was looking at me as if he were doing me a favor or himself a favor by suggesting I shoot him in the process of—most likely—missing the dove, which we watched as it lit in a locust at the field's southwest corner. I thought, What the hell.

I remembered now the old Dodge dually flatbed parked in the weeds not far behind me. It was out of sight of the gravel road where I was parked and where most who hunt Wickline's field park. I had noticed it earlier because I drive a Dodge pickup of similar vintage and because his had farm-use tags and was parked in that odd place, as though concealed.

The man approached. He moved with a wearisome motion. I sensed annoyance. He had a big, distended belly. The rest of him wasn't small. He reminded me of heavy equipment—a skidder, a dozer—that somebody was keeping running, less for use than to sell some day. He stopped ten feet from me. He reminded me of a bull. I still hadn't decided whether to say anything about his shot at the low bird. "You kill any?" he growled. He didn't look at me. He looked at his gun like it was a cat, a stray that he was going to drown.

"Couple," I said. He reached in his pocket. I wondered if he'd offer me a piece of gum. In a sudden and violent motion he tossed a handful of spent cartridges, cheap Dale Earnhardt 8's, in the weeds that formed the point where I sat. The man was close to fifty, I guessed. I remembered the first day I hunted Wickline's, how a fellow who was sitting where I was now reminded me to pick up my shells. He'd said Wickline had lost a cow because it ingested a shell the combine must have picked up. I had a sudden hunch this guy used to work for Wickline and had been fired.

"I hadn't hit shit," he spat. "My boys yonder tearing through boxes, a waste." His teeth were bad. They looked like fake bad teeth people wear at Halloween, only better, more artificial somehow. The overbite reminded me of rock climbing. I wondered if he was into the meth; I'd seen how the meth did that to teeth after time.

I nodded, continued scanning the horizon. Another wave of nighthawks worked their way up from the road. "Alrighty," the man said. I watched him start back again towards the old Dodge. The air smelled like dust and tasted that way too. It reminded me of the breath of a man who has cancer but doesn't know it. The highway was visible in stretches over the man's left shoulder. I watched the trucks for a while. There was something beautiful and terrible about all that speed and mass being far away and also very, very close.

There was a shot behind me now, it felt like inside me. I craned to southerly. The man's gun was still raised. I followed the vector of its barrel to a wing-crippled nighthawk. The bird dropped too slowly, like a caricature of itself. The man turned from it and opened the door of his truck.

I remained on the stool. The sun dropped and the air cooled. Over the Blue Ridge, the clouds resembled bad Easter candy. Later, I took the state road home. There were birds everywhere I didn't look and everywhere I did.

Fishing Torega

Three wild rainbows fill the skillet now, chunks of good butter between their ribs. They were alive an hour ago. We cook them briefly and then break half a dozen eggs on the hot black iron.

"Can I have the cheeks?" Sophie asks.

"You get some and Mama and me the others," I say. My daughter smiles. Somewhere she knows, better than I, that as the creek has shared, so will we.

Any time is a busy time at our place, but Septembers have an elegiac grittiness with last firewood to split and stack, last mowings, fall planting, summer's harvest. While Sophie and I cook, Kirsten hangs woolens we hauled in crates from the attic last evening. It is that time of year again. 8:30 A.M. and the mist is almost diffuse. You can see the soft outlines of late-summer mountains in the distance. A plume of fog rises over the James River, as though the land has exhaled.

Torega is not the creek's name but that's what I'm calling it, and in the mile open to fishing you crouch fifteen feet from a major interstate and cast to limestone chalk water, so focused on fly and motion that you almost aren't aware of the billboard up the opposite bank–halogen light searing the mist, Viacom label below letters large and yellow enough that a small nymph seems like the right choice of fly.

I try to take five fish a month from this creek. Five fish is one meal's worth for the immediate family. Plus roughage for the chicks and compost too. Last month, we traded two trout for several Masons of peach chutney and salsa and pickled okra. Friends had made the yummy concoctions with goods from our garden. If there is better eating, please show me.

The trout are not stocked, the creek rarely, if ever, fished. The father of an acquaintance bought rights to the water in the Twenties.

You can do this in Virginia, something to do with a King's Grant, some very old legal matter. Luckily, I have permission to fish the mile between the highway and the Department of Transportation work station. Before Torega culverts under the highway, it tumbles through a valley that would make those with a fetish for the pastoral tremor and go dizzy from shortness of breath. If anybody has fished that upper stretch of water, he's been a poacher and I salute and curse him.

I'm glad there are streams off limits to fishing. That the trout, bugs, birds, and plants in this creek do not know the influence of anglers treading its banks and channels feels right to me. I sense something pure when I travel the road along that stretch of creek, looking over, watching it run, and I go dizzy from shortness of breath. Something pure in the way a pawpaw fruit still on the tree is pure. It isn't about potential so much as preservation. But that's not it either. The word "wildness" comes to mind. Who knows what wildness is or what is meant by that word. It is a feeling. You can cast all day for definitions. You can see them, feeding. You know they are there but landing one is out of the question. Even a strike is a far reach. I wish there were more streams like this.

Normally I fish catch and release with the brook trout I like to stalk in the surrounding hills. I do it that way because there aren't many of these fish left. They've had a rough go with acid rain and silt and warming water temperatures due to loss of shade from dying hemlocks and many other factors. Still, a part of me grows very envious when I hear of old-timers dropping off the Blue Ridge Parkway with crickets or worms for bait, filling spackle buckets with brookies to pickle in Masons, to eat all winter long.

I remember a day last April, one of those busy spring ones when it is best to drop everything and go after brook trout. Around here in April, the mountains don their icing of foliage like so many mountains in springtime, the green arch and shrill and very yellow and not yet on the highest ridges, which are still brown and gray and violet, depending on the time of day and light, the crags visible through all those gaps. The buzzards are over the pasture and even the carport as though more curious than hungry. One gets the impression they're checking up on you, taking your pulse from sixty feet and some velocity. Maybe they're lost.

This was a Sunday after a couple of days of guests and festivities, followed by cleanup and a hazy, sweet kind of letdown, and I was headed east over the proverbial Blue Ridge. There were repairs to make on a rental house in North Carolina, preparations for and meetings with prospective tenants. Among the power and hand tools, I'd packed the two weight, another sort of tool. Its hardware, the nuts and bolts of flies and leaders, were encased in a Russell Kelly hand-me-down Woolrich fishing vest. It could be said, cheesily and not without truth, that such items are like levels and chalk lines; they help me plumb and true a place, and they plumb and true me in the process.

Water is needed, too, wild, tumbling water. Stony Creek where it schisms between slopes to the Otter River in Bedford County isn't as out of the way as one can get around here, but it's close. Out of the way, anyhow, is a state of mind that has to do with being in the way by being out of it. Something like that.

Being a warm weekend, the Blue Ridge Parkway was an artery thick with Harleys, motor homes, and all other manner of petroleum fix. A few spandex types on high-geared bicycles rounded out the mix. I parked on the shoulder a few miles from the Fallingwater Cascades trailhead, a mile or so past an overlook. Rigging up is always a fulsome affair, and it felt especially silly and wonderful to be fiddling with my little graphite rod in that place. I was thinking about the construction of the parkway, which snakes the ridge from northern Virginia nearly to Georgia, its pavement shimmering and oddly inconsequential among the expanse of woods and slopes and sky. It was humbling to wonder what the people who'd cut and laid that road had seen and done and felt. Who and what they'd displaced could almost be overlooked. Today there were groves of Mayapple and bluebells. The trees and shrubs seemed to carry electricity with their limbs adjusting to the new weight and shear of leaf, insect, spidersilk, birds, and song.

Having only studied Stony Creek on a map, I had some definite notions about its course and the promise of fish. For all I'd hoped, the creek could be sterile from some prior mineral or timber extraction. Maybe from toxins in the rain. Some of us have a weakness for worst-case scenarios.

The creek appeared three feet wide when I spotted it on my descent from the road. Heavily littered with deadfall and aphid-felled hemlocks and quick-running over a flat micro-valley, there appeared little habitat for the six-inch lunkers I hoped to fool with a parachute Adams. Looking downstream, however, I saw the bottom drop out on the valley. Literally, there was a chasm. I imagined the drops and at the bottom of the drops, silky, fishy pools.

The woods there, the poplar and oak and tiger maple and all the rest, the duff, the hellebore, the moss and foamflower, are part of the Jefferson National Forest. Another boundary, marked by small signs on trees, designated the Blue Ridge Parkway corridor, within which it is unlawful to hunt. I thought of all the trappings that mark the Peaks of Otter past which I'd sped—the lodge with its king crab buffet, the manmade pond, the visitor center, the maintenance area near where a friend used to harvest pounds of ginseng when he wasn't gathering hellgrammites on the James to sell at bait shops. I was glad for that place, this place, and the preservation and use of it. Glad, too, because I knew that on weekdays, especially in colder months, no one much poked around up here, except the deer and turkey, grouse and bugs and birds and bear.

It's never the individual plants and trees and critters that pique my delight at romping around in the hills. The sum of it, the interplay of breeze and color, shape and relation—that's what hooks me. There was a dry breeze. It moved through the pipe organ of all those branches and leaves and patterns patterning it even as it was shaped by those shapes and slopes. I felt present at the invention of rhythm as well as of green.

Where we live on the west slope of the Blue Ridge, we have a view of similar drainages and slopes, and the view can be a little maddening some days, because you want to be out there, deep in what you're looking at, invisible, shrouded, part and parcel and privy to those rhythms.

The creek began to drop. There were pools. It was all a rapid breathing and slippery rocks and big and small and fallen trees. Casting was a matter of slingshotting the fly or shuffling it out through the small pockets free of branch and their tangles. Trout rocketed to the fly. As if from the center of the earth. I'm not kidding. If they were small, they were thick. They channeled a disdain for captivity straight from the origins of these very hills. It was scary to catch them, release them. I felt as though all my species' betrayals, as well as my own shortcomings, were about to be devoured as consequence and by something that lived in these fish's eyes and flanks and brawn.

One fish, smaller than the rest but no less lively, seemed by the marking on its abdomen to have been tattooed with Tabasco sauce. Two rings of the most brilliant, polished orange flanked its girth. My senses went nuts. I tasted, all at once, the synapse and strobe of shadow and wave as well as the ferns nodding and fruit-dotted among the seeps. It was time to get my line on the water again.

Though you are only fifteen feet from the highway when you fish Torega, the sycamore and locust and other trees and shrubs keep you, in leafy months, mostly obscured from drivers' views. Of course, you feel and hear the traffic's vibrations in your very marrow, as the fish must. You smell exhaust, rubber, and other chemicals, tanker fumes and Lord knows what else. Over four thousand trucks pass that spot each day; twenty-two-wheel tractor-trailers are not uncommon.

I drive the highway to work during the school year. The highway is very convenient and traveling on it as exciting as contemplating suicide. I tend to crank a bad classic rock station and zip in our seventeen-year-old Jetta until I find a bubble between traffic, then I pop whatever's kicking around in the cassette deck, never certain the eject will give it back. The mind wandering all the while. Returning home from work, I take the state route; it is better for everyone involved.

Torega's best pool earns that title by virtue of its fish. It is also a soothing place, despite the industrial influence. The creek runs straight and there's a small sluice at the head of the pool. A spring enters, fanning over a vegetative clump of tufa—moldy, malformed, lovely biscuit of a limestone landform. Fish hold at the confluence. The water is cold. In summer, we fill glass jugs, old beer growlers and cider jugs on the other side of the highway, at a point where the spring exits mountain, along the frontage road there. Our well and pump and softener work fine; we just like the ritual, the taste of the water.

The pool is twenty feet long and milky in the manner of limestone creeks. I tried a #16 sulfur dun first this morning, my favorite fly. The reason was simple: the fly was still tied to the tippet from last month's trip and the trout had liked it then.

The trout were less than interested today. I crouched lower, both knees in a sandy place on the highway side of the creek. For a few moments, I was acutely aware of the noise—Harley, rumble strip, downshift. A Stimulator with rubber, cricket-like legs was my next offering. First cast a strike. And miss. A couple of more strikes suggested they were small fish and I started thinking nymph. I think about nymphs the way I think about needing help.

Fishing in an industrial setting is familiar to me. In Atlanta, the Chattahoochee and the golf course ponds had a similar feel. As a kid it pleased me that my home stretches of water did not resemble the photos in the fishing magazines. It gave me the illusion of being unique. From my place wading the Hooch, I liked seeing I-285, the traffic gridlocked there. The mirrored glass office complexes at Peachtree-Dunwoody lent the scene a toxicity that felt harmonious with the river and the times. For several years, when Dad offered to teach me fly-fishing, I said no thanks and fished with corn or spinners. It felt more genuine.

Despite Torega's surroundings, the trout are still trout—wild rainbows—and they go crazy, gracefully, when hooked. Eventually, the first of three keepers took a bead-head nymph. The mist felt lighter then, particles of moisture drifting apart. Rising from my knees, I was not conscious of the highway or billboard. I was trout conscious, rod conscious.

The rainbow was thin, the colors less vibrant than in prior months. Holding it, removing the nymph, my thoughts went elsewhere, to recent encounters, small things—a grasshopper on a can of Schlitz, milkweed fuzz solvent-bound to shotgun barrel, Sophie decorating the playhouse we'd made of stacked locust, split and golden.

I brained the fish on a chunk of limestone, slid it in a plastic grocery bag, and put the package in my pocket. For a while I stood there, considering the appetite of a fly fisherman who once spouted at me that lament about how Brad Pitt in *A River Runs Through It* had ruined the sport. Truck noise grew monstrous in the dilating light. As I began casting to the pool again, I remembered passing a semi a few mornings back. It was a mobile hatchery, tilapia I suppose. The largest indoor aquaculture project in the world, claimed the lettering on the door. Many things are less significant than they seem at the time, I decided a few moments later, watching my nymph hang, tangled in a spider web.

Beyond the Barn

A hawk screeched. Leaves fell. Dawn spilled its red tide through the branches. The understory had a dim, burnished glow. The trees were gray and black and many other colors, their limbs chaotic and askew and mostly leafless, yet they were patterned, definitely patterned with that thirst for sun. They reminded me—in texture and in form—of the limestone outcrops above the sinkhole a few hundred yards upslope.

Squirrels had been making their ruckus since first light. There must have been a half-dozen fluff tails in that area, working the duff for acorns. Perhaps they'd watched my headlamped figure tie the gun, a .50 caliber muzzleloader, to the haul line, climb the stand, buckle harness to tree, sit, fetch the weapon, pop a primer on its cap, and sit some more—light off—head turning as owl-like as possible.

Deer are quieter than squirrels. It may seem self-explanatory and obvious to you, but not to me. Deer hooves sometimes make a noise of leaf crunch or stick crack. Most often what I hear is a feeling, a sense of weight and pressure, a sensation that comes through the air and through the ground.

The first deer was a doe and larger than the yearling behind her. They passed the cedar with the rub, about fifty yards off, and were moving away from me at an angle that brought them closer. They hardly paused as they moved. They seemed spooked. The wind was blowing my scent towards them, the weather northwesterly, high pressure following the night's brief rain.

I heard our roosters doing their thing. The metal barn roof was visible in places through the limbs. I wondered if Sophie had already milked the goats. Listening had rarely felt so aerobic.

The third deer moved in sight. Spike buck. It was closer than the others, within range, and had stopped. There was a limb in the way of a clean shot, but if he moved another ten feet, things would be different.

The buck looked ahead, as if for the two does. It was looking with its nose, the nose a black wick on the long candle of head and neck. Or it was looking with its glands. His neck was swollen with the rut. But it was the ears I saw most, not the stained tarsals at the leg joints, not the tines or the outline of veins on its flank. The ears were erect, swively, a miniature in shape, ovate, of the head itself.

Deer look awkward standing still, pale tail flicking, legs so much for speed they seem to work harder not moving. I thought of the butterfly bushes on the side porch, roots exposed, before Kirsten transplanted them. I thought of other things, too, but mostly I felt. I felt good in a somber way, felt settled in an anxious way. The deer took another three or four steps, tense symmetry, and then stopped just as the wind picked up. I watched the one eye I could see. The buck wasn't small for its age. It stared ahead again and then it nibbled on a sapling. I think I saw its tongue.

My stomach was more relaxed now. Breath came easier. The roosters sounded like metal springs in the moment of breaking, shrill vibrations. There was something comforting about it. A vulture glided east and north across the wind.

I raised the gun to my shoulder and cocked the hammer with a click that sounded much too loud. The highway noise, general on the knoll that time of year, came into my ears' crosshairs, and I resisted it. This would be my first shot from the fifty-dollar ladder stand. Everything felt too easy, though I'd learned that when it comes to hunting deer or the hunting that's general to living, it is best not to trust some feelings.

There had been three shots in the vicinity that morning, one towards the Sinks' place a couple of miles up ridge, another from Edwin Dennis's place on the level across the gulch, and the third from Diamond

Hill to the south. Other shots, further away, had peppered the air off and on, giving the first Saturday of muzzleloader a weird holiday sound, a sound that made me think of meat.

I walk these woods year-round, attentive to the patterns of deer and wind and other things. I look for—and cut—dead oaks, cherry, locust, and hickory for firewood and construction projects. Walking helps me sort things out, put them in perspective—the rising cost of feed, the well-intentioned fiasco of the ethanol initiatives, Kirsten's gutsy measures to grow the farm, homeschool our kid, her focus and planning and work, and my own haphazard juggling of work and politics at the college with work and play at home on the farm and in the hills and streams. Walking, hunting, I find, at the glad expense of any resolution, something like wonder, abundance. Or it finds me.

I mean that without these walks, I don't feel right. I feel lost. Or I feel too found. I think it is the same for Kirsten with our garden and barnyard, kitchen and child. A dynamic, responsible woman, she keeps track of things all the time, yet loses herself to them, too, her consciousness tied to the soil and pastures, the soul of our place and our child and us, the beds and paths, seeds and plants, bugs and rotations.

When you live in the country and have a hand in gathering much of the food you eat, it's good to feel a sense of control. Even if that sense is an illusion. The feeling, a mix of effort and grace, will and abandon, is as simple as it is complex, like cooking a pot of rice in broth and coconut milk. I mean, it nourishes tongue and soul and bone. But it also erodes you, erodes you hard, softens you harder.

I saw the buck leap after the explosion of primer and powder. I saw the buck leap and then there were the trees and leaves and leaves and sky, the rough and tender emptiness called November. Where the smoke from the powder went was where I went—somewhere else, here.

After a minute there was a movement over the crest of the ridge, in the direction of a tangle of blowdowns, thirty or so yards from where I shot. I watched the area but saw only stillness. There was a calm in that stillness—I let there be. Really, it was a calm born of tiredness, a tiredness with not a little fatigue. The wind picked up again. I swayed with the stand in the tree, a middle-aged red oak. The squirrels resumed their foraging, and they clucked and chattered as ever. I looked around from tree to tree and from between the trees to between the trees, a mix of proximity and distance that can get dizzying unless you close your eyes now and then, or look at something close—the gunstock's grain, the stitches and stains on your gloves.

The way the buck had leapt—straight up like a cat that's been spooked—sent me cruising the coasts of hope and dread and the country between. Meantime, I dumped a hundred grains of Pyrodex from a film canister down the barrel, then worked a Sabot into place with the rod, butt of the stock on the stand's metal mesh footrest. A deer sounded its alarm of a bark from somewhere over the ridge, not too far away. I pressed another primer onto the cap and waited.

I waited for the buck to die. Time stretched out. The red in the sky was going gold, no, paler than gold. All the trees seemed to be looking another direction. I noted a few more landmarks—stump, ledge, shrub—that reminded me where I'd fired. The place the buck had stood was thirty-five yards away. I hoped for what you hope for, a clean miss or a clean kill.

A few minutes later, I heard our stainless milk bucket's handle clanging on the basin rim. There wasn't the quiet morning voice of my daughter talking Nellie through a smooth milking session—they were downwind—but I heard it all the same. I thought of a day in late June, a Sunday, sunflowers in blossom, Sophie steadying Tika as I tweezed ticks from his belly, Kirsten mulching the garden with old bedding from the goat shed. There were bluebirds lighting on the white oak tomato stakes that day. It was sunny, muggy, thunderstorms overnight, the rain barrels full. Later, we'd head to Buena Vista so Sophie could play her dulcimer with the musicians gathered by the Maury River for a festival. So we could listen, tap our feet. Later than that, we'd cook a venison loin over a cedar fire, watch the sun going down farther to the right—northwest—of Purgatory Mountain than it does all year.

It was time now. I scraped the primer from the cap and tied the gun to the haul and lowered it. And then I lowered myself foot and hand by foot and hand down the cold metal ladder. Before walking to look for the deer, I refastened the primer cap on the gun. The squirrels were scrambling in the leaves, burying or unburying acorns or who knows what. Their gurgly, ratchety voices made the highway noise feel less invasive. All the trees looked very purple. I stretched my blaze orange neck gaiter to full exposure. It was clear from the shots at varying intervals and distances that all the meat grubbers were out today.

The blood was the blood of a lung shot—oxygenated, bubbly, with pale mucus flecks. This gave me hope that the deer was dead and not far away. Indeed, the trail was much more than a trail. I tried not to step in that scent, that stain.

The woods felt especially vibrant now. It had to do with attention. Instead of scanning, as hunting requires, that looking by not looking, I was in focus. There was a destination, or the promise of one, and a trail. Under a persimmon tree that I'd walked by a hundred times without noticing, there were persimmons. I found one with no blood on it and put it in my mouth. The taste sent all my clouds to burst as it mingled with the coffee and coconut macaroon breakfast still hitched to my gums and teeth. I think I heard a chickadee. I definitely heard a titmouse.

The buck lay on its side among a tangle of fox grape and greenbrier. In places the leaves had been rubbed to expose dirt, perhaps by these deer or others on previous passes. Maybe it was the squirrels. I heard my daughter talking to the goat, her voice not her words. Was she singing? I was closer to the barn now, which stood in broadaxed pine-log rustication a hundred yards downslope. All the oak leaves in this copse had fallen, but they were still very green, too green.

The deer wasn't much to look at with its eyes gone dull, the blood on the leaves at its mouth, that hole below its shoulder. And yet it was the world for now, for I had killed it. My finger on the trigger as it crossed on a path it had crossed many times. I didn't think, as some propose, that the deer came to me, that it was ready to die. Nor did I believe that it was sent, a gift from the beyond. We had simply crossed paths, as the trees cross paths when one falls in the direction of another—who in the end can say why.

We hope for, and have been lucky enough to get, four deer a year. I'm not after trophy bucks but burger, stock, stew, loins, and steaks. Our chickens peck clean the ribs and spine. Our dogs eat the scrap side meat and gnaw for days on other parts—bones, sinew. The barn cats get what they can. The bones and hoofs go to the stockpot, the heart and liver to skillet or grill. Each year we talk about tanning hides, but so far bugs and others have taken care of the pelts.

Besides our love for the taste of venison and for the butchering ritual—the primal creativity at the heart of the act, how it brings us together from solitary ventures in various nooks of the farm—we like the fact that the only feed costs involved are the ammo and other gear. I hunt with a hundred-dollar, used Thompson muzzleloader. No scope or sling, no scentless clothing, mostly the same old warm clothes I'd wear paddling whitewater this time of year—skullie instead of helmet, and instead of a lifejacket, a gray, slightly battered but duct-taped winter coat that's kept me warm since the eleventh grade.

In this area the prior night, I'd heard a bobcat screaming its alto yelp. The critter had started from the bottom below Arcadia Road and worked up the cedar thicket, come behind the barn, and then proceeded up the ridge, calling at a mate, I suppose, or just the wondrous pain of existence. I don't sleep well and listened, haunted by the sound, as the puppy barked and the rain fell and the guinea fowl simulated something metal and weight-bearing in need of oil.

There's much rare and graceful and sane and wild and playful and serious about a bobcat's sound. And a deer, when you have your arms in

162

its gut, up to the elbows, that heat is not the heat of a bobcat's call, but it is not so different. Gratitude is an act as much as a feeling, and to say that there isn't dread involved would be, for me, a lie. When I feel thankful, I have worked to prepare for such a feeling. I have accepted that the world is, despite its vast and grand indifference, capable of ruining me at any moment. And when I keep this in mind, however tenuously, every minute I am not in ruins is a gift. Such a view is simple, but I've found it hard to remember more times than I care to admit.

The stomach popped as I rolled the steaming innards onto the leaves. The rancid smell was sudden and explosive and made me gag and want to order pizzas for the next year and quit this homesteader nonsense. For a moment, I forgot our three chest freezers full of pork and venison, beef and fowl, bread and veggies. I forgot the pride and pleasure we took in working up the meat, the intimacy of a small family gathered among cutting boards, a dance of knives and flesh, something good on the stereo. I longed for the ordered, Muzaky flirtations of a grocery store.

Luckily, none of the stomach goop splattered to taint the meat. I'd read of the nutritional value of the partly digested roughage, of folks who eat the contents of the stomach. We're not that hardcore, but our dogs are, always finding the gut piles and dragging them, along with bones we give them, to the grassy place around the trampoline, the first place visitors see and children go when they come to the house, a kind of welcome mat.

Sooner than it seemed, the gutting part was done. I sat in the leaves and looked around, feeling profound for feeling foolish or foolish for feeling profound—something. Restlessness better be a gift or your ass is grass, I thought a little later as I bent the deer's forelegs around back the head, tied a bit of rope there. With the other end of the rope bent over my shoulder, plastic bag of heart and liver in one hand, I dragged the deer down ridge and through the gate and past the sheep, who seemed more or less curious. They saw, in other words, that this was not a bucket of grain.

Chance, maybe. I'd been walking these woods for a while, watching for, among other things, deer and signs of travel. I'd chosen the tree for the stand according to a hunch that solidified after a bow season spent hunting on the ground, taking a few steps and waiting, watching, then another few steps. I'd sighted the peeps on the muzzleloader, fired it at an old cardboard box. There are patterns in this world and it felt good to have evidence of them. The deer now hanging head down in the shed among the scrap lumber, the surfboard, the hams, and salvaged enamel sinks made these patterns tangible.

Better yet was the evidence that I had been graced to be among those patterns, and if I'd altered them, that change felt like part of the design. I left the deer hanging, its meat to cool, and started through the garden towards the porch. There was a buzzard coming over the ridge from the James, mist like a shawl on Cove Mountain and Flat Top beyond. Kirsten and Sophie could tell from my face how things had gone and they smiled. They were by the woodpile, gathering heat for the day, and I joined them. Later, I peeled off my boots and went inside and washed my hands real well. I was ready to go back to bed, but there was an hour before my freshman seminar. That week, we were reading Silko's *Ceremony*.

A Hog Butchering

It's two below this morning, but there's no wind. The woods look scraped and desolate in the sunlight, and I want to take a long walk in there. But today is not for that. There are chores. I carry warm water to the animals. I load the wheelbarrow with firewood and then reload the cookstove, a hulky Amish-made number that also heats our house. Later, after banging some minor repairs on the fence, I check on the greens in the hothouse and cold frames—mosh, arugula, radish, and a frilled, red-edged lettuce called, sensually enough, Lollo Rossa. It stills me to see they have survived another frigid night.

A little after nine and the thermometer reads ten degrees. Having grained and hayed them, our daughter Sophie hops around with her Nubian doelings. Homeschool is in session. I watch them in the near pasture. She is large with clothing. They are playing queen of the stump. The little goats seem too frisky for such weather. Up Arcadia Road in National Forest, the waterfalls, frozen for nearly a week, contain more than enough ice to fill our house and barn. It is the colors of the ice that we love, the milky greens and blues, as much as their shapes. But today is for other colors, other flows.

At ten or so, Donnie rumbles up in the flatbed with Pepper—aka Steve, aka Pepperoni Sandwich—and the tools.

"You ready?" Donnie says.

"Yes," I say. "How's the fire?"

"It was ice in the hogpot all the way through," Donnie says. "But it's getting there."

I take our truck around and back it to the hog pen and set the rollers in place—conveyer belt salvage. Meanwhile, Pepper and Donnie and Sophie rustle the goats and dogs shut up in a shed off the barn where they won't be in the way. Sophie heads back to join Kirsten in the house while Donnie and Pepper meet me at the hog pen.

In the shade where the shed adjacent to the hog pen blocks the sun, Donnie bolts a .22 long in his Winchester. He might as well be answering the phone he is so matter of fact about it. We enter the gate, and Pepper and I watch as Donnie—hawklike as ever with his sharp nose—crouches towards the hog real slow and talking hard but soft somehow. The hog, he's not sure what the deal is, sniffing the barrel, snorting, eventually standing quiet. I'm looking and holding the knife and feeling caves collapse in my belly as Donnie and Pepper and the hog must be, too.

I see length, the steady line of the back, no saddle only a slight rise when the hog's nose is down. And somewhere closer than the back of my mind, I see beneath his skin, his insides like a memory trace. I don't have a good memory, but we butchered his brother last Saturday in weather much warmer than this—the images remain.

Hardly any lips on this hog, his jaw long, as if in proportion to the backbone. The permanent grin in the curve of his mouth is unsettling. And that nose—deep-nostriled, quivering and flinching as he sniffs at Donnie, at the gun's snout—the nose looks too sensitive in its moist pinkness to be so practical, scraped along the ground like a plow. The jowl beneath, where head transitions to neck, is bulbous and flared, the cloven hoofs of the forelegs never far beneath, though he kneels to relax. His russet bristles appear longest below the eyes, at the snout's high side—there's flourish in that look, a sense of style, though it probably has more to do with vision, protection from dust, flies.

His belly has five little nipples on either side of his penis, what's left of it, this being a barrow, a castrated hog. The bristles are at their thinnest on the belly. This hog is speckled, and the black patches are the places where the skin is dark, rather than pale pink skin where his hair grows dirty beige.

The tail, with that curl three inches aft, skinny and short in proportion to the body, seems like an afterthought, though a longer, thicker, bristlier tail would likely interfere. It has been said—and

166

measured—that a one-hundred-and-ten-pound pig produces a ton of manure a year, enough to grow plenty of grain.

I see why football people call down lineman hogs. By definition, one calls swine over a hundred twenty pounds a hog; under that weight, it is still a pig. Yet the ears are lovely with the virile attraction of some mammoth tropical foliage. The ears, to me, are the hog's most expressive feature, the eyes being hard to see among the bristles, thick jowls, and mouth. The ears flop over foreword, as if winking, when he relaxes, and they stand up in banana leaf splendor when he listens, alert, which he's doing now.

It always takes a while for Donnie to get the shot he likes—point blank between the eyes, proper angle critical—but it happens and the hog falls and kicks those stumpy, powerful legs. Quick I hand Donnie the knife and then grab the forelegs with Pepperoni Sandwich, all of us watching not to get our heads kicked by the hind ones as Donnie sticks the hog's neck in the right spot and the blood goes gushing in that wild red way with the twisting and flailing not about to stop but soon.

I think back to early June when we drove out 43 past Saltpetre Cave nearly to Eagle Rock, eating ice cream from the Hilltop Grocery, the sun low over the long Alleghenies to the west, a recent thundershower bearing mist and smells of heat and cut hay. We're talking a little, old houses going by, green fields, green woods. We go out to Travis's and he sells us our barrow shoats and we poke around a good while, admiring his new barn, the lumber he's cut and milled, and then we take an even longer, quieter way home in the dusk and twilight than we came.

And there was all the foraging and feeding and watering as we moved the pigs from plot to plot to graze and root and plow. How they fattened by the week, growing longer and wider, summer stretching on with more and more garden trimmings, whey from goat cheese, cracked chicken eggs, table and canning scraps, old bread, fish parts, the volunteer pumpkins and corn and squash grown enough in the hog pen by September to turn the pigs out there, where they stayed nights as colder weather came and with it other foods—deer and lamb parts, corn, hay for bedding, anything, really, they being omnivores with no dilemmas, and water: water from rain barrels under the gutters, and water when without rain from buckets, and water when freezing warm from the tap.

It was good to see them run in the pasture with the Pyrenees pups and the goats and sheep, how the hogs kicked it up with those short legs and big ears—rough and pushy and surprisingly quick, elegant animals. We watched them but not too close, because winter was always creeping from the equator with its various miracles and fates. We didn't name them, either—not anymore—not Country Ham, not Pig, not Hog or Hog 1 or Hog 2. And somehow they were closer to us for it—rooting in our sleep and in our bellies when we snacked on liver pudding or relished grilled loin those spring evenings of birds and buds and grace.

We drag the hog by the handles on the hook in its mouth. Unlike last Saturday, when this was a sloggy, messy operation, it's too cold for mud today. But friction happens. We drag him one hump at a time on the board and then up the rollers onto the truck bed where the blood will darken and coagulate in the shapes, roughly, of tongues by the time I back up to the table by the hog pot over Furnace way.

A mile down Arcadia road from our place is the James River, and not far up the river from the bridge, there's a creek coming in from the right bank. You could follow that creek—a pretty go, not too far— scramble up the slick, ancient bed and scale the big falls along Bearwallow Road and continue up where the creek cuts along Route 435, under Route 435, and then under Route 436, a distance of three miles or so. You'd come out along Furnace Hollow Road.

After a tangled, grapeviney stretch of woods, Ginger, an old roan Appaloosa, roams the pasture on the left, and a small house sits in the yard adjoining. The springbox, cement, spews a steady stream from a branch before the driveway bridge; up that branch in late December, but more regularly in January, there's likely to be smoke coming from a place between sheds. You might hear some guinea fowl making their fuss, a rooster or two, a dog or three, a cat snarling—all part of Donnie's outfit.

Backing the truck up to the table, I see Donnie swashing the thermometer in the scurfy, steaming liquid before taking a read. The smoke's from a fire going under a cut-in-half old water tank. The black steel tub sits up on cinderblock and is chinked with mud around the base. There's a piece of stovepipe jutting out the one end, but the smoke is emerging as steam from the water as much as from the pipe.

Pepper and I drag the hog from the truck bed's gate to a table flush to the pot's west edge. Pepper helps with the butchering each year. He's attentive and quiet in a tragic way, and I always feel something complicated when, working close to him, the acrid reek of vodka and cigarettes not just on his breath blends with the hog stench. He and Donnie grew up together on Furnace Hollow. If not sixty, Pepper must be approaching it. His beard, it's like another country—not as white as Donnie's but longer, more frizzy. In some lights he's a ropey man, in others drawn, but in all lights he works with a kind of care and endurance I'll probably never know.

When the water's 150, the hog goes in on a length of woven wire that serves as a ladle, a four-person ladle, taller folks—Pepperoni and me—on the branch side of the pot, others on the table. There's a solemn and careful kind of attention in the way we slosh the hog up and down and roll it side to side where it lays, almost floats, on the fence in the hot, nasty water. Now and then, Donnie'll yank the scruff on its haunches and ear, gauging when the coat's ready to be scraped.

It doesn't take long. We heave the fence just so while squatting, table-bound, on its west end, and the pig rolls with the wire from vat to oak boards. There's smoke and breath and steam going all over in the cold, but you hardly notice with the activity until you're coughing. Sophie's already handing me a scraper, a wood and metal sort of mushroomy thing, because it's time to barber those hog bristles, which scrape in mats, some places easier than others.

We go fifteen or twenty minutes on each side before the hog is shining white as a snowball, to use Donnie's words. We all step back each time Kirsten dumps a five-gallon from the pot to keep hog hot and good for scraping, but we scoot back in there because this is no time for chilling—a life's been taken and there's another one yet to take. And plenty to do with both of them.

There's a cross between a possum and mole and a horse in a hog. There are the origins of squat. There is bloated tick or there is swollen. It has to do with bulk. It has to do with transport—hog, pig—the expansive breath of h and o versus the shrill, quick p and diminutive little i. The snout does it, maybe, or the jowls, give swine that knowing, detached look.

But they're not tragic, hogs, made for eating as they are, and they are even less heroic. People call them smart. It is strange for a thing to be smart and to be built so well, every part, for being consumed. Eating just anything might make you smart in the sense of adaptable. And not providing wool and not being harnessable or cuddleable or milkable might be smart in terms of being left alone. But having an intuitive face doesn't mean you're smart. Fools often own intuitive faces, just as smart people often bear foolish, maudlin faces.

This is our second winter butchering with Donnie. We do it because we like it and we like it because it is satisfying, bringing us together at a time of year when a person can use that sort of thing. We enjoy raising pigs from summer through early winter. And we like having good pork throughout the year—some to sell, a bit for trade, a lot for eating. But, most of all, we do it because we feel a sweet strength being with Donnie. He's a capable, kind man who loves what he does, which in the manner of a countryman is a thousand things a day; loving them, he does them well and treats us, a couple years new to these parts, almost as though we're family.

Something, certainly, has been lost in our regard for the animals by butchering them, but as much, if not more, has been gained. We look at a hog and see meat. We look and, in seeing meat, we feel a hard kind of gratitude—it happens without us knowing, affection and remorse and gratitude and other feelings, too, a sort of automatic prayer even as we reckon on its taste, the proportion of lard to lean, the diameter of its loin, the color and volume of grease its sausage might leave in the pan.

But, in the end, we look and we thank because we have to, we can't help ourselves, and not because thanking is a more expansive way of seeing than looking the way I too often look, looking to have looked and not seen, a gesture more than a habitation.

Out here by the hog pot, there's nobody thinking about intimacy, not intimacy with nature, not intimacy with these hogs or with each other or with all the generations who've been working up hogs since way back. Nobody's pondering their carbon footprint or the price of gas or the oxymoronic possibilities of the term "sustainable development," either.

People are just trying not to do anything stupid, trying not to get hurt or hurt anyone else. A hog's as much weight as there's sharpness on these blades and slick, busy ground. There's a lot of ways to fall and some bad hot water and icy boards and frozen and blood-dark ruts. Everybody's keeping eyes out, playing it safe, looking for how to help whether how means getting in or out of or just being the way. By the time we're feeding this hog through grinder or slicer, we'll have lifted it several times, each time heavier, each time making us feel more and less human, more like lard, a way I like to feel.

But it's happening, a messy, smelly, nourishing intimacy. And the wood under the hog pot, it's from a dead pine that fell in high winds two weeks ago, the pine that, when its dust was flying all perfumey from the Stihl, was as beautiful, its bark and rings and limbs and tensions, as any place on the Sierra Club calendar.

Under the hog pot and under the fire under it and under the table and the sheds, the roots of an oak tree hold things together, and I'm looking up the bole of that scraggly dead tree, wondering what it's going to smoosh when it falls just as Donnie says grab that ear and let's slide this hog over on the board. So I grab the bald ear at its root and reach under the jowl with my other flipper and yank and the hog doesn't move much, dead weight being what it is, but it moves enough. There's a hard little wind starting to come up from the south, hitched to a raft of quilty, undulant clouds. Donnie cuts a slit behind the tendon of each hock and threads a steel hook in those before we roll hog down the salvaged conveyer where the three poles are laid out with bolts and swiveling so far up.

It takes some finagling and heaving, but soon the hog's long snout's off the gravel and Sophie shouts, as she likes to do every year, "Hog on a pole," the three old locust rails nearly humming with the weight. Donnie swipes file on blade as Pepperoni plugs in the Sawzall, and Sophie asks me to hold some baling twine which she slices with her knife, the smaller one of her two, both of them gifts last Christmas from Donnie, knives she won't let a file touch, she honors them so, thus are sharpened on a diamond stone.

Everyone settles for a spell. Somebody offers Pepsi. I feel a chill from the sweat under my layers. A hawk screams from the hill across Furnace, the creek rimmed with ice. A black and white cat lingers off the side of the hog pot. Rows of fruit trees look too skinny to be alive, but are. Kirsten and I, our dirty hands—we hold them over the hole at top of stovepipe. There are hog bristles and dark, gummy mats of skinstuff on our sleeves and on our pants. Behind the shed, the sudden, blunt crack of a .22 and then snorting, though higher than snorting, salvation and terror being the same pitch—not pretty and not not pretty. It's Sophie and Kirsten and me and the first hog, our hog, the hog that never called us his—the last to work up this winter—hanging on the pole, massive with stillness, a loud red staining its undersnout from the neck's spiked place, a two-inch gash.

There had been twenty minutes there—where did they go but into cold dirt, cold air—when we worked sharpened knives from the hocks down, shaving what remaining scruff as well as any grime from the hanging hog. We scraped tail, hams, joints, folds, belly, nipples, chin, ear—every inch. And we dumped hot water over it. And, later, we dumped cold. It almost gleams in the low winter light, the hog, more monkish in its girthy baldness than any of us with hoodies drawn thick over wool hats.

"Let's get a hand," Donnie yells, so I hustle around the shed to his hog pen and wrap a hand on the hook's handle and help haul the hog on the conveyer to and up on the table for another scalding on the woven wire, everyone real careful not to fall in the pot or take a mouthful from the frequent splashes.

Two hogs on a pole now, the second paler fleshed than the first and a little longer. "Three-fifty," Donnie says. Around three hundred pounds, everyone agrees, is the first.

Sophie sidles closer than any of us to watch the next part. Her excitement, I suppose, is natural for an eight-year-old who doesn't find work like this outdated or irrelevant or disgusting. She watches close because, in part, she wants to memorize the process—she's the kind of kid who looks forward to doing this herself.

First Donnie takes the long, pointy knife, thin from many bites of the bastard file, and cuts around the anus. He cinches the opening with baling twine and then scribes an incision longways down the center on belly-and-spine side. Next, a careful mix of knife and Sawzall work reveals a steaming mass of coiled and bulbous innards that slough into a washtub—Donnie catching the liver and heart, though all will find a use—the stomach matter, partly digested roughage, a chicken's delicacy. We'll render lard, scramble brains in eggs, and boil various pieces into puddings and stocks. For other parts, there are other nourishments, not solely human, though human enough considering who the dogs, cats, and chickens are served by and serve. Those who say, "With a hog, you use everything but the squeal," are wrong—the eyeballs don't amount to much.

There is a solid way of standing now that's not just a result of a winter day spent among good woods and animals and water and people who feel closer to them by working them. Something of my head is removed when the hog's head is taken to hang by steel hook in the same distant shed where the spine and side meat are laid on butcher's paper. My various aches and pains throb more perfectly. And I feel privy, as I know Kirsten and Sophie do as well, to an ancient kind of progress watching Donnie slice, carve, almost whittling at times, the spine away from the loin, the hog soon enough in halves. If the varieties of red in the meat and the equal shades of pale in the lard and flesh and bone aren't touching us way down, they will touch us all the way through as we spend the coming days chopping, slicing, grinding.

There are hours to go cutting the halves in threes, removing the leaf lard, ribs, loin, shoulder, side meat, and ham—hauling them to the sheds where it all hangs overnight to cool; and then a day tomorrow, a ten-hour day of bacon, loin, jowl—hauling and slicing and grinding and spicing, keeping it all tidy while working two masses of sausage meat, 136 pounds from one hog, 123 from the other, the masses worked by hand, many clean, chilly hands, one mass at a time on a table in Donnie's basement, a down-home and lovely little butcher shop. As you might figure, that's a lot of meat on a table and a lot of sage and other spices and handwork to get right, and plenty of tasting to make sure.

The third day, we pack sausage. We pack one pound per quart bag, all the air out, a thin brick, the meat pressed with care to fill each corner of the bag, the kind Donnie likes best—because they work best—the kind with the zipper seal. And, later, we rub salt and brown sugar and then more salt on and into the hams, sprinkling them with black and red pepper to keep the mice off as the hams cure on the rough poplar shelves in the shed. Later, they'll spend the summer hanging in a double wrap of pillowcase and feed sack, cinched up tight, a sprinkling of Borax for critter control.

Hours to go and days, but first there's another hog on a pole, and Donnie's already working what isn't magic so much as experience and love and care and intention—and, also, I think, a kind of rebellion—the spark of any true artisan. There's a need in him deeper than heritage, deeper even than love. It's good to be around that. Lord knows, it's easy enough to find a store to sell you some overmedicated, big company pork for a third of the price of an hour of such skilled labor.

There is a lull now as Donnie does his thing. We watch him in the cold. Though I haven't mastered the art of standing around while others work, especially when chilly, I've come to accept that Donnie won't let anybody else do the dirtiest, most intricate deeds—the killing and sticking and disemboweling. Donnie runs the show with an intense kind of cheer. It is a pleasure to see. You can see it from a mile off in the way he stands there, in his hunkered, earthen gait; in the sparkle of his eyes, the curve and heft of his fingers. He's been doing this longer than Kirsten, Sophie, and I have been breathing, and it's become as necessary to him and as hard to explain as any very serious passion.

Once again, the guts go where they go. The head goes, and the spine. When we look between the three locust poles now, we no longer see a hog—we see parts, we see tasks, we see use. It is wealth we see.

And if we see and feel something of ourselves, too, and something outside ourselves, it's because work like this at the end of the day has a climax, and in that stage, on some level deeper than awareness, we start seeing what we've seen and haven't seen all day: each other and all the others—every drover and dirt farmer and homesteader from Bavaria to China to Botetourt to New Guinea to the lands between, every hog hunted, raised, and sacrificed throughout the ages, all the hogs and habitats and foragings of everyone and everything now and then and to come. Contact is like that. Far-reaching. Hopeful. Scary. And a part of me, it happens every year—for a minute, maybe more—never wants to eat pork again.

"Here," Donnie says, as he steps back from the table, knife in one hand, strip of leaf lard in the other. Beyond him, the wind carries a weak plume of steam from the hog pot. He's finished cutting another side.

Sophie hefts the tapestry of ribs. Kirsten shoulders the shoulder. Pepper opens his arms to the square of side meat, which folds as he cradles it. The last slice of sun is beneath the clouds now and pouring some wild juice through the woods. Ham slung over my good shoulder, I follow the procession to the meat shed, thinking of waterfalls and ice, but mostly of home, a crackling cookstove.

Pepper is strolling back to the table when I catch up with Kirsten and give her a peck. Her cheek is red and tastes of cold. There are hog quarters on our shoulders. There's a world of grime and stench and germs in our clothes and hands. It isn't unromantic. "What do you want for dinner," I ask.

Her right eye squinches as she thinks. It is a serious question for my wife, what to have for dinner—holy even. I watch as she watches a laying hen, a lustrous Australorp, scratch in the leaves next to the meat shed. Meanwhile, Sophie, banging around that little room of steel hooks, of pinks and reds and pales, still does not want our help hooking up the bulky web of ribs.

"Fresh greens," Kirsten says at last. "A little salad," she continues. "A white bowl. Arugula, goat cheese, lots of herbs."

Yondering

We drove up Buffalo Road and then cut on good gravel over Garden Mountain, wound around Sugarloaf and Painter—way out past the old Dudley place, sky a raw milk, cold enough for the rime to stay in blossom all day, rhododendron leaves curled up, too. We ended over Mill Creek way, at the top by Smith Branch, hugged in among Middle and Brushy and Sandbank, mountains that look more gentle than they feel when you're in them, hunting tangles where the grouse might be.

It was a day in December, my friend Greg Whitt and his dog Lily and me. The woods were a lake of leaves and deadfall and stone. Not everywhere was the water stiff with cold. It dropped in places too quickly for that.

This was shale country, the Alleghany front. Picture a centipede and you'll see, scaled down, how the water drained for miles, how it ran together. This was cutover paper company land. This was the line where the counties changed names—Rockbridge, Botetourt. This wasn't nowhere, but it was as close as we could get without having to go real far.

Lily's a German shorthair, a year old the past October—she's Greg's first. He's been training her according to books and local knowledge, but like a lot of young dogs, she hasn't seen enough birds. We hoped to help fix that today. I said as much to her as we wound around another long curve, brown mass of mountains, the sky ponderous and lovely, Greg all fired up by a grapevine mass close to pulling its host tree down.

"It's like a vineyard in there," he said. Lily, as if in response, stole up between the buckets from the backseat, her nutty, fierce eyes, ears tuned to the song of rocks under tire, and she gave Greg a little lick on the neck without looking at him, saying let's get there, I care about you and those grapevines, sure, but I want to run those woods, I want to follow my nose. She turned then and slipped aft. I glanced back and saw the lean dog, rump foreword. She was rubbing her snout in my coat, which reminded me it hadn't been washed since the hog butchering a few days prior.

Lily's liver-ticked the way shorthairs are, and she moves like a grasshopper, lean and trotty, bouncing and leaping and galloping, prancing or trancing, almost flying, too, when necessary. Her brown patches are islands among an archipelago of smaller brown spots, the white a kind of sea. She's a walking mural of gingerbread cookies, in other words. My favorite patch is two circles joined like an eight, a solid one, with a little three-quarter circle, also solid liver, bulging off of it.

We were descending a long curve now. Greg was taking it pretty fast. For a while, you could see so far to the north I wondered if we hadn't paid an admission fee.

"Greg," I said.

"Yo."

"You have a beautiful dog," I said. "But her tail reminds me of a scrap of PVC. There's one in our toolshed—same length and width—but I couldn't find it the other day."

"That's it," he said. "Sorry, I meant to tell you."

Solemnity has a thin bladder, and we had punctured it. The miraculous thing is, she has more than one. This was shaping up to be a fine day.

Where we parked by the National Forest gate at Smith Flats, there were two trucks, steel cages in the beds—bear hunters. Lily, eager to get going, slashed about the woods while we geared up and chatted with one of the bear guys, a big bearded man. He was friendly. When Lily returned and was checking the scent on this new human, he gave her some loving, clearly admiring. And we were friendly back to the man, especially when he started in with reconnaissance. "Flushed two yonder," he said, looking at us over Lily's ear. "A few days ago, but it was right up there not even a mile."

"We won't be in your way?" Greg asked.

"No," he said. "Billy's off the other direction. Our hounds treed a sow and cub." His voice was flatter now, a bit lackluster, like he'd been hoping for a big boar. I don't know much about hunting bear, except the few cuts of bear meat I've eaten over the years were delicious, nutty and of a texture and taste that seemed a rendering of the mountains' very essence.

Behind the man, off the gravel in a pile of dumped brush, lay a coyote, stiff, its upper lip upfurled. I looked at it from a distance while Greg and the bear hunter kept talking. It was a big animal, darker than grey, fifty pounds or so. It seemed to have been dead a while and yet it looked as if it could pounce on us at any moment. The bear hunter didn't acknowledge it. Greg didn't either, not until later when Lily showed a nervous interest in the brush pile.

We hunted then. We went where the man said they'd flushed two. No grouse emerged. We went another yonder and then another few yonders. I like yondering, when where you're going isn't all planned out but figured on the fly, something to do with a tip and the terrain and the dog and her nose and the promise of game. Your pace determines it, to a small extent, and the weather and season, too. Most of what puts you where you are is so close to the heart as to be illegible and perfect. Any time is good for yondering, but winter has its perks, especially in the wooded uplands of Western Virginia—there's more room.

You could see North Mountain and Ad Cox Knob and Bearwallow Mountain, too, but mostly we saw a lot of brush and leaves and limbs and moss where we were stepping, where we were crackling the lobes and veins, looking out for greenbrier and grapevines and ankle twisters, steep ground, the dog's bell clanging, our whistles now and then calling her to stay close, work this way, slash that, her tail docked and tense, wagging now and then, up even then like a fin for balance.

We walked up and we walked down. Hours passed. The sun stayed behind the clouds, and the earth moved, and we moved across a small, vast part of it. We walked across and down and up and up and across and down. We backtracked. We looped. We sat down against trees and we drank water and ate bread and cheese and spoke a little, mostly to the dog, to Lily, saying good girl, stay close, find a bird.

The walking was good. It was all about picturing everywhere you ever will and won't be and were and are at all times of day and night and year. How else can you look for something unless in every corner of experience. How else can you find that something when you likely never will.

Lily kept stopping. Her bell would quit and Greg and I would tense up in expectation. Then we'd see her. She'd be squatting the way female dogs do. She stopped often, every twenty minutes or so. She was in heat. Greg said it made her a little erratic. I couldn't tell. I know dirt about bird dogs except I like them. I go out there with Lily and Greg because I like to tromp around in woods that are new to me. New woods are new woods, good in their own right, and also good for renewing one's appreciation for the old, regular haunts.

A person is many things and many feelings, but I've come to feel an intoxicating satisfaction upon returning, after a day or more in wild country, to the rituals of care that raising food demands, all the surprises among the routines that grow, over time, a little more intimate—the crunch of an old coffee can digging in a feed bin, water in the rain barrel slopping into an old spackle bucket, all the grunts and mews, quacks and clucks. Lately, the feel and sound of manure and mulch slipping off our shovels onto the garden beds had taken the sting off of a hard situation at my job. That situation was way off the radar today; in our first mile of walking, it was sighted somewhere south of Cape Horn, among the icebergs.

Of course, I like carrying the old over and under, knowing it's loaded, my fingertip aware of where the safety is, each of the two triggers. The promise of firing on game is forever a strong and personal pull, but seeing some new country, seeing a lot of wonders, even if it doesn't amount to seeing a grouse or shouldering the stock, releases the safety on the senses and on desire, which are always tangled up in memory. Several times as we worked those woods, as they worked us, I heard the drumming of grouse in my head, way down between the ears, those lawnmower-like eruptions I hadn't heard since fishing the Jackson the prior spring.

The trees, by the way, were not a chorus. Except for the broken ones. The more a tree grows, the more it reaches down, night the only foliage one would ever care to count on.

For days—and I had a sense of this then—my knees' pockets would be full of shale. It was hard walking, usually is on these outings. Every smile had some grimace. Look, I wanted to tell you a story about grouse and now you've got one that's not about where everything is coming from or where it is going, the stones sewing new jackets from the cloud's whittlings.

At some point, Greg said, "It's wild country this way for days, two hundred miles—maybe more."

"Any roads?" I asked. We were stopped on a flat, a kind of false summit. Greg finished drinking some water and offered me the canteen.

"A few," he said.

I trust Greg's knowledge of the region. He's fished and hunted all over Botetourt and Craig County since childhood, and his appetite for local history, gleaned from books and locals, runs as deep as he wears it gently. He often travels the back roads of Western Virginia in his work as an environmental engineer, sampling soil and water and overseeing the remediation of contaminated grounds—healthcare for the land. Essential, it seems, to his doing good work are the relationships he strikes up with people on the jobsite and in the small towns, his infectious love of nature and culture regularly inspiring them to relate stories about their own places and people. Greg often shares snippets of these experiences with me, but the spring he was involved in the cleanup after the Virginia Tech shootings, he said very little, except that he was there.

The day was progressing nicely. Those who claim that a scarcity of game inspires you to hunt harder are on to something; whether you hunt better is another story. The clouds seemed to share their thickness and endurance with us, but they kept their heaviness to themselves. And though the dirt was frozen, you could fall all the same. I busted my butt a few times. It was that steep in places. You had to use your hand, the one not holding the gun. The grip of the ground was the grip of the cold. We went and we went, and for a map we looked at Lily and we looked at the trees, at the bark, the limbs, all the joinery.

Every now and then, I had to imagine living there forever. Not to do so would have been irresponsible.

We were squirming through the dense new growth of a clear-cut when I came into a small opening and discovered the skeleton of a buck. Many of the bones were missing, but the upper part of the skull was intact, the two outermost of the six thick tines gnawed a fair bit by mice. I couldn't see or hear Greg through the trees. It was a damp place, a seep, golden sedges matted every which way. I squatted there and let my breathing subside to regular. There's no good place to die, but this looked as fine a place as any. I thought of the coyote and figured it and this buck had probably known each other, at least by scent. It seemed we weren't that far from the truck, having circled around, but there was something intensely private and remote about the spot now. My eyes went from the knobby base of the tines to a small beech, its leaves sharp, parchmenty. I wanted to linger but had to get going. Being a collector of sorts, I hung the skull by its rack through the straps of my game vest and starting walking again, awkward with the new bulk. Lily's bell clanged not too far ahead.

More hours passed. You still couldn't see the sun or its outline behind the dense and darkening clouds, but the big star was lower on the horizon—the quality of light said so, and the light seemed an accurate meter for the remaining energy in our legs. We had pushed a lot of covers with no points from Lily and no grouse. My gun seemed to be putting on weight. Snow began to drop, big flakes. Greg said, "This is last summer's burn." We had come over some ridge or other and were out on a rise between drainages—just over from some old iron mines where we'd paused for a look, little caves and stone piles that Greg connected with a furnace on Mill Creek he said was operated until the 1850s by the Tredegar Iron Works out of Richmond. Where we stood on the rise, it was hard to look at the burn line on the stumps without imagining the heat. Greg was still to my left—him a righty with the gun and me the opposite. Lily, meanwhile, worked the scarred ground roughly thirty yards out, tail tight back and forth, bell the sound of something later than old.

"Not much food in here," I said.

"Not much," Greg said. We'd been working the burn for a little while. Where we'd brushed them, charred sticks and stumps had smeared our boots and pants with black marks. What greenbrier remained was yellow. "Let's cut across the contour—find the edge of this," Greg went on. "They could be piled up in there."

We hunted the edge with new degrees of hope. The cover was good there—a recent clear-cut, some grapevine, laurel, and greenbrier among the young trees. Turkeys had been scratching the duff—dark, rich soil littered with acorn husks—and a few deer prints were frozen in one of the cleared spots.

The snow didn't last long. And there were purples, yes, but even the gray could not speak of them. I mean we were lucky sometimes and we saw each tree as its taproot sees the crown. But we were luckiest because for much of that day we were unknown to ourselves. We wanted nothing, least of all the smell of pollen.

Later, there was a grouse. It flushed sixty yards off, from down in a gulch beyond the edge of a clear-cut, far from where we were headed and far from Lily. We turned and went the yonder it had flown. We crossed the bottom and walked edgeways across the contour up the slope. Soon, we heard it flush again. It was a ways off, beyond the dog. We heard it, we both said so. And we saw things in that hearing and in that saying so. There were big oaks in there, some poplar.

Dark April Light

Life—or spring, who knows—was kicking my butt, at least in my head. I was jonesing bad. So I went to the boat shed, a rundown summer kitchen, shouldered my pig of a Dagger Cascade decked canoe, and slid it in the truck. It was Saturday, early April, as good a time as any for a dose of truancy in the form of whitewater paddling.

We'd had a leisurely morning of farm chores and then eaten grits with gobs of butter, duck eggs (over easy), and sausage from the winter's last hog, the one that put up a real fuss at the end, requiring two bullets. The forsythia was starting to drop its petals. The grass needed mowed. There were fences to repair, papers to read, seeds to start, bills to pay, a president to elect, a climate to save, and so on—no problem. With all that deliciousness in the air, I kissed my wife and hugged my daughter and then rolled on down the gravel drive a little too fast. It was just after ten.

The rain had stopped Friday morning, but I knew the Maury was holding at a fair level. We'd had a wet March, and the trees were not yet drinking the rain the way they would when they leafed out in a few weeks. My regular paddling partner had obligations that entailed a hospital room and people who might become his in-laws. He was doing the right thing. I was doing what I was doing—going to get lost and found to the feel of the river in my body again—and I hoped to run into someone else doing the same thing.

The boat was in the truck's bed along with a trio of garbage cans; the two plastic ones, in fact, had been salvaged from the banks of the James on random canoe trips. I dumped the contents of the motley cans in the motlier bins at the wayside near Natural Bridge and then hopped on I-81. The road wasn't crowded, the old Dodge running smooth. It was fine to be out of the office and away from the homestead. I thought of the nine puppies on our Great Pyrenees' teats in the mudroom, a mass of warmth and squirm on old blankets and towels against a crate where two Nubian goat kids, born the prior morning, slept off their morning milk. I thought of them and many other things because they were beautiful and a handful and going to the river is as good a time as any to revel in beauty and handfuls.

It was hard to watch the road with the clouds veiling the Blue Ridge, but I persevered and then snaked through the pastoralia outside Lexington on Route 39. The sky was a mussel shell, clouds glossy and purled. The meat of this front wouldn't hit us until that evening, bringing the rivers up once again. The thick light accentuated the color starting on the trees. Redbuds were at their shrillest voltage. Clumps of anemone blossomed along the road's shoulder. I didn't even consider listening to music. There were songs everywhere and everywhere else there was music.

At some point in the drive, while reviewing the list of supplies I needed to fetch at the hardware store in Lexington before heading home, I made a couple of phone calls to prospective tenants of our rental property and probably scared the people on the line with the buzz of expectation and excitement in my voice. I do not apologize for being fired up.

There were no cars at the take-out above Rockbridge Baths. There was nobody at the picnic area or at the overlooks stonewalled on cliffs above the gorge. The Webster Springs Whitewater Festival in West Virginia must have drawn a lot of the regulars, I thought. It seemed I'd be paddling alone or else waiting for a group to appear. I didn't want to paddle alone, but I didn't want to wait. At four-thirty, I was needed to help a neighbor hump a front-loader washer down a winding stairway. It was already going on eleven.

So I zoomed past the monument to Matthew Fontaine Maury, for whom the river was renamed in 1968. Maury, known as the "pathfinder of the seas" for his trade-enhancing work charting winds and tides in the early nineteenth century as director of the U.S. Naval Observatory, is one of those figures from history whose accomplishments and honors feel dizzyingly consequential, if not abstract. In addition to shaving weeks off the sailing lines and inventing torpedoes to harass the Union navy when he quit his post in D.C. to serve the Confederate cause, the guy published a dozen books on geography, helped to create the U.S. Naval Academy, The Virginia Technological and Agricultural Institute, and was asked to be president of William & Mary and VMI. I don't know how many roads and buildings in Virginia bear his name. In a recent blip of fortune, Pat Robertson honored him as a scientist of faith.

I prefer to think of Maury in the image of him as a young man traveling from Virginia to Tennessee, when he first visited Lexington via canal boat on the then-named North River after coming up the James from Richmond along the Kanawha and James River Canal. I like to think of him admiring the river, perhaps aware that later in life when he taught at VMI and came to better know the river and land it shapes, he'd request his remains be carried through Goshen Pass when the laurel was in bloom. They were.

At a certain elevation the skunk cabbage was visible, freckling the ground through the woods along the road like small green mammals. Mountain cherries in blossom, serviceberry, too—the river splashed and gurfled, and even at forty miles per hour I could hear it with the window cracked.

I was turning off 39 on the gravel road to the put-in when glimpses of unnatural color—plastic—appeared through the trees. There were boats, lots of boats and cars and people gearing up for a river trip. The word "playdate" came to mind.

There was a woman, I kid you not, with her dry suit unzipped to the waist, going from vehicle to vehicle, person to person, offering home-baked chocolate cookies from a Tupperware so large a monkey could have paddled it down the river. Her name was, I forget her name. Like me, she paddled an old Dagger. Most in that party paddled boats from another era. The eras had been accelerating in recent years, but everyone knows this.

I tend to be the old guy on the water. Today, it appeared that at thirty-six I was younger than each of these folks by at least ten years. To ponder why this felt so exciting went, thankfully, against my latest religion.

"Are you in charge?" I asked a guy with a beard like a muskie fly.

"Am I in charge?" he laughed. "I can't even find my lifejacket." He seemed a little blown away, but I tried not to project.

"I'm wondering if I could join this group," I said to the lady with the cookies. "Is it one group?"

"Indeed," she said. Her hair was gray and her eyes reminded me of fruit juice. I've always been unusually attracted to people who use the word indeed. "Check with that guy over there," she said. I bit into her cookie, looked at the guy. He was walking towards us. He, too, wore a dry suit unzipped to the waist. I wondered if they thought I was underdressed. I wore pile pants and a couple of those recycled soda-pop shirts that retain your worst odors even after you wash them in the latest earth-friendly detergent.

"You're welcome to join us," the guy said. We introduced ourselves. Chris, Scott—I forgot his name. I thanked the lady for the cookies. She looked a little too pleased. I tried to guess which of the crew might be her husband. The other fellow confirmed that, indeed, he had left his lifejacket at home.

"Is he from Vermont, too?" I asked Scott or Chris.

"No," Scott or Chris said. "He's not with us. He was going to join us, like you."

"I wish I had an extra vest to lend him," I said, hoping I'd remembered mine.

There were eighteen boats in the party. It was a group from Connecticut and Vermont I'd joined. We looked ridiculous on the river—many paddlers do—like waste from an overturned toy truck, but there was something thrilling and beautiful about it, too. Not long after we put on the river, I stared upstream from my place on the river near the front of the pack and what I saw and what I felt were so distinctly different, I knew there was a moral in the moment that I'd never understand. I think it involved civilization and twilight. I carved into a micro-eddy then. Yes, I did, and then I peeled out with a flourish, feeling the entire watershed of that river join the watershed of every river I hadn't paddled and every river I had. Waves, I'm talking about waves.

The Maury is a sandstone river. Due to mysteries of origin and form, the rock is chunkier than the bed on other sandstone rivers in the region. They say the flood of 1985 turned a lot of the Maury's boulders, and I think this also may account for the harsher, sharper aspect to the bed. In Goshen Pass, the rocks are gray and pink and yellow and purple and every other color, too. Lichen mottles it and so do the splash marks in some chemical fashion in addition to the smears of wet. Looking at the river, I always wish there was a geologist present to read me the story of the long and sloping, stacked cliffs along the banks. Sometimes these cliffs run parallel to the river, but mostly they run at all angles. I like it when they curve and fold down the slope and into the water like some massive hieroglyph that represents gravity and fate.

The river flows primarily west to east. Just above the put-in, the Little Calfpasture River and the Calfpasture proper, running north to south along the long Allegheny ridges, bend and join to form the Maury, which runs forty miles—through Lexington and Buena Vista and Glasgow—before it dumps into the James at Balcony Falls. I've been lucky to experience the watershed from several angles. I've paddled the final stretch into Balcony Falls many times and fished Buffalo Creek's forks near Collierstown and hunted deer and helped with a buddy's maple syrup operation along several tributaries in the Kerr's and Walker's Creek neck of the forks. Before our animals rooted us to be home each evening and morning for chores, my family spent a yearly May weekend camping in the Ramsey's Draft Wilderness west of Staunton, where we hacked around and fished for brook trout, hardly aware of how that cool, hemlocky stream was destined for the Maury.

More than just alder and laurel and rhododendron grow along the banks in Goshen Pass. There's flood debris, wild contortions of driftwood and leaves hung in the saplings. The slopes along the gorge vary from mixed hardwood to laurel hells to pine. Some of the south-facing slopes on the river-left bank, being drier and rockier, are especially scrubby. As with mountain rivers in general, the whole is a sum of contrasts—dry and wet, concrete and fluid, inert and alive.

The rapids at all but a flood level do not surpass Class IV in difficulty. Goshen Pass is a good stretch of river for experienced paddlers to hone their edges. There tend to be many alternative lines in addition to the main one. There are creeky slots and choked chutes all over. To map the menagerie of routes through the rapids at any level would produce a doodle not unlike those that sometimes emerge from long meetings where for all the overeducated, expert talk nothing gets accomplished. You could run any rapid fifteen different ways and catch upwards of thirty eddies a shot. When time and my bad shoulder allows, I prefer to catch as many eddies as possible in a rapid. Blasting through the maw of a wave train is great, but carving in and out from the pockets of swirly behind rocks gives a rapid another few dimensions. For one thing, you get to look back upstream and at the banks, and you feel the rapid in all its dazzling, disinterested intricacy. The torso twists as the paddle blade plants and the boat pivots. You feel too dizzy to feel dizzy.

When paddling in a group, catching eddies allows you to see who might be entering the rapid next. You can watch her run. Maybe she'll join you in the eddy. Sometimes the eddy is too small for two boats and she joins you all the same. I love it when that happens, as long as I'm on the receiving end. A tricky rapid gets trickier. If shit happens, too, being in an eddy mid-rapid lets you assist in a rescue more quickly.

The craziest big group paddling experience I remember was on Overflow Creek, a steep tributary of the Chattooga's West Fork. There were nine boats. The creek was high. Six of the crew was on our first trip down the creek. We broke into groups of three. I followed a good buddy who in the eddy above a horizon line would mumble instructions and then peel out and disappear over the drop in a manner opposite what he'd mumbled. Another friend mentioned later that my friend was dyslexic.

These days, I think and talk about paddling more than I do it. In three years of living forty minutes from it, this was my sixth trip on the Maury. Recently, I discovered that my gear apparently reflects my vague orientation as a paddler. A group of twenty-somethings I paddled with on a high water Balcony Falls trip in February tagged me the Junkyard Paddler. To them, my gear was beyond vintage; to me, it is my gear and it is old and tattered and leaky with stories, not the least of which is the one that explores how keeping old gear alive says a darling Fuck You to the global economy. Someday I will give it all up and swim the rapids, preferably naked. It is the river's essence I'm after when I paddle. Nothing tells you a river's essence like swimming it naked.

But I paddle in order not to swim. I paddle because I like rivers and boats and paddles and the interplay of hull and body and blade with each other as the water demands whatever it demands. The craft and setting of it interests me. I've been in a lot of boats over the years and I've used several kinds of paddles. Each one lives in muscle memory like an old friend, and the rivers we navigated together are inseparable from that intimate history.

The clouds broke not long after we put on the Maury. The air was in the high fifties. I was comfortable—not too warm, not cold—and the boat and the river felt familiar under me. I enjoyed being with the group. Somehow the impersonal, individual nature of the sport mixed with the intimacy of the shared experience in ways that brought the river closer. It was fun to see who among the seventeen other folks stayed together and who were the lone rangers. I noticed there were two couples, one of which stayed near one another on the river and the other of which roamed. A gray-haired man in one of the new kayaks always ran sweep and a man in a big canoe who must have been seventy often ran first. We were a little society of nomads wearing goofy helmets and neoprene skirts. We were going downstream for no reason other than pleasure.

Paddling is not a spectator sport unless you are in the mix and take the time to watch the others. I've always liked that aspect of running rivers. The extreme paddling competitions that I hear are broadcast on television I've never seen, but I've blown a little time watching paddling videos on YouTube, feeling dirty afterwards for reasons that are simple— I mean you can air paddle all you want as you stare at a computer screen, but you're not going to feel the river in your bones or smell its clean, wet reek or hear its heavy rock and froth and swirl.

A mile into the run, we encountered the approach to Devil's Kitchen. The rocks were larger, here and there bus-sized. You could no longer see the river downstream, only a congestion of boulders. The volume grew. Water broke in more places and with more force as the gradient increased. I wasn't the only one ready to stretch my legs when we eddied out above it. There was a guy with a Grateful Dead sticker on his boat. He had introduced himself to me, but I did not catch his name. He lived in Southern Vermont and had the look, a pencil mustache, smiley, twinkly eyes. I thought of Ben & Jerry's Chubby Hubby.

"Here we go," I said, not knowing what to say. What do you say above a rapid called Devil's Kitchen—"Let's put on our aprons, big guy!" No. I mean here was this total stranger in a helmet, lifejacket, and neoprene skirt. I think he was wearing gloves, too.

The sky was starting to clear. The clouds that layered the morning were more diffuse. Now and then there were patches of sun. I pulled my boat high on the bank, though there was little chance the river was rising. The high-water line was a couple of inches on the rocks; staring at it, I decided the rate of evaporation must be slower than the rate of the river level dropping.

We peopled the rocks along the rapid, scouting our routes. The walking wasn't simple on the roots and stone and mud. My legs were stiff from kneeling in the decked canoe, and I was happy to feel them under me, stretched, the blood moving. Why I chose to kneel in a canoe, decked or open, twenty years ago when I started to paddle had something to do with it being easier to roll from that position and with one blade instead of two, but it also had to do with visibility and power. Being on your knees allows a higher vantage and more torque per stroke. Despite sincere intentions otherwise, I've always been more inclined to power more than to subtlety and grace.

Devil's Kitchen resembled a maze. I remembered running it the first time at very high water with a bloody nose. I was living in Charlottesville, romping into a life of an outdoorsy poet, carpenter, husband, father, a life that my wife labeled with comic accuracy as: mountain man, the video game. In recent years, we'd taken the label to new strides, settling on a small acreage, growing our food, and homeschooling the kid. To pay the mortgage and insurance, I help tend a flock of aspiring writers at a small college. It's good coming home from the desk and classroom work to cut wood for heat, work plants for roughage, chickens for eggs, and goats for milk, and to kill deer and hogs and meat birds for the main course. Now, standing on the bank, it seemed I was staring as much at the rapid as at a blueprint of any typical day on the farm or at the school—tangly, expansive, dreadful, wondrous—something exciting no matter which route you choose.

The cleanest line required entering the rapid with a left to right angle, dropping over a small ledge, jamming right over another ledge, and continuing right over several larger ledges with progressively larger holes below each drop. I had a good feeling about the rapid today. From my place ten feet up a boulder, I could visualize a clean line each time I looked at the rapid, and I stayed there a while, letting the feelings of confidence open my eyes to more subtle aspects of Devil's Kitchen—a branch hung between two rocks, a hatch of insects drifting in the misty shine over the river's surface, the topographic bark pattern of a big sycamore tree.

As I stood there, a boat entered the rapid. The fellow paddling it had a red chubby face. It seemed the neck gasket on his drytop was too tight for him. A lot of blood appeared stuck in his head. I wondered if his head might pop. He looked silly, which reminded me that I looked just as, if not more, silly in my yellow egg of a fiberglass helmet, tattered old paddling jacket, and neoprene booties.

Like his run, mine was clean but not graceful. Devil's Kitchen is not conducive to clean runs. I muscled through the moves a little too amped. When I eddied out below the last drop, I realized I had no memory of the rapid as a whole, save a few select glances as I powerstroked off the various ledges. My bad shoulder felt strong, which pleased me since it had been nothing but trouble since I dislocated it on a lazy low brace on the Upper Yough six years prior, at a rapid named Cheeseburger Falls.

The eddy pulsed with its orbits. I drew occasional strokes to keep from spinning. Matthew Maury came to mind. I wondered what he would think if he saw us plowing our way through slots between sandstone in rotomolded plastic we wore fastened to our waists by neoprene skirts.

The guy with the Grateful Dead sticker ran the Kitchen not long after I did. He was more casual than I thought he could get away with, drifting over the ledges with hardly a stroke. I think he was chewing gum. The river pushed his boat and him around a good bit, but he made it. This guy clearly was not an aggro, hyper type.

I thought about carrying my boat up the bank and running Devil's Kitchen again, this time with more presence. I wondered if anyone had attained the rapid. Attainment paddling means paddling upstream, gaining ground against the gradient by ferrying from eddy to eddy with bursts of power and finesse. It is a delicate, forceful act. Sometimes I practice attainment on the James down the road from our home. From the put-in at the Arcadia Road bridge, it's fun to attain up through two rapids and pools to a place where Jennings Creek enters the James. I like to get out of my canoe at the cobbled mouth and poke around, looking for driftwood and other surprises.

Not one of the eighteen boats flipped at Devil's Kitchen. I didn't run it again. Five or six people portaged. Somebody who ran early stood on a boulder and shot video with a hand-held. I sat in the eddy on river-right, below the cliffs and Route 39. I was already thinking about the slot move at Corner Rapid. The slot at Corner reminds me of Left Crack on the Chattooga below Corkscrew, though without the consequences. There is no finer sort of move in whitewater paddling. You have a line and you can't be off it by much; finesse and precision are all you have, and you have the approach to have them in, that's all.

The man in the big canoe who always ran first was asleep on a rock next to the river when the last boat came through the Kitchen. The Grateful Dead guy floated in the eddy with me, and I said, "I doubt the Devil cooks. You think?" I figured this guy is from Vermont and he likes the Grateful Dead so he might be theologically inclined.

He didn't smile. He looked at his paddle blade and then at me and said, "There's a Devil's Kitchen in the UK, in the Canyonlands, and in Australia. Either there's a lot of Devils or dude's got a lot of kitchens."

We continued bobbing up and down and side to side between a boulder and the faster current off the eddyline. Another sycamore tree dominated the bank over the guy's helmet. It was starting to bud out and show a vibrant green, though overall the tree still resembled winter more than spring.

"Have you ever heard of Devil's Courthouse in Pisgah, down North Carolina?" I asked the guy, apparently a world traveler or Google-head.

He shook his head, negative. Something about his eyes and the lazy way he'd run the rapid, I wondered if he was stoned. He peeled out of the eddy then and caught another one a little ways downstream. On the back of his helmet, one of those little green stickers that suggest our country is a conglomerate of many smaller countries advertised Vermont—VT.

The group continued downstream through the ledges above Laurel Run. We all beached our boats at the picnic area and took a lunch break. It wasn't my idea of a lunch place, with port-a-johns and picnic tables and Route 39 right there. I wanted to eat in a nondescript tangle along the river where a spring trickled from an outcrop, a few bloodroot in petalled splendor, a chance to see salamanders.

But I ended up chatting with a fellow about trips through Grand Canyon and on the Selway in Idaho, which was pleasant. We discussed the permit system for running long trips out West and our various experiences on rivers throughout that region. I munched on nuts and berries, and he ate an MTO from Sheetz.

"Can't you put on the Middle Fork after August first without a permit?" I asked.

"No," he said. "But you can on the Selway."

"What's the Selway like at low water? I ran it early season, when it was high."

"It's lovely," he said in such a way that suggested anything you said about the Selway would be an understatement, which is true.

When we got rolling on the river again, my mind was on food. Lunch had been unsatisfactory and the run through Devil's Kitchen had conjured thoughts of our own kitchen. The prior night I'd chopped red onion, garlic, shitake, chard, and carrot, sautéed them in coconut oil, and then added strips of venison heart. There was sea salt and black pepper, balsamic and soy sauce and asofoetida to bolster the flavor. To add a pinch of asofoetida is always thrilling, since the stuff reeks of dirty socks before it mellows to an earthy, truffley taste as it cooks into the other ingredients. Kirsten had strained and chilled a fresh batch of kombucha, a beverage I always find hard not to chug. A mache salad, still dirty from the garden, finished the meal, each bite a splash of early spring's green wave in mouth, throat, stomach.

I was in the eddy above the slot at Corner Rapid when I came back to that present where because you're aware of being present, you aren't really present. I am no foreigner to such space and trusted the rapid and the task of running it wouldn't let me stay there for long. I stared at the place I hoped to drive the boat, a tongue of water licking a big boulder's right flank. There was another boulder three feet away, which formed the slot. The water folded in a powerful, endive-translucent crease in the middle of the slot. I'd run the crease once and didn't want to go there again, no matter how beautiful it was to see. Meltdown moves—where the boat disappears and you with it—are for younger folks than me.

Hardly a drop of water landed on my boat's deck when I landed the launch. My last stroke, at the lip, was well timed and had enough juice. I skirted the crease and launched the slot move. The rapid had mercy on me, or the approach to it. Really, there's little you can do to correct your angle after the approach except mutter something exclamatory. I eddied on the right and watched the rest of the group run the left side. The Grateful Dead guy carved into the eddy with me. He'd been worked a bit by Hematoma Hole, a juicy hydraulic left of the boulder, and he was smiling from getting through it.

"How was your run?" he asked.

"Clean," I said. "I ran the slot."

"You know," he said. "I asked my buddy if running the slot took big balls." He paused, adjusted the strap on his helmet and then his drytop wrist gasket.

"What'd he say?" I said.

"He said it takes having been here a few times."

"It's smooth if you hit it right, a sneak line," I said, but he was already peeling out. A canoe entered Hematoma Hole right then. The guy's mouth was wide open, primal.

It was getting late and I had to leave the group. They were surfing the waves and holes in the small rapids that began after Corner and pulsed nearly continuous all the way to the take-out. I said thanks and goodbye and paddled the last couple of miles straight, no eddies, no surfing, just the rhythm of the water and the body with the strokes to keep the boat in the right place, forward. There would be time to pick up supplies at the hardware store and help Cleatus and Morgan move the washing machine and be home in time for evening chores and to cook dinner, maybe get a few licks on my daughter's dulcimer. I closed my eyes and saw the river and trees and rocks. This was a calm place between rapids. Somewhere close, a waterthrush was doing gymnastics with its throat, and for a moment I knew what Wallace Stevens meant when he wrote, "My titillations have no foot-notes."

Sparks

The light on the river sheds another skin. It's not really evening, nor is it dusk. Listen, not even hard, and one can feel the ghosts of old loggers, oxen, and road builders all around. They are in the birds' throats and wings, colors and trajectories. They are in the hellebore. In seep-drip and moss. Buffalo, wolf, elk—there are other ghosts, all commingled, half this, half that, voice a blend of voice and presence.

The map is open on my pack. Jakes Creek, Miry Ridge, Sugarland Mountain. Over there, across the river, beyond the logjam and the big boulder with moss ten feet up—that's Goshen Prong. Low to the ground and in great numbers, the trillium are up, all broad leaf and bud, just hints of their burgundy petals, slivers. Hickory shoots test out their fingers. There are a few clouds and they are slightly strawberry. The map says all this, too—in its contour lines.

The air is giving its heat back to the sun. A slight breeze moves downstream, as if rolling down Clingman's Dome, where the river starts, so many trickles fresh and mossy. The sweet haze of early spring is general, alchemy of bud, pollen, light. I'm near Rough Creek's confluence with the Little River. This is East Tennessee, nearly as east as you can get. None of this matters. Geography turns to so much flood debris up here.

I'm stiff from getting here. It was a good hike, and like good hikes, the rhythms and sights took me away from distance and time as I generally know it, quantifiably. Hiking in was always a kind of hiking out. And now, too, I have the feel of trout in my arms and eyes. Brook and rainbow trout, wild ones fooled by a fly, an Adams fastened to a 6X tippet. Maybe I was the one fooled. Maybe the trout knew what they were getting into and played me. You see, there'd have to be a kiss involved, a whole life of them, to explain the river's pressure on my legs as I waded, looking, casting.

Even if you don't sleep well in a sleeping bag next to a wild mountain river, you lie awake so wonderfully, watching the stars brighten like blossoms on the limbs of the hickory and oaks. And wake from spells of sleep to the familiar shape of the canopy, more familiar each time, the curly, peacock quality of the hemlock boughs, poplar, sycamore. At dusk there is a bat up there, maybe two. It comes, once, within six feet of you, but after that it remains sixty, eighty feet up.

You lie in what at high water must be the tail of an inlet-type eddy. Under the sleeping pad is a mat of sticks the water left when it fell. They crunch when you roll. The doghobble reaches over you in places with its sharp cones, waxy with shine and splotched with bug traffic.

There are thoughts of bear. And of downpours in the headwaters. You remember the time on the Ocholochonee River, outside of Tallahassee, in the Apalachicola National Forest, down there in the best part of Florida, its armpit. You had twelve kids in your care, among them a rapist, a barn burner, a teacher stabber, a crack dealer, and a chronic runner. They were on solo, each on a small, shallow island in that swamp. It was February, you and your co-instructor—now your wife— set up on a big island in the middle of them. It was cooler than on prior trips down there.

That time—cold morning, still dark—you woke to the wailing of a name. There was frost. The kids were only supposed to yell their names when there was a life-threatening emergency. You listened, watched your breath in the headlamp's smarts and heard the name again and then others. The boats, when you stumbled upon them, were no longer aground. Two feet higher was the river. The islands, the kids were under water. They'd been sleeping, or trying to, when the water came closer and then into their sleeping bags.

Two weeks ago, on Saturday, we were returning from my brother-in-law's wedding and stopped to pick up some goats that friends of friends were giving away—purebred Alpines, the mama in milk. This was in Warren County, North Carolina, east and north of Raleigh. Things were going well. We had mama goat in the back of the truck, under a cap with two three-month-old kids and a couple of square bales. Kirsten was next to me in the cab, Sophie next to her giggling as the seven-day-old buckling in her lap sucked her finger like it was a teat.

The Slant Six in Lillie Mae, our old Dodge, was thirsty, too, so we stopped for gas outside South Boston, a former tobacco town in Southside Virginia, an hour north of Durham. Kirsten and Sophie took the young kid to a grassy place adjacent the parking area. I had to use the restroom something fierce, so left the pump running and ran inside. The place was one of those new mini-marts where the light is like an X-ray and everything screams buy me in a way that's disgustingly seductive.

Anyway, I returned to the truck and the goats and peered under the cap. My plan was a simple one: replace the gas nozzle, check the oil, and then drive to the edge of the lot so these three goats could have a walk and a bite to eat.

But smoke was coming from one of the hay bales. It was a thin plume. Curious, I lifted the cap's rear window and moved the bale. The baling twine was broken and the bale sloughed. Flames leapt. Then more flames. The day skipped to a harder song.

An hour passed, a crazy, fateful hour made tender by the help of strangers. Then we were waiting for the vet, standing in the grass, the truck soaked and black, its cap melted, glass in shards. Sophie held the kid, offered it her finger, which it took, greedily. I watched the wind. I don't know what I watched. She asked me, "Daddy, when you were little, did you watch anything burn?"

"A house," I said after a pause. "But nobody was in it."

It is morning, birdnoise and foliage the only flood. The air is chilly. The Little runs an inch below its most recent high waterline. To hear the birds through the creek's voices reminds me how in and out of tune the world is all the time. I walk in the moist air and watch, hopeful, as the sun creeps over a distant ridge, lighting the one ridge visible to the west.

Soon it is coffee time. There is no better ritual than making coffee in the backcountry—the intricate simplicity, the reward. I soften the gasket on the old one-burner's pump, white gas hitching a ride on my index and thumb. The pump squeaks but pumps, pushes air. I open the pack to fetch the pot. I dig through the little that is there. I look around, in the weeds and roots. I dig again through the pack, the little that is there.

The rare times it gets real cold in Florida, they release water from the dam on the Ocholochonee to make power so people can juice their space heaters. We didn't know about the dam then. Nobody told us about a dam. We knew the kids were soaked, tearful, hypothermic, alive. We built a big fire. We boiled water for hot chocolate. None of the kids passed out from the cold. We figured the group would be tighter than ever now, and maybe they were—a few days later, we caught this kid, a really funny, good kid, cheeking his Ritalin, trading it for favors.

Now it is later. Sophie, off to check her chicken flock, has disappeared back of the barn. We sit on the porch, watching the mama goat that jumped from the truck in flames. She is rubbing against the fence back of the pasture. Her burnt hair has nearly been replaced by new growth, white and black. We discovered her charred udder had fallen off a week ago when we saw our dog using it as a chew toy. Her kid Willy hops on a square bale, bucks his head. We listen to the birds, distant traffic.

Kirsten asks about the conference in Maryville. I tell her of the Smokies, tell her of Mayapple and trillium, rich soil and lush groves, trout, sleeping by the river. She knows how much I need coffee and shakes her head as I describe holding the Vienna sausage can full of water and grounds over the one burner's blue with my multitool. "A demitasse," she mutters.

As usual, it is good to be home. But it is hard to look out on the ridges and drainages of the near range and not feel a yearning to explore them, see them in today's partly cloudy, early April balm. Many days, I am too restless to be anything more than a haphazard homesteader. As much as I love our animals and plants, the food and care they provide, I often grow claustrophobic at the routine, in and out of gates, fences, the regular milking, waterings, feedings, repairs.

Kirsten, graciously, interrupts my yearnings. She reminds me that Sophie is still waking in the night to dreams of fire. As she speaks, a barn kitten pokes through the knee-high peas. I try to say something comforting.

"Let's head down to North Creek," I suggest. "When Sophie returns from the barn."

"Okay," Kirsten says. She looks up from her hands. They are strong and dirt-grooved from her work in the garden and kitchen. "It's a good day for swim."

I look to the pasture again. Mama goat kneels on her forelegs, eats sparingly. I try not to wonder what dreams our daughter's dreams of fire have replaced and what dreams will replace them, if dreams can be said to replace and not, like ghosts, commingle. Willy, mama goat's kid, does a little goat dance, a hop and buck and shimmy. The grass is the color of nasturtium leaves. The redbuds are still in blossom, a garish purple. It feels like a front is approaching, something in the air, some pressure.

On the James

In summer heat and at summer flows, rivers can feel morningafterish—
edgy and sluggish and scattered and lovely. It is true of the James where
we live. There's the sun, humidity, and debris from the last high water,
old leaves and sticks and trash in limbs, driftwood and traffic cones and
picnic tables and other flood booty piled at the head of islands and at the
outside of bends. More than in the water, the energy is in the river's
potential and its bed and in the inhabitants. There are the wakes and fins
of minnows and of smallmouth bass chasing minnows. Sometimes
there's a muskie, a mink, an otter. It is never hard to see the bottom.

Even at its boniest, the river bears passage. There are rock
formations and assemblages, random as gravity and time, and between
some of them flows water enough for a canoe. The cobble bars distend
and make for fine poking about. Always the river's giddy, solemn babble.
Rocks to skip, crawdads to hunt—thoughts go where they go. The
birds—kingfisher and green and blue heron and osprey and sandpipers
and geese and ducks—seem larger. And the trees, heavy with foliage,
bugs, and birds, seem more significant, too, as if they hold as much, if
not more, water than the river—which they do.

I think often of the James. There is news of it most warm mornings
in the mist that rises from its corridor less than a mile from us and
envelops and lacquers and nourishes our place with moisture. But getting
on the water is not always possible, nor is it always desirable. We have
many animals and each other and a garden to tend. On most days, our
tasks feel like a part of the river, a river we are closer to because we are of
it, a part of it by our responsibilities and our work, rather than just on it.
But there are some days when my terminal need to escape, to explore
lands outside our fences, to which I am responsible in less responsible
ways, gets the better of me, and our life feels too busy then, like we're

trying to do too much, like we're tangled in loose ends, losing sight of what matters in the quest to live a life that matters.

Our little homestead, I'm trying to say, does not feel so little anymore. Working land, whether or not you care about leaving the place better than you found it, means having more to do than you can ever do and trusting that you'll get it done.

Nowadays, getting towards August, there is harvesting, canning, jam making. Dishes to wash, laundry to do—visitors come, arrive weekly, at times daily. The phone rings. The goats get parasites. They get coccidia. Foxes eat chickens. The fences need repair. Calls go unreturned. Always Sophie milks the goats morning and night, strains that white gold, bottle-feeds the kids. She goes to the barn humming and comes back singing and then she helps Kirsten make butter, cheese, kombucha, kefir, jam.

We are often tired, but we are filled with something good and indefinable. And we are rarely weary. I mean we are rich with care, with food and with work, friends and animals, plants and tools and play. We take our visitors, friends and family, to the creek. They help with chores. We swim with them. We feed them—Lord, how we cook and how we eat. And we feed our animals well, too, and our soil and the plants in the soil. Sometimes, late into the morning and again later in the morning, very early, I read, scratch words on paper, hoping—only later—that they are words wrung out of me by decent living. One day last week Kirsten asked, "What color do you want to paint the bedroom?" and though it wasn't the most intimate thing I'd heard from her in a while, it felt that way, and I said something ignorant instead of laughing or crying or taking some fresh water to the ducks and chickens. A few hours later, in a moment of tenderness—some might say weakness—Kirsten said, "Why don't you go to the river."

So I went. It was late July, morning, and when I crossed the bridge down the road, I saw the James was muddy and rising from rains of the prior evening. Three storms had converged over our area around seven.

They came from the west and south and north and met between Peaks of Otter and Troutville, drenching the land with a spectacle of sound and vision and damage. Over three inches of rain fell. Friends up Lithia Road, in the Mill Creek drainage, had their telephone and computer fried by a bolt. We learned this a week later. Apparently, they were in no hurry to fix them.

There's a rock midstream we use for a gauge, and I saw the rock was almost covered. For the last month, the rock, the size of a good woodstove, had been exposed almost in its entirety. When the rock is covered, the river level roughly correlates to four feet on the USGS gauge. I like knowing this. Four feet is the beginning of juicy paddling water on the James, especially downstream at the rapids in Balcony Falls, twenty minutes from our place.

I braked and crossed the railroad tracks real slow. Norfolk Southern runs on the river-right side of the James, CSX on the river left. I was on the right bank now, which is the east bank here. The James runs south to north from Buchanan to Natural Bridge before resuming its more general west to east meandering path to Richmond. A hundred yards later, I caught the first glimpse of Jennings Creek. It was up but not up enough for paddling. Jennings and North Creek had flashed overnight. They were both six inches too low now. The falls in Arcadia proper said so.

But the creeks had run, and I had missed them and felt giddy about that, especially since I'd been very awake at 4 A.M. after shooting in the vicinity of a stray dog who'd wakened all of us with his barking—deep bass, I think he was part German Shepherd—and had frightened our goats and sheep, kids and lambs. To think I could have taken that twelve-gauge energy to the creek, taken it paddling at dawn, juiced all my brainwaves, and I wanted to go for a ride right then, on a buffalo.

I parked at the confluence and walked along the bank, which was wet, the grasses and weeds pressed down from the recent water running over them, as if in supplication. It was not yet seven and already muggy, but there was the promise of cooler weather soon. I felt that mix of anxiety and elation that a good rain brings anybody who loves free-flowing rivers and streams. Something in the air—a weight, a pressure—suggested more boomers that afternoon. A front was breaking through the door of a hot week of weather.

I had a day of notching and seating logs on the cabin, a future play/guesthouse. But I vowed to get on Balcony that evening. Ideally, I'd get on the water as the front arrived in earnest. To be on the river just after a summer thunderstorm, especially at dusk, is to know a holy time. The hills, inhuman as they are, seem to strut their stuff with the contrails of mist and do it with a feisty mix of humility and pride. The foliage glimmers with a damp sheen. Everything feels fresh, even if it's not. Often the river is warmer than the air and a fog rises around and through you. Dusk erases forever, whatever forever is. And something about the pinks and peaches that the sun spits as the earth buries it, erases you, the parts you hope can be erased, and you too spit pinks and peaches.

Back at the house, Sophie was finishing the goat-milking routine. Kirsten was taking care of the pigs and rabbits and other things. The rain barrels were overflowing. Pearls of moisture hung from leaves, grasses, stems, webs, even petals, and the morning light refracted through them in liquid, lugubrious spectrums. I watered and fed the dogs and chickens and then us. Breakfast, in honor of the storms, was Gypsy Three Eyes. As I cut thick slices of walnut parmesan bread from one of the scrumptious, meat-like loaves from Breadcraft in Roanoke, I thought of Alex and Rebecca, owner and head baker respectively, and how they were going on ten hours of work at this point in their day. If I called them now and didn't hear a hint of grumpiness in their voices, it wouldn't stop me from trading duck eggs for their day-old bread. They use our duck eggs in their brioche, a treat that does to your mouth what first frost does to persimmon fruit, to tweak a Neruda trope.

In a skillet over medium heat went a cassette-sized chunk of butter, a bit of lemon, sprinklings of fresh ground black pepper, and salt. As those wonders did their thing, I ripped three holes in each slice of bread and then laid them in the skillet, top sides out to conform with the bend of the iron. A duck egg fit in one hole, a chicken egg in the other, a guinea egg in the smallest. Somebody blabbered smartly on the radio about the price of gas, and after a pleasurable while of failing to ignore him, I turned off the radio and flipped our meal in the skillet.

We ate and talked and we chewed and swallowed and said as much. The day trickled on, heavy and gentle as the drenched July hills. And we trickled on, crossing paths among the various tasks. After some time in the garden, Kirsten and Sophie put tomatoes and peaches by. I worked on the cabin, taking breaks from the chainsaw and chisel now and then to work a scythe against stickweed coming up in the pasture. Sharpening tools with files is lovely, but there's nothing quite like sharpening an old scythe that's been sharpened so many times the blade is very thin. You can't help but wonder what other bodies have felt the weight and motion of that tool, and how if you're lucky, you might feel something of the best and worst of them and all that in you.

The ground never really dried out before the sky turned moody and gruff with approaching storms. By three-thirty, I'd notched and set four more logs, bringing the cabin walls overhead, and I hadn't reorganized my face with the chainsaw. In fact, I'd had a good time, the attention and care bringing me closer, more at home in the tasks. Kirsten and I lay around for a little while, chatting and touching. It always surprises me how I learn as much about her day from the wild, rich smell and taste of her skin—it was tomatoes and sun and soil that day—as from anything she says about it. Sometime later, the sun over Fincastle-way, I outfitted an old Perception Slasher C-1 with thigh straps. I'd bought the vehicle a month prior off a fellow in Wytheville but hadn't paddled it yet. In 1991, I bought the same model new, the only new boat I've owned.

The Slasher is what's referred to, in whitewater parlance, as a longboat. And at twelve feet it is long. It is sleek, too, as its name implies. You can pivot the stern coming in and out of eddies, and the boat carves waves like a fillet knife. Like said knife, the boat, too, has a sharp kind of grace about it. None of the tricked-out hull design of the newer boats; paddling a Slasher, despite its silly name, bears similar sparks as coming upon a house with copper screens, gutters, roof— somebody kind and lovely inviting you in.

For thigh straps, I got the webbing and the Fastex buckles stitched haphazardly with a leather needle and dental floss and then lashed the boat to the rack of our econobox and headed out. The rain was still falling from the last storm, still some lightning and thunder, too. But there were patches of blue to the west and a cool breeze blew. I listened to the new Bruce Springsteen album, where he puts his brass and grit and heart to old songs Pete Seeger did up, like "Old Dan Tucker" and "John Henry" and "Jacob's Ladder." It suited my mood, even if the politics of the moment called for something like Bananarama's "Cruel, Cruel Summer."

You go north on Route 11 eight miles to Natural Bridge and then east on Route 130 another six miles to Glasgow. You go over small hills and streams, over Natural Bridge itself and past pastures and woods, mountains all around, and then down to the valley where the Maury River dumps into the James at Glasgow, the site of several big flood episodes. I was aghast at the new clear-cut adjacent the put-in on the Maury, just upstream of the confluence, and then I started thinking about firewood. There was plenty of gleaning opportunity here, I thought, driving on. At the dead end, two cars with racks were parked. This pleased me perhaps more than it should have. It meant somebody else was on the river, upstream or down I didn't know.

There'd been break-ins at this spot in the recent past. I'd met a guy one day on the river who'd lost a window and some gear to the vandals. He came back a week later and parked and waited in the bushes with a .357, but nobody showed up. Perhaps he was lucky. Like many such places, there was an abundance of litter and no trash can. I don't understand this and don't need to. I slipped my sprayskirt over shorts and zipped up the lifejacket and buckled on my brain bucket. Evidently, Rockbridge County had not received the rains of the prior night. The Maury gave the term "boneyard" another definition. This meant no running the first good rapid at the confluence, a juicy little flume at normal flows.

I knelt in the Slasher and strapped in the thighs and then snapped on the skirt. On one strap, the knot I'd tied—after getting impatient with the sewing process—promptly slipped, and I spent a frustrated few minutes trying to retie it without getting out of the boat. It's not bad being a numbskull, but you get bit in the butt sooner or later. Which you like or else why be that way.

The river was the color of coffee with a good amount of cream. You couldn't see the bottom at all, the snails and freshwater clams, cobble and pebbles. Too, subsurface rocks were harder to see with the silt. To avoid scraping, you watch for disruptions on the surface, dimples and boils and fret marks, and you learn to tell from the surface what's going on beneath it. They call this reading water. For me, it is the central pleasure of boating. People who fish rivers and streams rely on this skill, too, for knowing where the fish may be and for effective placement of their cast.

I can't help but imagine the worst when paddling alone. Of course, it is important to remember the consequences of a screw-up; there's nobody to bail you out. With the first few strokes, I'm always picturing myself in all sorts of ugly situations—pinned against a rock, skirt popped, water forcing me in the boat. Since I've spent a lot of time in boats on whitewater and have seen many ugly scenarios, they might as well be useful.

After running the first rapid and eddying out, I felt more confidence. It had been over ten years since I'd caught an eddy in a Slasher. The boat likes eddies. You lift and press your knee and plant your paddle at the right time, and with enough boat momentum and power to the eddy, you whip around with the boat forty-five degrees and face upstream. Catching and peeling out of eddies lets you taste the various syllables of the river's language, and you feel, too, the pauses and accelerations of its punctuation and syntax. Water level and season and weather and the lay of the bed and surrounding banks and hills are rhetorical concerns, unrelated to your boat but as important as breathing.

I'd like to say that I felt something good and true run through every part of me as, simultaneously, something else bad and false was running out or just being pushed aside. But that wasn't the case. The feeling I had was, in essence, the nature of the water, the way it carries its load, for better and for worse, moving with one purpose, undeterred by rocks or other obstructions but going around and filling in behind them, turning lovely shapes and holding and letting go of the light in as many myriad, not wholly random designs according to those shapes. But the feeling was also, I think, the nature of the rocks and the bed and the hills, the way they stand, altered or not by prior industry—logging, mining, canals, railroad—eroding slowly with the pressure of weather and water and development, the primary flow cleaner than in the past, but still polluted enough that most people don't even eat the fish they catch in the James.

From my place in the first eddy, drifting and bobbing, I watched the top edge of a wave pulse and break. The wave started at the head of the eddy and extended across the tongue of current to another eddy. It was muddy for sure, and I watched it the way one watches the stars upon waking under them, dreamily, as if in a trance. Soon I found myself maneuvering the boat onto the wave. It was an easy wave to catch and it held the boat gently. I dipped the boat's edges and carved back and forth, feeling the force of the water and its volume move under and around and downstream as I stayed there in one place, moving side to side, the boat a tongue wiping some upper lip. How lucky I felt, how truant and huge with puniness.

What happened next matters little to the history of the world; I paddled downstream. There were cliffs on the river right and mist like sponges wiping the ridges further up. The James is wide in Balcony Falls. The mountains rise on either side. They are mellow, old landforms, less peaks than long ridges. The trees in high summer foliage insulate them, make them feel unattainable and intimate both. There was a comforting sense that nobody could see you through all those limbs and leaves, even if they wanted to.

There's a power line running across the mountains on the left side of the river. To say it looks like a scar is a cliché, but it looks like one, one that keeps getting scratched, opened and ever running with pus. The James is not where you go for a wilderness river experience. There are places here and there where you feel out there, but you are never really out there.

Instead of wilderness, you feel a sense of history and commerce and settlement, and of prior wilderness. Route 130 is visible in places where it winds up and over the ridge, at least two overlooks providing travelers a tree-studded view into and across the gorge. On the river left were the remains of stone walls, big ones of huge rocks, hewn rectangular and stacked over twenty-feet high for the James River Company in the 1800s. You see the walls a short while after leaving the Maury at Confluence Rapid. The railroad tracks, which cross the Maury less than fifty yards from the James, continue down the gorge on the landward side of the wall. But the wall was built originally for the canal and the towpath.

It wasn't only George Washington I thought about that night in my little plastic boat, how he conceived the canal as a way to open trade routes to the west. I thought about what it was like to journey up (thirty-three hours from Richmond to Lynchburg, a five-dollar ticket) and down the river on the canal when it was completed sixty years after breaking ground, and how after the war the railroads trumped the canal for speed and efficiency, and the paths and other works fell into disrepair.

I thought, too, of the men who built the canal, and of the women and children who were left behind. I did not imagine the smell of black powder and granite dust, the heat and the cold, but I thought about it. And thought about the pleasures and hardships of the work, the diseases and triumphs and deaths, the hours and days and months of rhythm and grace, tedium and toil. I thought of the river running by them, and when and how they saw it and what was on the river then and how it looked and smelled and tasted. It is a shame that no books bear the testimony of these workers, but it is not impossible to hear the sound of their tools and voices in the river moving and breaking over and eroding the rocks.

I had shared a meal of venison burgers and cucumber salad with Kirsten and Sophie before leaving for the river, and as good as it felt to have that nourishment as I headed downstream, it felt as good to be missing my wife and daughter. There has always been something of the preservationist in the escapist in me. I don't really remember what's important when I get away from what's important and mess around on moving water, but I feel at home in ways that seem worth trying to bring home.

It was approaching eight P.M., and the sky was growing brighter. The storms and the clouds had moved east, clear skies behind them. I approached the rapid below the cobble bar with a somber tempo. I kept left of center with easy forward strokes. I listened to the rocks turning the water into bubbles and froth. Twenty feet above the drop, I saw paddle blades, a weird puppet show of them, popping, no, slicing over the horizon line. Kayakers were surfing the waves in the run-out.

Paddlers tend to be friendly people. There's a sense of camaraderie inherent in the sport, a sense not unlike that of churchgoers of similar denomination. Even so, my trance was no longer the same. There were other people here now. There were no deer or bear coming down to the banks for a drink. There wasn't even a blue heron. I wouldn't see the four otters—a family?—for another mile or so, the eagle until almost to the take-out.

I ran a clean, safe line through the drop. In the middle of it, planting a forward stroke and aiming for the eddy, I saw the three paddlers were a father and his two sons. You could see it in their faces, in the structure and the strain. I caught the eddy with a hard cross draw, pivoted, and paused. One of the boys, maybe thirteen-years-old and in a snazzy new kayak, was surfing the first and strongest of the run-out waves. His father yelled at him the way some fathers yell at their little leaguers. It was disheartening and exhilarating. The boy flipped over and blew his first roll. I started to paddle toward him in case he wanted a bow to right himself. The father approached, too, a little slower than me, and he shot me an annoyed glance. I nodded as friendly as I could, which was probably too friendly, just as the boy rolled up, his father yelling acidic instructional praise.

I had noticed other paddlers downstream and headed for them with more haste than was necessary. Something about the cliffs and big boulders downstream filled several holes in me. I looked from them to the water and back and so on, sometimes checking the position of my paddle blade. I chose the river-left channel and caught a few eddies, ferrying across the main flow, feeling the boat grow more familiar under me, a part of me. Indeed, I was wearing the thing; it was attached to the skirt that was attached a little too tightly to my thirty-something-year-old belly, and under that skirt my thighs were Fastexed to the hull as I knelt.

Slowly, I maneuvered to river right. There were two paddlers standing above their boats on the rocks above the next good rapid. I approached them and whipped a pivot turn against the current of a chute against the right bank, and then caught the eddy next to which they stood.

"Hello," I said.

"Nice boat," the guy with the mustache said. He was standing over a short boat, one of the newer models. I knew this was going to be one of those inane and delightful forays into small talk that happen among paddlers.

"Thanks," I said.

There was a pause. The river had gone away. The trees were just a bunch of trees. Only the rocks mattered.

"Do y'all have a car at the take-out?" I asked.

"Well, I've got a truck," the guy without the mustache said.

"Would you all mind giving me a ride back to the put-in?" I asked. The rapids grew louder now. "I don't mind riding in the bed," I added quickly.

"Alright," the guy said after a minute.
"That's perfect," I said. "See you down there."
"Yep," the guy without the mustache said.

I took off, cranking hard from eddy to eddy, river right to river left around the big boulders to line up for the next rapid, a left to right stairstep-like drop. Among many things, I thought of my daughter and her relationship with the river. Our random trips in the canoe and our swims in the falls and pools on North Creek—near daily in summer— felt like better training for the practice of loving rivers than gearing up in helmet, lifejacket, sprayskirt, paddle, and boat. And the fact that she wouldn't relinquish her position as queen of the goat-milking ritual, draining the udders of our four Nubians twice a day at 6:30, suggested she was learning plenty about water and craft.

I had the Lesans of Pothole Paddles on the Chattooga make Sophie a canoe paddle when she was born. Of course, it was as much for me as for her, with a Dynel edge on the cherry- and hickory-accented blade and a Dynel sleeve on the ash shaft. She grew into the paddle last year, and last September, when she and I canoed every Sunday morning of the month on the James from Buchanan to Arcadia, it seemed that she put the same kind of care into working the tool as the Lesans had put into making it, which pleased me more than anyone cares to know.

I carved into the eddy below the bus-sized boulder. Could you call such a rock a boulder? It was like a house, really, in shape and in bearing. I felt inhabited, the way a well-kept home can make you feel. I hoped, with more pride than was called for, that the cabin we were building might contain some of this energy. The colors of the stone were pale pinks and creams and peaches, mottled and striated and worn smooth and curvy by weather and water. Trees and shrubs and weeds grew in the crevices and depressions. It felt good to feel smaller than I already felt down there with the wide, bending river and mountains all around, the dusk accelerating, a chance of another storm. Things were fine. There was a wave off the boulder and I put the long, thin boat on it and surfed a while and then headed downstream. A long steep ridge loomed above the bend, band of cliffs three-quarters of the way of up. Everywhere the disturbed water was giving the softening light back in ways that seemed far from disturbed.

Recumbent Folds

We're playing fetch the keys in North Creek. There are ten keys on three rings and a Swiss Army with chunks of its red plastic handle missing. These are my keys, the ones that live in my pocket most every day. I throw the bundle again, watch them reflect the light before disappearing underwater, ten feet downstream of a waterfall.

The strangeness does not set in when Sophie dives, but when she emerges with them in her mouth, barking through the car, office, house, and shed keys as though she were a golden retriever. I want to fret when my daughter disappears under the water and then emerges, pretending she is a dog, fetching, but I cannot. Sophie is nine, a strong swimmer and great lover of dogs.

I glance at the monoliths of granite that buttress the falls. It has been dry this August and plants growing on the stone are slumped and brittle. The water trickles over the falls like someone about to quit a job. Now and then fingerling dace dart a few inches out of the water and slide back down the rock. Crickets and cicadas thrum as if inside your head.

We are a few hundred yards above North Creek's confluence with Jennings Creek and not far from the James River and our home up the west bank of it. This area is like a second backyard for us. The entire creek, from its source near the Blue Ridge Parkway, is in Jefferson National Forest, so we have free range. And it is rarely crowded, being a thirty-five minute drive from the nearest small city. Kirsten, Sophie, and I head down here a few times a week. After work and farm chores, we drive down and mess around in the water. To get outside the fences, not for long but long enough, is essential to our health and the health of the farm. Playing in the creek swirls us closer as a family, and as animals, bodies of water.

Sophie barks another funny imitation of golden retriever. Again I toss the keys with the old Swiss army on the ring and watch them disappear. To see her so delighted is beginning to tire me. We have been at the hole for over an hour, and Sophie has not taken a break. Her fingers and toes are raisins, wrinkly and pale. I look downstream where the creek courses nearly straight for a hundred yards. There are clumps of jewelweed, Joe Pye weed, and butterfly bush, big plants of late summer. In times of drought, creeks assume a frail and tender beauty. Swimming in them almost feels like trespassing. We try to be quieter, our motions and our voices. We worry about fish and bugs and plants. But we do not worry about the rocks. Drought is rock time. The banks grow monstrous. As a friend said recently, when asked why he bothered to paddle a certain river at low water, "It's a nice pile of rocks."

The same water snake we see each warm weather visit appears now between two pale blue boulders by the logjam on river right. Maybe it has been there a while. I don't know. It looks like an extension of the water itself, being born this very minute, with each swivel of its sleekness. Sophie pauses from our game of fetch to regard the skinny, two-foot snake. A seepage drains from the rich soil onto the largest and flattest of the boulders that frame the snake. To say the seep is flowing or even oozing is an overstatement, yet it finds the creek the way fog and mist find the territories beneath our flesh.

It seems there's always a confluence nearby, that its presence is felt whether you've seen or heard or noted it on a map. You feel it the way you feel it when kids fall into more primal rhythms of play. Like in cooking when you're making it up and all the spices and ingredients are coming together just right. Or in remodeling when you're not sure what's beneath the ceiling you're tearing down, but you know that however you replace it will bring more air and light as well as many small, lasting discoveries along the way.

As Sophie dives again—I swear she would keep playing this game for four more hours—I remember our visit here one day two Decembers back. The sky was the grey of a blue heron's feather. Sophie and her pal Eben were selling me skipping stones for a nickel a piece. They cared as little for where we were as for what you call those stones they were deep in the process of gathering—sandstone, limestone, greenstone, quartz. They weren't particularly concerned with the money they were making either. They wanted more skipping stones, and they wanted to make a transaction, to hand me something and for me to hand them something in return.

Pretty good money for seven-year-olds, I reckoned aloud, bargaining them down to five skippers for a penny. They'd taken all my nickels, you see, even the shiny, new buffalo nickel I'd been meaning to save.

Another skipper skittered like some young critter in flight along the still water towards the latticework of an old bridge piling. The kids poked among hemlock and sycamore roots and turned the largest rocks they could manage to turn in order to get at the talus beneath.

"Here's a good one," Eben announced.

"Yessir," I said, turning as another skipper sunk at the tail of its course.

"Look at this one," Sophie said to nobody in particular.

I was about to run out of pennies now and had my eye on a winter-dead butterfly bush, its twig-ends, as my next form of currency to exchange.

In no time, Sophie and Eben's attention shifted, and we found ourselves poking through the woods along the river-left bank towards a rapid we call Cauldron. This is trout country, stocked trout, and there was fishing line, wrens' nests of it, in the limbs and sometimes in the leaves and sticks on the ground. It was charming to see the kids regard the tangles as though they were something besides litter, acts of carelessness.

I started balancing a large rock on a boulder near the run-out of Cauldron. Eben and Sophie were digging in the sand. I heard Sophie yell, "Let's make a house here." They crawled into an alcove-like area between boulders. One of the boulders was the color of purple chalk, which isn't really purple, the way crows, seen up close and in the right light, are not really black. They delineated a kitchen and a bedroom. They started cooking sand pancakes and biscuits of stone.

The creek sounded like a bunch of telephones with muffled ringers and the whole world was calling and the rest of the world wasn't answering. A glance at the flow suggested that with an inch of rain, there'd be enough water for a paddling trip. There's a sharp move to the river-right you have to make as you drop through Cauldron in a boat, and it gives your breath back a little sharper and cleaner as you try to do that. But really Cauldron is the kind of place that helps you breathe whether you are in a boat or not. It is a fine place.

Once more I took a rock the bulk of a cinderblock but more svelte and held a point of it against a larger rock that was embedded in the cobble by water's edge. I palmed it in a slow turning motion, very slowly, until it felt as though it would stay on its own. The rock's size and shape, chill and hardness reminded me of the tension I'd felt in my wife's muscles and tendons the last time I rubbed her shoulders. I don't know how long I turned it or how many times around or on how many different places on the host rock. Eventually the rock stayed without the aid of my hands.

It looked like a priest or country on a map, the rock, how it was standing on that one point. There were creases and dimples in its rough, mottled face—all grays and rusts—and you could see many things in the way the light and shadows played along them. "My daddy's balancing rocks, look, Eben," I heard Sophie say. They vacated their new home and started doing the same.

I watched Sophie as she gave up on the point of one rock and turned it to another point. You could tell by the way she moved the rock that she was trying to force it. I looked away to keep from giving advice. Soon I heard her toss that rock and step to find another. Eben had already stood a couple of rocks by their edges, rather than by their points—it wasn't dramatic but it was a start. He was all business, like the sound of the water was in his body now and everything he did was getting it: downstream, downstream. I thought of watching our lamb

Pippi, then three weeks old, stare down a hay bale and then hop on it, tentatively at first and then a dozen more times with verve, not as though mastering the feat, but reveling in it.

A balanced rock is as temporary as a stone wall is permanent. It is not an act of resistance and fit and edges, the way stonework is, or masonry, or the way I parent when I'm tired and distracted. Balancing stone is an act of points and feel and grace. The longer a stone resists your balancing of it, the more opportunity you get to feel the energy of the rock as well as that of the rock on which you hope it will rest, precariously, as though defying gravity. It is an exercise in touch and in feeling. It is all about connection, the interplay of edges and materials and yet it is as much about not thinking and looking away or closing your eyes and letting your hands move against the rock as gingerly as a damselfy on the summer air, snow on the winter air.

Eben, buzzing about like an electron freed of its orbit, kicked over one of my more dramatic works. I heard it clack before I saw it fall. He didn't notice, I guess, and I cared little. The pleasure of it, after the process, is in realizing they fall down, all the rocks—some sooner, some later.

Now we three were clunking around the cobble beach, standing rocks on rocks and rocks on rocks on rocks on rocks, making cairns and figures that brought to mind gnomes and Easter Island and Matisse and many other shapes and places deeper than knowing.

Who knows how much water had passed by the time Sophie, Eben, and I had twenty or so rocks standing in a formation most certainly not designed by us. The lack of design, in many ways, is the joy of it for me. Balancing stones is an evolving act, but even so, it always looks like some ritual place or burial ground more than the erratic play of a man, his daughter, and a friend of his daughter's. What ground isn't burial ground, I wondered to myself.

I noticed two large trout holding in a deep pocket near the tail of the pool where the creek recomposes itself after the tantrum of Cauldron. Eben and Sophie saw them, too. I watched them watching and as I watched, wondered if it wasn't the same muscles required in the act of watching trout as in the act of balancing stone. You look by not looking. You balance by not balancing. The rock stands on its point when you've stopped willing it, the way the trout appear once you're looking at the entire world of the creek and thinking less of trout than of what a trout's skin has to say about the creation of the world.

"Each of y'all grab five throwing stones," I said to the kids. "It's time to knock those suckers down." I was being a little dramatic now, and why not?—spending time by a creek, playing with kids and rocks: this fires me up.

Eben, being our guest, threw first. I toed a line in the sand ten feet from the nearest balanced stone for the kids, and then made a line thirty feet back for me. On his third throw, Eben knocked over a rock that had been balanced rather like a duck. We all hooted, probably stirred some hibernator with our noise. It was his only hit. Sophie, too, sent one of the rocks to another, more random, place among the rocks. I missed on all five throws and felt a little funny about that. After throwing two more rounds of five rocks apiece, sixteen of the original twenty rocks were still standing.

"Free for all," I shouted. The kids knew exactly what I meant. We stayed behind our lines and chunked stone after stone and then sticks and sometimes three or four smaller stones in a spray pattern.

Maybe it took forty-five minutes to knock down all the stones. I'm not sure. It felt like a long time, but even so, we balanced more stones for the next round and threw well into the patient winter dusk.

Sophie brings me the keys again. They dangle from her mouth, Swiss army between her teeth. "Ruff Ruff," she spouts and then shakes her bottom as though she had a tail. I toss them, imagine what she sees as she dives. Now and then she throws the keys, and I go after them, recover them from the rocks at the bottom, subaqueous world peaceful and strange and off-limits for more than brief, dream-like gulps of breath. We do this over and over, connecting, Sophie and I and the creek and even the keys, tools critical for our transportation and security. Sophie is always connecting, but often I need her help, and the water's, to unlock doors, free me from rooms of superficial nonsense I tend to place far too much stock in.

Our game of fetch is on hiatus now. I am swimming with Sophie on my back, but really I'm crawling. It is too shallow as we approach the falls, so I drag us with my hands gripping stone on the creek's bed. Sophie's delight courses through her body wherever it touches mine and this gives me a second wind, a third and fourth. I cannot imagine a better place to be in this world right now.

When you hack around with kids, there are times when the activities, wholly unplanned, build upon one another with effortless grace. This often happens in the presence of water, running water especially. It is akin to good conversation, one anecdote spawning the next anecdote, idea, or inquiry, sweet force of intimacy in charge. "Underwater tea party," Sophie yelps. I follow her under. We are in a hole, a scour hole at the base of the falls. The white, aerated water swirls above us like magic insects—dragonflies and gnats. You can see the fuzzy outline of trees and sky through the current-disturbed surface of the creek. At home, Sophie likes to set up tea parties for her dolls. Those are more involved than our underwater party, which is quick and sloppy and perfect. We mime the pouring and sipping of tea while struggling to stay under the surface and hold our breath.

We share a few rounds of tea before leaning against the bedrock of the falls, getting our heads, necks, and shoulders massaged by the downward course of water. Nirvana, whatever nirvana is, feels more than attainable now. So what if I am tired and have a lot to do, both at the farm and the school where I teach, another semester about to begin. I watch sunlight ooze through the hemlocks and sycamores to the west, hints of autumn in that light. The water is cold but the air heavy and hot enough to make the wet feel refreshing even after a long time.

There is an angled groove in the stone that forms the falls, and the water runs down that crack, meeting the water that curtains down the falls where we are standing. These channels join in a frothy maelstrom. At floodwater it would be a bad place to swim. After a good rain, we come here and watch logs recirculate, as they do for hours in the hydraulic, letting our memories of the creek at low water enrich the wonders and mysteries of the place in flood.

We scramble up the falls by its slightest flank and slide down the angled crack with its flume. The momentum dunks us briefly, thrillingly, into the carbonated-looking pool at the base. We slide twice more. Since the water is low, the rock abrades our fannies more than usual. At higher water, we often slide a dozen or so times, yelping with glee, but not today.

"Let's skip stones, Daddy," Sophie says, already swimming away, towards the beach with all the little stones and grit and sometimes cigarette butts from the folks who visit here and, well, you know. So I am swimming after Sophie. I am following her, being the golden retriever now, being a good, happy, obedient dog. The mind is a big eddy on days like this. It is April again, just as it is December, just as the mind and heart are one and more than one organ and my daughter and I as much a part of this creek, indeed this whole lovely, beleaguered world, as it is possible to be before we die.

One day this past April, Sophie, who'd be turning nine in a week, said she wanted her friends to paint stones at her birthday party, so I offered to go to the creek with her and gather them from its rocky shore. It was Saturday, the air so clear it seemed hyperbolic, as though you could feel every organism down to its smallest cell. I figured we'd grab a dozen or so rocks and head back home.

We parked in a gravel wayside along North Creek and as we stumbled through the shrubs to the creek's bank, we stopped to regard the fire pink in blossom. I've always loved how the fire pink's deep red color contrasts with its thin petals, as well as its name. There's nothing pink at all about fire pink, and it is so red as to surpass all that's meant by the word red. Something, too, about the flower's shape suggests it has been gnawed by an insect, even though it hasn't. Perhaps that shape is a sort of defense mechanism against being eaten.

"How many rocks will we need?" I asked. The fire pink was behind us now. Sophie was squatting among the cobble, flipping and handling rocks.

"Ten," she said, matter of fact. "Like this. Flat on one side. Not too big." I studied the rock in her hand. It was the size of a small paperback book and vaguely heart-shaped. It looked like a rock that with a little luck you could skip.

"Ten it is," I said, thinking twelve would be better, just in case. I was watching a trout hold at the tail of a pool just off the bank. The water was emerald-colored and looked cold. The terrain was right for gathering stone, as we were a few inches below normal rainfall and the creek was running low.

How sweet the feel of creek stone in your hand. There's something about the grit and the weight that's calming. I hear the sound of water running over rock perhaps more fully when I'm down low like that, handling stone; and the birds—I think there was a veery somewhere up the opposite bank—the birds through their songs feel very present.

I hefted a couple of rocks that seemed to fit Sophie's ideal and piled them on top of her finds. There was a good deal of culling required in order to find the right size stone. As I shuffled and squatted among the rock, lifting and turning them, life slipped into perspective. Whatever small, private pains I had at the time began to tickle. Here I was with my daughter gathering stones for her birthday party. For a moment I wanted to scream, but I let the feeling—some blend of joy and fear—dissipate, become something closer, perhaps, to what the experts call happiness.

Sophie smiled when she saw me smiling at her. She had moved to another place, and when I approached her new spot at the head of an island, I saw she had a twig and was poking a stonefly larva. "Stonefly," she said. I nodded. She stood and reached for my hand, and as I reached for hers, I saw my daughter more fully than in some time. And I saw that Kirsten had been right a few days before when she'd said that Sophie was growing up now, vertically, that she'd been going in phases, growing out then up.

We walked down the island together, her in the lead and nimble. A monarch flitted upstream. A truck crossed the bridge fifty yards below. We found several more painting rocks among the boulders and driftwood of the island. There was no hurry about the way we looked. Now and then one of us would squat or kneel and run our hand over several specimens. It was still too cold to really worry about snakes.

We had twelve or fourteen painting stones now, and I carried them in separate trips to the truck. As this was National Forest and I wasn't sure of the Forest Service's policy on gathering stone, I piled the rocks on the floor of the passenger seat instead of in the bed. The pile wouldn't bother Sophie, since she still traveled in a booster, lower legs dangling off the edge of the bench like a couple of strange, hearty vines.

It was too pretty an evening to leave the creek so soon. Sophie was tossing small stones, Frisbee-style, when I caught up with her along the shore. "Come skip rocks," she said. "Come on." So I joined in, skipping rocks on the pool where the trout had been. The creek was thirty feet across there, and it was easy to skip a well-shaped, flat rock across it. But Sophie was not having any success coaxing her rocks to skip. Her Frisbee-tosses resulted in the rocks plunking into the water. I wondered whether to give her some pointers.

It must have been fun for her to see the rocks splash and then disappear under water. There's a sense of power in moving stone, no matter how large it is or how you go about it. That power feels almost as good as the powerlessness you feel when sliding down waterfalls, being dunked in the hydraulic at the base. Sophie watched me skip another rock and then she tried herself, but she didn't seem to want to imitate the motion that was working for me.

I couldn't remember learning to skip stones. There must have been a day when the motion came together. There must have been a rocky stream or pond. Maybe somebody offered a few pointers. I'm not sure. I wanted to remember that day, but it wasn't available. "Try it like this," I said. Sophie watched with some skepticism as I gripped a stone between thumb and index. "It's in the wrist." The rock skipped a few times, as though the water had hardened, turned to ice. "Here you go," I said, handing her a rock that resembled a piece of pine bark. There was a smell on the air then, very strong, of a tree or shrub or flower, or many trees and shrubs and flowers in blossom. Squeaky birdsong, as of warbler, seemed to surround us and surround the sound of the water, too.

Sophie gripped the rock just right and flicked it, and it fell a foot from her onto a half-submerged, grayish blue stone. "That's the idea," I said. Sophie didn't look convinced. I handed her another one. "Get more of your arm into it. And your hips. Hips, arm, wrist—that's the motion." As I acted the form in slow motion, I remembered my high school shot-put coach, Bob Neu. Coach Neu emphasized form over mass. He loved to study video. We watched world-class shot putters Randy Barnes and Ulf Timmerman. Over and over we watched them throw, studied their motion. Though I was small by shot-putter standards, I was able to score our track team points because Neu was a good, patient, and obsessed teacher of form. He seemed to love nothing else more than watching me, at two hundred pounds, outthrow opponents who weighed two-fifty or more.

As though still fixated on the wrist motion, Sophie again dudded her next attempt. But she had the grip right, and the wrist. "That's the idea," I said. A crow passed over the creek just then, headed upstream. It didn't make a sound, but the shadow of its motion caught our eyes, and we both watched it. Meanwhile, I repeated the mantra, "Hips, arm, wrist."

I lost count of how many skips Sophie's throw made then; whether ten or fifteen, the rock crossed the creek and settled in the moss of a boulder's crease. A saxifrage was blooming there, all veins and stars and cling. I yelped with glee. Sophie smiled like a kid smiles who has pleased her dad. The smile disarmed me. I hoped her pleasure was more for her sake than my own.

Probably Sophie would have moved on to something else had I not showed her a way to skip rocks. And with her I would have moved too. Maybe we'd be stacking stones into a cairn shape. Or balancing rocks as we had with Eben and many times afterward. Maybe, since we'd both worn bathing suits, we'd be dunking ourselves in the creek, flailing about in the cold water.

But I had showed her how to skip rocks. I had given her some pointers, and now she was fairly obsessed. I vowed to keep my mouth shut for a while. No more "hips, arms, wrist"—no more of the words anyway.

Sophie's next few attempts were mixed. A few skips, a few plunks. She was ecstatic with the new skill and very focused. After a little time of being maybe too excited, almost every throw sent stones skipping. I had joined in the fracas myself. It was trickier than we noticed, standing on the tops of rocks, balancing so as to keep our shoes dry. We threw dozens of rocks. Once each batch disappeared, it took us longer to find new rocks with that smooth, somewhat flat shape.

Compared to looking for painting stones, looking for skipping stones was as different as looking for thrush is to looking for hawks. As I squatted by the creek, fingers combing its bed, I thought about Sophie's birthday party in a week, how much that party meant to her, how pleased I was that pieces of the creek would be present there.

It's getting late now. We are skipping rocks across the pool where earlier we dove for keys. There are many flies and they are as busy and various as the splotches of light reflected on the shrubs, rocks, and flood-smooth logs along the bank. Busy as we are hunting rocks to skip, flicking them with our wrists, arms, hips. There are flies and there is still the falls and it appears friendly with the low flow. It is a conventional falls in the sense water drops vertically and unbroken with the slope of the boulder. The angled groove where we slide, that channel—there are only two channels—makes the main drop even more compelling. There's a cavern on the left side, immediately below the falls, a cavern large enough to keep a dozen people dry in a rainstorm, though they'd be wet to their knees at normal water levels. The cavern, along with the abundance of stone and the angled slot and sound of water not falling but landing, lends to the place an arena, chasm-like quality.

The rocks have a soothing quality all the same. Despite their hardness, erosion has rounded their edges and faces, and it isn't hard to find on the boulders and stones a comfortable place to recline. To one lying on the rocks, a nap comes quickly, especially when the sun is out and the rocks heat up and you have been playing too long in the cold water.

But Sophie and I are not napping. We will head home soon enough, will slide key in ignition and drive up the road. We are skipping a few more rocks first. Sometimes we flick them and they do not skip but sink more slowly than the keys did. We skip the stones so they skip off boulders that form the borders of the pool, and often they fly into the air, as if off a ramp, and break upon landing on another boulder. The boulders, God they are pretty, the muted hues, pastel violets and tans, greens and grays and peaches. Lichen splotches, white to pale lime, cover fifty percent of their exposed surfaces. Ferns and grasses and flowers root in crevices, in minimal soil. As we continue to skip rocks, I remember how at spring's peak, we counted five different wildflowers simultaneously in bloom on the west cliff, the largest boulder, rooted in a thin carpet of soil—rue anemone, toothwort, Dutchman's-breeches, pussytoes, fire pink—their common names less important than their color, grouping, shape, size, all the manners of relation. And for weeks then, giddy with spring, we hunted morels in the strip of bottomland between the bank and the slope to the road. We didn't find them there. We found them upstream, when we weren't looking.